The Structure of Modern Commerce

The Structure of Modern Commerce
An Introductory Course for Business Studies

J. L. Hanson
MA, MEd, PhD, BSc(Econ) (London)
Formerly Senior Lecturer in charge of Economics
Huddersfield College of Technology
(now Huddersfield Polytechnic)

Seventh Edition

Revised by
E. W. Orchard
BSc(Econ), MSc(Econ)
Senior Lecturer in Economics, Bolton Institute of Higher Education

and

J. Buckman
BA, PhD
Sometime Economic Consultant to the OECD

PITMAN
150 YEARS

PITMAN PUBLISHING
128 Long Acre London WC2E 9AN

© Pitman Publishing Limited 1986

Seventh edition first published in Great Britain 1986
Reprinted 1987

British Library Cataloguing in Publication Data
Hanson, J.L.
  The structure of modern commerce : an introductory
  course for business studies.——7th ed.
  1. Commerce
  I. Title II. Orchard, E.W. III. Buckman, J.
  380.1   HF1008

ISBN 0-273-02532-5
ISBN ISE 0-273-02618-6

Produced by Longman Group (FE) Ltd
Printed in Hong Kong

Contents

Examination Questions

The following abbreviations are used to acknowledge the sources of
examination questions:

RSA	Royal Society of Arts.
UEI	Union of Educational Institutes.
WR	West Riding of Yorkshire Education Department.
NCTEC	Northern Counties Technical Examinations Council.
LCCI	London Chamber of Commerce and Industry.
WJEC	Welsh Joint Education Committee.
GCE JMB	GCE (Ordinary Level) of the Joint Matriculation Board of the Universities of Manchester, Liverpool, Leeds, Sheffield and Birmingham.
GCE Camb.	GCE (Ordinary Level) of the University of Cambridge Local Examinations Syndicate.

Preface to the Seventh Edition

This revised edition is intended to provide for the needs of students reading the subject of commerce in preparation for the General Certificate of Secondary Education (GCSE) and other examinations of a similar standard, such as that of the Royal Society of Arts. It is also a useful introductory course covering the needs of students preparing for the examinations of the Business and Technician Education Council at the General and First Level. The book should also be of great use to those who wish to know something of the organisation of modern commerce, but who are not necessarily preparing for an examination in the subject.

Commerce is very closely related to economics, treating as it does a similar range of variables such as the firm, the consumer, the transaction, income, costs, revenues and profits. Thus a course in commerce forms an excellent setting and background to the study of economics, and this revision has been reshaped to constitute a convenient companion volume to *Economics for Students*.

The high frequency of change in the world of economics and commerce has necessitated a thorough updating and revision of the previous edition. All statistical tables and information have been carefully brought as up to date as the latest official figures will permit, while the many institutional changes affecting commerce in recent years have been accounted for. Much additional information has been provided, for example on markets, retail trade, the Stock Exchange, foreign trade and the balance of payments. The increasing significance of the European Economic Community has been recognised by the addition of a completely new chapter on this subject. The sequence of chapters has been reorganised so that the book falls into four logical and convenient parts. At the same time, every effort has been made to retain the very solid merits of the previous edition, much of which has been retained on the grounds of its utility to the student.

Our thanks are due to the following bodies: the Export Credits Guarantee Department, Her Majesty's Stationery Office, the European Commission, the Co-operative Union, Lloyd's of London, the Banking Information Service, the Baltic Exchange, the Bank of England, Barclaycard, Visa and Access. Tables drawn from the *Bank of England Quarterly Bulletin* are reproduced with the permission of the Bank of England.

We would also like to thank the following examination bodies for permission to reprint questions set by them: the Royal Society of Arts, the London Chamber of Commerce and Industry, the Northern Counties Technical Examinations Council, the Welsh Joint Education Committee, the Joint Matriculation Board and the Cambridge Local Examinations Syndicate. Finally thanks also to H. R.

1986   E.W.O.
                                          J.B.

Part One
The Background of Commerce

1 The Scope of Commerce

1 Complexity of production and distribution

At one time all forms of production were on a small scale, generally dependent on local raw materials and often carried out by the workers in their own homes. During the past two hundred years, however, both production and business organisation have become increasingly complex. As a result, at the present day the manufacture and distribution of goods form a vast, complicated, often world-wide process.

Consider the boot and shoe industry. Although a few isolated firms have established themselves in other parts of this country, boots and shoes are mostly manufactured in a relatively small area of Northamptonshire. The boot and shoe factories have to be supplied with leather, most of which has to be imported from abroad; footwear manufactured in this district has to be supplied to people living in all parts of Britain, and in addition large quantities are exported to other countries. Other industries display a similar complexity of organisation.

An immense and varied assortment of goods is produced at the present time. Yet in countries like Britain it is possible to enter the appropriate type of shop, put a sum of money on the counter and obtain in exchange commodities which have been brought from the furthermost corners of the earth – coffee from Brazil, tea from India, a suit made in Italy, wine produced in France, bacon from Denmark, furs from Northern Canada or Siberia, or jewellery made from gold mined in South Africa. Commerce is responsible for all these products being available to the people who want to buy them at the time when they require them.

Commerce, then, is concerned with the distribution of commodities of all kinds – raw materials, foodstuffs, manufactured goods. Under modern conditions the business of distribution has become as complex as production.

2 The branches of commerce

The work of commerce can be illustrated by a simple commercial transaction. Any transaction is commercial in character if it involves exchange, whether of goods for goods, which we call barter, or of goods for money.

Suppose that John Smith requires a carpet. He will seek out a shop which deals in such goods, and expect to be shown a selection of carpets from which he can make his choice. After examining them he decides to purchase one. This, the final stage in the business of distribution, enables the commodity to reach the person who actually wants it for his own use, that is, the consumer. This is the function of the retail trade. Most people's commercial transactions are limited to deals with retailers. This, then, is one branch of commerce.

The student of commerce, however, must pursue his enquiries further. From what sources, he may ask, does the retailer obtain supplies of the goods he sells? Many retailers obtain their stock from wholesalers. The retailer who sold a carpet to John Smith probably obtained it from a wholesale carpet merchant. This is a commercial transaction involving a retailer and a wholesaler. The wholesale trade is thus a second branch of commerce. The wholesaler in his turn probably bought his stock of carpets from manufacturers in Halifax or Kidderminster. Here, then, is a third commercial transaction, this time involving a wholesaler and a manufacturer.

The manufacturer bought the raw wool from which the carpet was made at a wool auction in London or Melbourne. If the wool was sold at a London auction it would be consigned to an importer in

London, who would have to arrange for its warehousing between the time when it was unloaded from the ship which had brought it from Australia and the time of its sale at the wool market. At the wool auction the carpet manufacturer probably employed a specialist buying broker to act for him; the importer, too, would employ a selling broker to undertake the sale. All these people are engaged in commercial occupations. The import trade forms, then, the third branch of commerce.

Since a country cannot import goods from abroad unless it can sell some of its own products to other countries, there must also be another group of merchants – those who are engaged in the export trade, the fourth branch of commerce.

The four branches of commerce which we have considered so far are all concerned with the buying and selling of goods, and so comprise different kinds of trade. The basic commercial activity, therefore, is trade, but commerce embraces much more than trade. Certain other services are necessary to the carrying on of trade. The first of these is transport. The transfer of goods from one place to another would clearly be impossible without some means of transport. Indeed, the extent of both home and foreign trade depends upon the efficacy of the means of transport that are available, the expansion of trade having gone hand in hand with the development of transport. Before the coming of the railway and the steamship the volume of world trade was of very small proportions compared with what it is today. Transport is vital to trade, and so it forms an important branch of commerce.

There are also two financial services which are important ancillaries to commerce – banking and insurance. Banks assist commerce by providing businessmen with convenient means of payment for both internal and international transactions. They also help merchants and others to finance the holding of stocks. Insurance relieves those engaged in all kinds of business of many of the risks associated with the movement and holding of stocks of goods. Sales are often stimulated by advertising. The expansion of trade owes a great deal to the development of efficient banking, insurance and advertising facilities. These, then, are all important commercial occupations.

The four kinds of trade, together with transport, banking, insurance and advertising, form the main divisions of commerce. A study of these is required of the student, for they comprise the subject-matter of that branch of knowledge to which we now give the name commerce.

3 Commerce and economics

To some extent the two subjects commerce and economics overlap, but the similarity is more superficial than real. Economics is concerned with problems arising from the production and distribution of goods and services. Both the student of commerce and the economist, therefore, are interested in the distribution of goods, just as they are both interested in money and banking. Where they differ, however, is in the way they approach these questions.

The first thing which the student of economics learns is that all things are scarce relative to the demand for them. This is so because the economic resources required for their production – land, labour and capital – are themselves limited in supply. Obviously, if a piece of land is being used for cattle-rearing it cannot at the same time be used for growing wheat; if more labour is drawn into manufacturing industry there is clearly less labour available for farming; if a country wishes to increase its production of armaments its people will have to make do with fewer other goods than they would otherwise have been able to enjoy. From the simple fact that everything is limited in supply the chief problems of economics arise: how shall the various economic resources be shared out among the many kinds of production which compete for them? What people themselves want are the things we call consumers' goods – food, clothing, household goods, motor cars, etc. What quantity of each shall be produced? These are the questions economists try to answer.

Some economists, however, appear to have little interest in the actual problems of economic life. They prefer to analyse the working of the system, so that for them economics becomes a highly theoretical study. They seek only to understand the principles underlying economic activity, and although such study may often seem to be quite unrelated to real conditions, the tools of economic analysis have proved to be invaluable instruments for the solution of practical problems.

Commerce, in sharp contrast to much of economics, has no place for theory. It takes economic facts as they are. The student of commerce will not be asked why firms in one industry are large and why in another industry they are small; why a certain price rules in the market; why different parts of the country specialise in the production of different commodities; or why restrictions are sometimes placed on imports. These questions do not concern him. It is sufficient for him to know the facts: that in some industries most firms are large; that specialisation of production exists; that restrictions on trade have been imposed.

Commerce, as we have seen, is concerned with the distribution of goods, and the student of commerce must know how retail and wholesale trade is carried on, how goods are imported and marketed and how they are exported. Then he must know how transport, banking and insurance assist distribution. Thus he is more concerned with the 'how' than the 'why' of economic activity.

4 Why study commerce?

The student of commerce should know how his own particular occupation fits into the general scheme of commerce. A study of commerce, therefore, is useful for all who are engaged in commercial occupations, whether it be in trade or in one of the services ancillary to trade. Commerce as a subject of study can, however, fulfil a wider purpose than the merely utilitarian; it can provide a valuable introduction to a later study of economics, in which students are often handicapped by lack of knowledge of the facts of commerce.

Questions

1. Show how the various branches of commerce are related to one another.

2. What is the purpose of studying commerce?

3. The term commerce includes occupations other than that of trade. What are they, and in what ways are they connected with trade?   (RSA)

4. Explain the purpose and scope of commerce.   (GCE Camb.)

5. (a) What is the meaning of 'trade'?

(b) Describe (i) the main branches of trade and (ii) the main aids to trade.   (LCCI)

6. (a) Explain briefly the meaning of 'commerce'.

(b) Describe, with examples, how commercial activities assist industry.   (LCCI)

7. (a) Explain the meaning of the terms: (i) production; (ii) commerce.

(b) Describe the relationship between production and commerce.   (LCCI)

2 The Relationship Between Commerce and Production

1 Direct and indirect production

The main purpose of production is to satisfy man's wants. In early times people's wants were mainly for food, clothing, shelter and little else, for it took all their time and effort to satisfy even these wants to a very moderate extent. As people became more skilful at producing things it became easier for them to satisfy these basic wants. As time went on production expanded, but with every expansion of production people's wants also increased. The satisfaction of wants can be accomplished either directly or indirectly.

(*a*) *Direct production*. This occurs when someone attempts to satisfy his wants entirely by his own efforts. He may grow his own food, make his own clothing and build himself a place in which to live. If he tries to do everything for himself he will probably have to be satisfied with little more than the bare necessaries of life. In some countries, for example India, most of the people still do a great deal directly for themselves, and as a result have to accept a low standard of living.

(*b*) *Indirect production*. In this case a man spends his time at one occupation and then exchanges some of the things which he has made for goods made by other people. Exchange, therefore, is indirect production. In early days it took the form of barter, but exchange was greatly simplified by the use of money, which made possible the production of the vast and varied range of goods we

enjoy today. People nowadays work for money payments which we
call wages or salary, afterwards using the money they have earned to
purchase things made by other people. Indirect production may
take the form of producing goods for export or the provision of
services – for example, transport – for foreign countries, and
importing things from other countries in exchange. As indirect
production has increased, so has the range of man's wants, and the
countries where the people enjoy a high standard of living are those
in which indirect production has been developed to the greatest
extent.

2   Types of wants

Wants fall into two main categories.

(a) *Goods.* People require food, clothing and shelter if they are to
keep themselves alive. These are their primary wants, and until
these have been reasonably well satisfied other wants will not press
very heavily upon them. Once, however, men have satisfied their
basic needs the horizon of their wants widens, and they begin to seek
other things. At the present day a great variety of commodities is
produced, but not a year passes without some new things being put
on the market.

(b) *Services.* People's wants are not completely satisfied by
material things. In a modern community there are also many
services which they wish to have performed for them. For instance,
they like retail service to be available at conveniently situated shops
where they can buy the goods they want; they find banks useful in
assisting them to make payments and in providing other services; in
sickness they require medical services; where legal problems face
them they expect to be able to find solicitors who can advise them;
for the protection of their persons and the safeguarding of their
property they require the police; and to minister to their spiritual
welfare there are the clergy.

The production of both goods and services is undertaken to
satisfy people's wants. Economists, therefore, regard the provision
of services as a form of production.

3   What do we mean by production?

Economists recognise three different kinds of production in relation to goods.

(a) *Changing the form of a commodity*. By this we mean taking raw materials and turning them into finished articles – the sort of production we all easily recognise.

(b) *Changing the situation of a commodity*. Two things, identical in appearance, quality and structure, are not alike economically if one is in Leeds and the other in London. Clearly, it is of little use to a man in Stornoway who is in need of a raincoat to know there is a good supply in Manchester! Those people engaged in this kind of production are concerned with the transfer of goods from their place of manufacture to the consumer.

(c) *Changing the position of the commodity in time*. A bushel of wheat in February is not the same as a bushel of similar wheat in September. In order to enable us to buy commodities at the time when we want them, it is necessary for someone to build up stocks when the goods are in plentiful supply and hold them until consumers want them. This is one of the main functions of wholesalers and to a lesser degree of retailers.

Most people would probably regard only the changing of the form of the commodity as being a productive process, but production is not really completed until the goods have reached the people who actually want to consume them, so that changing the geographical situation of a commodity or the time of its availability are essentially the final stages of production, and economically they are of equal importance to changing raw materials into finished products.

We may be tempted to argue that the second and third forms of production are commercial services performed on behalf of producers, but, as we have already seen, production includes the provision of services as well as goods. In fact, all production really consists of the provision of services. When we say that certain goods – a length of cloth, a piece of china or a television set – have been manufactured we do not mean that something has actually been created. All that has happened is that the form of something has been changed: the raw wool has been spun and woven into cloth, spinners and weavers having performed these services; the form of the china clay has been changed by modelling and firing in an oven into a cup or a plate as a result of the potter's services; the television set has merely been assembled from a large number of small components by men who were paid for providing these services.

4   Consumers' and producers' goods

Finally, we may notice that the production of the commodity we want may itself be direct or indirect. What we all want are consumers' goods, that is, things which we desire for their own sake – all kinds of food, household goods, clothing, etc. The output of all these things is greatly increased if capital goods, such as machinery, are used to assist their manufacture. Capital goods, however, wear out or become out of date, and so have to be replaced. A large proportion of the total output of goods consists of capital goods or, as they are frequently called, producers' goods. These are clearly not wanted for their own sake, but only to make possible a greater production of consumers' goods. In this category, besides machinery, we should also include raw materials, partly finished goods, factory buildings and means of transport. Thus two main classes of goods are produced: consumers' goods and producers' goods.

5   Classification of productive occupations

All occupations are productive of goods or services, but only those for which payment is made are of economic importance.

Some people take up hobbies – building model yachts, for example, or model railway engines – but though such activities may occupy a great deal of their time, the work is undertaken entirely for pleasure, the articles they make not being for sale. Others spend some of their leisure in their gardens and perhaps grow fruit or a few vegetables, which they consume themselves. Many people too do odd jobs in their own houses, such as repairing a gate or a fence or papering the walls of a room. People also frequently perform similar services for friends or neighbours, payment often taking the form of a return service on another occasion. Probably, however, the largest group of people doing 'unpaid' work comprises housewives. Unpaid services of all kinds are completely ignored when the total volume of production of a country is calculated, and so they must be excluded from any classification of production.

In the following chart showing the various types of production only paid services, therefore, are included.

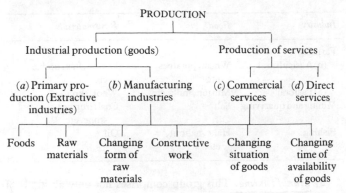

PRODUCTION

Industrial production (goods) — Production of services

(a) Primary production (Extractive industries) (b) Manufacturing industries (c) Commercial services (d) Direct services

Foods Raw materials Changing form of raw materials Constructive work Changing situation of goods Changing time of availability of goods

Thus it will be seen that there are four main branches of production. Two of these are described as industrial, one being concerned with the production of food or raw materials (primary production). The second branch of production uses the raw materials of the primary producers and turns them into finished articles. Both the third and fourth branches of production comprise two groups of services. The third branch of production comprises all services which assist the distribution of industrial products among the people who want them. These three branches all have to do with the satisfaction of material wants. In the fourth group all other paid services are included.

6   The four branches of production

(a) *Primary production*. This form of production includes all kinds of work concerned with the extraction of the fruits of the earth or sea, that is, the extractive occupations (*see* table below). In this group, therefore, we find all types of farming or associated occupations – the many branches of agriculture, the rearing of animals, market gardening and lumbering; all types of mining and quarrying; and fishing. Primary production includes occupations that have been carried on from the dawn of history – those that provide us with food and raw materials.

Industry	Food	Raw materials
Farming		
(a) Agricultural	Wheat, potatoes, etc.	Cotton, flax, timber, etc.
(b) Pastoral	Mutton, milk, etc.	Wool, skins, etc.
Mining and quarrying	Salt	Coal, iron ore, stone, etc.
Fishing	Hake, halibut, etc.	Oil

(b) *Manufacturing*. This group comprises not only all kinds of manufacturing, but also constructive work. Each of the important industries – textiles, micro electronics, computer hardware and software, chemicals, motor vehicles, etc. – provides an extensive list of occupations. For example, in the wool-textile industry there are wool scourers, sorters, twisters, spinners, weavers, dyers, finishers, bleachers, warp dressers, loom tuners, designers, burlers, menders, perchers, drawers, fettlers, feeders, pieceners. Constructive occupations include all those connected with the building and construction of roads, railways, bridges, tunnels, reservoirs and other public works.

(c) *Commercial services*. These are all services associated with the final stage of the production of goods, that is, their movement from the place of production to the final consumers or the storage of goods until consumers want them. These functions together comprise the business of distribution. The following diagram shows the relationship to one another of the various commercial occupations.

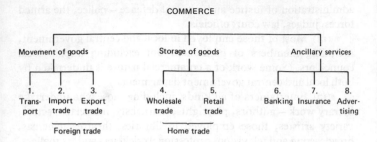

Thus, there are eight main branches of commerce – the four divisions of trade (retail, wholesale, import and export), together with transport and the three ancillary services of banking, insurance and advertising. Import and export trade are concerned with the exchange of goods (and services) with foreign countries.

The wholesaler acts between the producer (or importer if the goods come from abroad) and the retailer. The movement of goods would clearly be impossible without transport. Insurance assists those engaged in trade by relieving them of some of the risk to which goods both in transit and in store are liable. Banking, as will be seen later, offers many services to businessmen, including the provision of convenient means of payment. Advertising has become a large industry. The huge increase in the output of goods which has taken place in the past one hundred and fifty years has resulted in an even greater expansion of commerce. The number of people employed in commercial occupations tends to increase relatively to the number employed in industry.

(*d*) *Direct services*. In a highly developed society there will be many non-material wants to be satisfied, and so there will be many people whose business it is to provide services which are unconnected with the transfer or storage of goods. These are classed as direct services, since many of them are of a direct, personal nature. In this category there is a great variety of occupations, of which the following list is merely a selection.

(*i*) Those who provide personal services, such as doctors, dentists, nurses, teachers, clergy, solicitors, barristers.

(*ii*) Those engaged in the maintenance of law and order, the

administration of justice and external defence – police, the armed
forces, judges, law court officials.

(*iii*) Most of those employed in local and central government,
including members of parliament but excluding unpaid local
councillors. (Some work of a commercial nature is undertaken by
both local and central government departments.)

(*iv*) Entertainers of all kinds, including those who undertake
literary work – authors, playrights, journalists, musicians, actors,
variety artistes, those employed in libraries, theatres, cinemas,
broadcasting and television, professional cricketers and footballers,
etc.

(*v*) Domestic servants and hotel employees.

7   Distribution of labour according to occupation

The table on p. 17 shows the number of people in the United
Kingdom who are employed in different occupations.

It is unfortunately not possible to use this table to calculate the
numbers employed in the four branches of production, since some
of the above groups include people from more than one branch. Of
those listed, for example, as performing professional and financial
services some are engaged in commercial, others in direct, services.
The extractive industries, however, are more clearly defined, and
these now employ only 3½ per cent of the working population as
compared with 5 per cent ten years earlier. It is of interest to note
that even in Australia, which we are apt to regard as being principally
a primary producer, only 12 per cent of the people work at extractive
occupations, as against 28 per cent in manufacturing, the remaining
60 per cent being almost equally divided between commerce and
direct services.

The higher the standard of economic life reached by a community,
the greater will be the number of people it can afford to employ on
direct services. In the United Kingdom, as in Australia, about 30
per cent of the working population is employed in this way. The
basic wants of these people, however, have to be met by the efforts
and exertions of those engaged in the production and distribution of
goods. The maintenance of a large number of people on direct
services is therefore impossible unless society has attained a fairly

advanced level of economic development. It seems reasonable, then, to conclude that both Britain and Australia enjoy a high standard of living.

Distribution of employment in Britain, 1977 and 1981

Occupation	1977 (000)	1981 (000)
Total, all industries and services	22,126	20,729
Total, all manufacturing industries	7,150	5,926
Agriculture, forestry and fishing	378	352
Mining and quarrying	348	331
Food, drink and tobacco	689	613
Coal and petroleum products	36	37
Chemicals and allied industries	433	393
Metal manufacture	483	326
Mechanical engineering	915	742
Instrument engineering	148	123
Electrical engineering	745	649
Shipbuilding and marine engineering	172	137
Vehicles	739	626
Metal goods not elsewhere specified	532	426
Textiles	480	343
Clothing and footwear	410	330
Bricks, pottery, glass, cement, etc.	258	212
Timber, furniture, etc.	253	223
Paper, printing and publishing	531	488
Other manufacturing industries	324	258
Construction	1,232	1,105
Gas, electricity and water	337	331
Transport and communication	1,447	1,420
Distributive trades	2,700	2,583
Insurance, banking, finance and business services	1,128	1,213
Professional and scientific services	3,546	3,586
Miscellaneous services	2,294	2,357
National government services	621	584
Local government services	943	942
HM Forces	327	334
Unemployed	1,390	2,577

Source: *Annual Abstract of Statistics*, 1983.

8   The volume of production

If we add together the output of goods and services which result
from the efforts of all the people engaged in the four groups of
occupations during a particular year we arrive at the total volume of
production for that year. One difficulty in computing such a total is
at once apparent: how are we to add together this heterogeneous
mass of items? We might, as has been done in Britain on one or two
occasions, compile a list giving the quantities of the different kinds
of goods produced during a selected year. This would show how
many tonnes of coal were mined, how many metres of cloth were
woven, how many pairs of boots and shoes were made, how many
ships were built, how many tonnes of wheat were produced and so
on. This would be a census of production.

9   The national income

A census of production, however, does not show a complete total of
production in the sense the word has been used in this chapter, since
it takes no account of all the various services supplied during the
period. This is a very serious omission, since in countries such as
Britain a quarter or more of the working population is employed on
direct services. But if these services are to be included how are they
to be reckoned – as so many hours of work? A comprehensive total
can be computed only if we cease calculating in terms of tonnes,
metres, square metres, litres, pairs, hours, and use the common
measure of money. This again unfortunately has a serious drawback:
unlike the metre or litre, it is not itself a fixed measure, for a certain
amount of money will buy different quantities of goods at dif-
erent times. Yet this is the only means by which such a varied
mass of goods can be added together. As a result great care
has to be exercised if comparison is made between one year and
another.

So far the term 'volume of production' has been used to indicate the total goods and services produced in a year. The money value of this production constitutes a country's national income. It is an important indicator of a country's economic health and a measure of its economic progress. Variations in its size and its growth have implications for the levels of employment, investment, consumer expenditure, and so on – in fact, all aspects of commerce.

All governments collect information from several different sources in order to measure their national incomes. In the UK the national income is calculated by the Central Statistical Office (CSO) and the figures are published annually in the *Blue Book of National Income and Expenditure*. National income statistics are useful for several reasons:

(a) to assist the government in planning and managing the economy;

(b) to assist firms in making decisions concerning their future levels of sales, for example, whether they increase or reduce production;

(c) to guide the trade unions in formulating their wage claims for the year ahead;

(d) to provide information useful in making inter-temporal comparisons of the standard of living;

(e) to enable international comparisons of the standard of living to be made; and

(f) to provide the information necessary for the calculation of a country's contributions to international organisations such as the IMF and the OECD.

A country's national income measures not only the value of total output over a given period; it is also a measure of (a) all the incomes received in that period of time, and (b) all the different types of expenditure made in that period of time. Hence national income is measured in three ways: the expenditure method, the income method and the output method. These three methods reflect the fact that an economic transaction (i.e. one involving the exchange of money) embodies three aspects. For example, if A pays B £20 to cut his lawn, A spends £20 (total expenditure = £20), B provides £20 worth of services (total output or product = £20), and B receives income of £20 (total income = £20). Extending this to the whole economy, the following identity emerges:

national expenditure ≡ national product ≡ national income.

These three related concepts will now be considered in turn.

(a) *The expenditure method.* The first step is to measure the various components of domestic expenditure and add them together. Various adjustments are then made to this total to provide an estimate of national income. These adjustments include international trade, the effects of taxes and subsidies, and depreciation of capital equipment (known as capital consumption). The final figure, which is known as *net national expenditure at factor cost*, is the national income. In 1982 the national income as measured by the expenditure method was as shown in the table opposite.

(b) *The output method.* Here, the value of the output of goods and services of the various industries is calculated; for example, agriculture, forestry and fishing; manufacturing; construction; education and so on. Once again, adjustments are made to the total, including one (the 'residual error') which arises from the use of different sources of information (data). This approach provides a useful measure of the changing structure of the economy. For example, a comparison of the estimates of the percentage of the gross domestic product (GDP) attributable to manufacturing indicates that the relative importance of manufacturing has declined for several years. The national income as measured by the output method for 1982 was as shown in the table on p. 22.

(c) *The income method.* In this approach to national income the various types of incomes received are added together and a number of adjustments are made to the total to give a third measure. Transfer payments are omitted as these are merely transfers of income from taxpayers to groups such as pensioners, students, the sick and the unemployed. There is no corresponding production of goods and services in such cases. The residual error of £50 million is again taken into account in order to bring the total derived by this method into line with that derived by the other two methods. As a result, the totals calculated by the three different methods will be the same. The national income for 1982 calculated by the income method is shown on p. 23. It can be seen that the total is consistent with the totals arrived at by the other two methods of calculation, hence the identity stated on p. 20.

National income: the expenditure method (1982)

		£ million
Consumers' expenditure		167,128
Government expenditure:		
central government	36,675	
local authorities	23,407	60,082
Gross domestic fixed capital formation		42,172
Value of physical increase in stocks and work-in-progress		−1,162
Total domestic expenditure		268,220
Exports of goods and services		73,128
Total final expenditure		341,348
Less imports of goods and services		−67,165
Gross domestic product at market prices		274,183
Less taxes on expenditure		−47,082
Plus subsidies		5,452
Gross domestic product at factor cost		232,553
Add net property income from abroad		1,577
Gross national product at factor cost		234,130
Less capital consumption		−33,057
National income (net national expenditure at factor cost)		201,073

Source: *National Income and Expenditure*, HMSO 1983.

National income: the output method (1982)

	£ million
Agriculture, forestry and fishing	5,752
Energy and water supply	26,307
Manufacturing	55,222
Construction	13,480
Distribution, hotels and catering, repairs	29,971
Transport	10,311
Communications	6,853
Banking, finance, insurance, business services, leasing	16,782
Ownership of dwellings	14,690
Public administration, national defence, social security	16,724
Education and health services	20,868
Other services	15,543
Total output	232,503
Residual error	50
Gross domestic product at factor cost	232,553
Net property income from abroad	1,577
Gross national product at factor cost	234,130
Less capital consumption	−33,057
National income (net national product at factor cost)	201,073

Source: *National Income and Expenditure*, HMSO 1983.

National income: the income method (1982)

	£ million
Income from employment	155,133
Income from self-employment	20,068
Gross trading profits of companies	33,344
Gross trading surplus of public corporations	9,068
Gross trading surplus of government enterprises	124
Rent	16,166
Imputed charge for consumption of non-trading capital	2,507
Total domestic income	236,410
Less stock appreciation	−3,907
Gross domestic product (income-based)	232,503
Residual error	50
Gross domestic product (expenditure-based)	232,553
Net property income from abroad	1,577
Gross national product at factor cost	234,130
Less capital consumption	33,057
National income (net national *income* at factor cost)	201,073

Source: *National Income and Expenditure*, HMSO 1983.

Questions

1. What is meant by 'indirect' production? Describe briefly the various forms of production.

2. Distinguish between consumers' and producers' goods. What is the importance of making this distinction?

3. Show how occupations can be classified. Into which groups would you put the following: (*a*) coal miners; (*b*) shopkeepers; (*c*) railway engine drivers; (*d*) cotton spinners; (*e*) a concert violinist?

4. Make a list of the eight main branches of commerce and show how each assists the fulfilment of the purpose of commerce.

5. What do you understand by the terms (a) production and (b) commerce? How are the two connected?   (RSA)

6. Into what general classification should each of the following occupations be put: miner, weaver, farmer, typist, actor, shop-keeper?   (WR)

7. Describe the main classes of occupation which are concerned with the production and distribution of goods. Show clearly the various kinds of commercial occupation.   (NCTEC)

8. Explain carefully the differences between commerce and industry, and illustrate to what extent they are interdependent.   (NCTEC)

9. It is said that commercial workers act as a connecting link. Explain fully what is meant by this.   (LCCI)

10. It is sometimes stated that persons engaged in commercial occupations are non-productive. How far do you agree with this view?   (WJEC)

11. Distinguish between industry, commerce and direct services.
                                                                  (GCEJMB)

12. Describe (a) the main commercial occupations and (b) their role in the work of production.   (LCCI)

13. (a) Classify industrial occupations and explain their contribution to production.

(b) Explain why banking and insurance can be described as productive occupations.   (LCCI)

14. Select four commercial occupations and explain the part they play in the working of the economy.   (LCCI)

15. In December 1981 in the UK there were 700,000 people employed in primary production. There were about 16 million employed in the private sector and about 4.5 million employed in the public sector including 2 million in local government. Trade union membership was about 13 million.

(a) Explain the underlined terms. Give examples to illustrate your answer.   (8 marks)

(b) State two main purposes of trade unions.   (4 marks)

(c) The number of employees in a company is one way of describing its size. Give two other methods which could also be used to compare the size of companies.   (2 marks)

(d) Explain two ways in which a public limited company differs from a public corporation.   (6 marks)
                                                              (RSA Elem.)

3 Expansion of Commerce

1 Production without exchange

In the simplest type of community there would be no commerce. An individual living entirely alone and with no contact with the outside world would be entirely dependent for his livelihood upon his own exertions. Consider the case of Alexander Selkirk, an eighteenth-century mariner, who had a disagreement with the captain of his ship as a result of which he asked to be put ashore on the uninhabited island of Juan Fernandez, some miles off the coast of Ecuador. There he lived quite alone for over four years before he was eventually picked up. (It was this remarkable adventure of Alexander Selkirk that prompted Defoe to write *Robinson Crusoe*.)

While he was on the island Selkirk might proudly declare: 'I am monarch of all I survey', but only those of his wants which he could satisfy by his own unaided efforts could receive attention. When hungry he had to go out and gather wild fruit, kill an animal or a bird, or catch fish. If he was in need of clothing he had to make it himself from the skins of the animals he had killed. For shelter he built himself a simple log cabin. In such circumstances there was no possibility of his making an exchange of goods with anyone. Since he had to do everything for himself, he would probably be able to satisfy only the most pressing of his basic wants; he would be so preoccupied with providing himself with food, clothing and shelter that he would have little time for anything else.

The simplest type of community in normal circumstances,

however, was the family. Like the solitary mariner, the main concern in a primitive society was with the business of keeping oneself alive, and even this was a hard struggle. Much would depend on the natural resources of the region and the people's own capabilities. A certain measure of division of labour would probably prevail, the mother looking after the home and children, the father and the older children taking over responsibility for providing food and, if necessary, undertaking the defence of the homestead. The tribe was simply an expansion of the family, but it made possible a greater degree of division of labour, freeing perhaps one or two members from the business of seeking food - the headman and his immediate followers and in some cases also a small group of special warriors. With the development of agriculture the women often took over the cultivation of the land, thereby giving the men more time to devote to fighting. There was still no commerce, however, for the tribe was self-sufficient, except for any goods which might be obtained by force from a rival tribe. (Compare the cattle-stealing raids which Highland clansmen used to make on Scottish farmers of the Lowlands.)

2 The first commerce

It was not until peaceful contact between different groups of people became possible that the first commercial transactions took place. For this a certain level of civilisation had to be reached. The Vikings of Scandinavia took to the sea to seek out other peoples, but only to rob and pillage or to found new homes for themselves. On the other hand, early traders like the Phoenicians sailed to other lands in search of things they could not obtain in their homelands, taking with them some of their own handiwork to offer in exchange.

The earliest forms of exchange, therefore, would be by barter, that is, by the exchange of goods for goods. Similarly, as community life developed it became possible for those people with the necessary ability or aptitude to specialise in certain occupations, in this way acquiring even greater skill. So craftsmen emerged. Once this stage had been reached exchange became essential, for a man could specialise in his craft only if he knew he could exchange some of the things he had made for food and other necessaries.

3   Drawbacks to barter

There are, however, three serious drawbacks to barter.

(a) Before a transaction can take place it is necessary not merely to find someone who can offer what the other person requires, but someone who is at the same time willing to accept what is offered in exchange; i.e. there must be a 'double coincidence of wants'.

(b) The exchange of large for small commodities is difficult, since the person with the large commodity may not want a large amount of the smaller commodity.

(c) Even when these two difficulties have been overcome it remains to be decided how much of one thing is to be given in exchange for a quantity of the other, i.e. what is to be the rate of exchange.

4   The use of money

It was to overcome the drawbacks of barter that money came to be used as a medium of exchange. Many different commodities have served this purpose, e.g. cattle and cowrie shells. In fact, anything that is generally acceptable can serve as money. In early days the commodity selected as the medium of exchange was always something which was regarded as valuable for its own sake, so that if it ceased to function as money it could still be used for its original purpose. The precious metals (gold and silver) were soon found to perform the functions of money more satisfactorily than other commodities – small quantities of them had considerable value, the supply was limited, they were easily divisible for making small payments, they could be carried about without difficulty (portable) and they were durable.

The use of money made possible even greater specialisation of production, and as a consequence both a greater variety of goods and increasing quantities of them became available for exchange. Money overcame all three drawbacks to barter. After money came into use it was sufficient for (say) Jones to seek out someone capable of supplying him with what he wanted; no longer was it necessary for the supplier to be willing to take what Jones had to offer in exchange.

Money simplified the transaction. Jones merely handed over a sum of money which Brown, the seller, could himself use at a convenient time to purchase something he wanted. Money also facilitated the transaction in another way: Brown could assign prices to the goods he was offering for sale. Though Jones and Brown might still haggle over the price, this was a simpler matter than trying to determine how many eggs should be given in exchange for a pair of shoes. Exchange having become easier, more transactions could take place than when such a clumsy method as barter was employed. Even more specialisation, therefore, became possible.

Thus, exchange becomes an indirect method of production. Jones can make himself a chair or he can devote himself to some other pursuit for which he has a special aptitude, and then perhaps make an exchange with Brown, who is more skilful than he is at furniture making. From what has already been said it should be clear now that the greater the extent of specialisation or division of labour, the greater the amount of exchange, that is, the greater the extent of commerce.

5   Advantages of specialisation

The chief advantage of specialisation is that it enables a man to work at that occupation for which he has a natural bent. By spending the whole of his working time at one trade he becomes more skilful at it than others and capable not only of producing a better chair or piece of cloth but also of doing the work more quickly. Thus, specialisation results in a greater volume of production. But the greater the extent of specialisation, that is, the fewer things a man does for himself, the greater the amount of exchange required to distribute goods among those wanting them. Increasing specialisation, therefore, brought about a corresponding expansion of commerce.

6 Extension of division of labour

At first, then, every person did everything for himself. The first stage in the division of labour occurred when men began to specialise in particular trades, and for the first time exchange became necessary.

The second stage in the development of division of labour was reached when the various processes in the production of a commodity were undertaken by different men, each of whom acquired skill in the performance of a single operation. Although every process was still carried out by hand, as when one man did the whole of the work, a huge increase in total output was achieved. Adam Smith, the first great writer on economics, was amazed at the effect on output of division of labour, and in his book, *The Wealth of Nations*, he devotes many pages to this topic. To support his argument he quotes the case of making pins, showing that before division of labour was introduced each man made on an average only 20 pins a day, whereas afterwards the average per man rose to the huge total of 4,800 pins a day. Once the stage was reached where a man undertook a single process in the manufacture of a commodity the time was ripe for the introduction of machinery.

7 Effect of the Industrial Revolution

The revolution in industry, which occurred during the late eighteenth and early nineteenth centuries, was brought about by the invention of machinery and the application of power to drive it – at first water-power and then steam. As a result, industry came to be concentrated on the coalfields, and in time most of the domestic industries, carried on in the homes of the workers, died out. Thus, the cotton industry came to be centred in South Lancashire, the woollen industry in the West Riding of Yorkshire, the manufacture of cutlery in Sheffield, pottery manufacture in North Staffordshire, the manufacture of bicycles – and later, motor cars – in the West Midland area, and so on. The use of power-driven machinery still further increased the output of all kinds of goods, increased division of labour later making possible the mass production of a great variety of cheap goods well within the reach of most wage-earners.

The concentration of industries in particular areas made possible a third stage in the development of the division of labour – the specialisation of individual firms in particular processes. The localisation of industries and the huge increase in the quantity of goods produced required a correspondingly vast increase in the work of distribution. As a result of the Industrial Revolution there was, therefore, also a great expansion of commerce.

8   International division of labour

The fourth stage in the division of labour takes us into the international field. If all countries specialise in the production of those commodities for which they have the greatest advantages compared with other countries, the output of all commodities, taking the world as a whole, will be much greater than if countries pursue aims of self-sufficiency by attempting to produce as great a variety of goods as possible. As the student will learn later, many difficulties stand in the way of the complete development of international division of labour. For example, in the case of some things countries are generally unwilling to become dependent on others for the satisfaction of their wants: food production may be encouraged even though it could be obtained more cheaply from abroad, because of fear of starvation if subjected to enemy blockade in time of war. Nevertheless, some countries by reason of climate or geology are capable of producing certain things which others cannot produce: most jute is grown in north-east India: most nickel comes from Canada. Commodities in this category were the first to enter into international trade, the Phoenicians, for example, seeking to trade with other peoples who could supply them with the things which they could not produce themselves.

Each widening of the range of specialisation makes possible a greater output of goods than could be produced previously, and at lower cost, but as specialisation increases so does the work of distribution. An expansion of commerce has, therefore, followed every increase of specialisation. Specialisation in the international sphere has brought into being an interdependent world.

At the present day no country can make economic progress if it attempts to supply all its own needs itself. Britain is largely dependent on Australia, New Zealand and South Africa for raw wool; on the United States, India and Egypt for cotton; on Brazil and Kenya for coffee; on Sweden for iron ore and so on. In return Britain supplies many countries with manufactured goods. Within the borders of the United Kingdom people are dependent on Teeside for chemicals, on West Yorkshire for worsteds and woollens and on the East Midlands for boots and shoes. The greater the extent to which division of labour is carried, the greater is our dependence upon other people for the satisfaction of our wants.

9 The ancillaries of commerce

The huge expansion of trade during the past hundred and fifty years would not have been possible, however, without a corresponding development of the various services that in many ways assist trade – transport, banking and insurance. Chief perhaps among these was transport. Side by side with industrial development went improvement in means of transport. Roads and canals were built, railways and new harbours and docks constructed, larger and faster ships made their appearance on the oceans of the world. Industrial expansion and transport development had to go hand in hand, because otherwise it would have been impossible to distribute the huge output of goods that flowed from large-scale industry.

In banking the development of the use of the cheque as a means of payment greatly facilitated the carrying to completion of commercial transactions; methods of transferring sums of money from one part of the world to another were also developed. Bankers, as we shall see later, also helped to finance industrial development.

Insurance has lessened the risks associated with the carrying on of most kinds of economic activity – the risk that goods will be lost at sea, that they may be damaged during transit or during storage, the risk of fire and so on. By accepting these risks in return for a relatively small premium, insurance assisted the expansion of both manufacturing and commerce by making businessmen more willing to undertake risky enterprises, and so still further helped to increase industry and trade. Large-scale production required an expansion of distribution, and both these necessitated a more efficient transport system, better banking and wider insurance facilities, so that all these developments were linked together.

Questions

1. Is existence possible without commerce?

2. What are the chief drawbacks to barter?

3. How did the use of money assist the development of commerce?

4. What were the main stages in the development of the division of labour? What are the advantages of the division of labour?

5. Show how the expansion of industry and commerce are linked together.

6. 'Without money we should have to return to a system of bartering.'

(a) Why would this method of exchange be undesirable?

(b) Describe the functions of money in a modern economy.   (LCCI)

7. 'Money is a medium, a measure, a standard and a store.' Describe the functions of money in relation to this statement.   (LCCI)

8. (a) What are the main benefits of the division of labour?

(b) Explain briefly how the division of labour operates in a modern industrial economy.   (LCCI)

9. (a) Explain the term 'division of labour'.

(b) Illustrate, with examples, the advantages and disadvantages of this method of industrial organisation in a large manufacturing firm.   (LCCI)

4   The Business Unit

1   Types of business unit

At the present day many different forms of business unit exist side by side. At one extreme there is the small 'one-man' business, employing perhaps only a few thousand pounds' worth of capital; at the other end of the scale are the giant public companies and the public corporations with capital assets running into thousands of millions of pounds.

As the scale of production has increased, new forms of business enterprise have been developed. Nevertheless, in many lines of industrial and commercial activity the small business still survives. As a result business units do not conform to a standard pattern, various forms of organisation being available to meet the varying needs of different kinds of firm. It is necessary, therefore, to consider the different types of organisation, their advantages and disadvantages. The following are the main types of business unit.

(a) The sole proprietor.
(b) Partnerships.
(c) The private company.
(d) The public company.
(e) The public corporation (*see* Chapter 5).

2   The sole proprietor

In this type of business one person is solely responsible for providing the capital and for bearing the risks of the enterprise. He is its sole owner and upon his shoulders alone falls the burden of management. His success or failure depends upon himself; he takes the profit or stands the losses.

In some cases the proprietor may employ no one but himself, with the possible exception of an errand-boy or an apprentice. These are the smallest firms, but it is not a necessary feature of the business of a sole proprietor that it should be a 'one-man' business in this narrow sense. The essential condition is that one man should be responsible for the provision of the capital and the management of the undertaking. Though generally small at the start, many businesses of this kind have developed into large firms, employing hundreds of workpeople, and have still retained this form of organisation, though more frequently expansion of a firm has led to – or been the result of – its being turned into a partnership or a limited company.

Until 1982 sole proprietors, as well as other types of business units trading under names other than their own, had to supply details of ownership to the Registry of Business Names. In 1982 this was abolished so that today if a sole proprietor or other type of business unit trades under a name other than his own, his actual name and address must be shown on invoices, letter headings and any other stationery and displayed at the business address.

Sole proprietors remain the most common form of business unit in the UK and they are a vital part of the country's business structure. Two of the areas of commercial activity in which sole proprietorships are most commonly to be found are retailing and building. Both of these activities tend to be labour-intensive rather than capital-intensive. Nevertheless, in terms of capital and numbers of persons employed, sole proprietorships are of limited importance. In recent years there has been a steady fall in the number of sole proprietors for several reasons, for example:

(a) lack of capital to invest in new premises and equipment;

(b) competition from the large stores and other forms of larger business units which are able to benefit from various economies of scale;

(c) changes in shopping patterns caused by an increase in married women at work and a rise in car ownership;

(*d*) higher overheads and administrative costs caused by increased rates and costs of VAT collection.

3 Advantages and disadvantages of the sole proprietor

(*a*) *Advantages.* The following are some of the chief advantages that the sole proprietor enjoys.

(*i*) It is in his own interest to make his business efficient and successful. Self-interest can be a powerful driving force, and a sole proprietor will often put more effort into his work than a man working for someone else.

(*ii*) Decisions can be made and put into effect at once without the necessity to consult others and convince them of the wisdom of the proposal.

(*iii*) The smallness of the business makes it possible for the proprietor personally to keep in touch with every side of its activity, and this makes for greater efficiency.

(*iv*) A more personal relationship is possible between the employer and his employees who as a result understand better one another's point of view.

(*v*) The sole proprietor too can take a personal interest in his customers and so meet their requirements more easily and more fully. This is of particular importance if he is prepared to allow credit.

(*b*) *Disadvantages.* There are, however, serious drawbacks to this type of business, of which the following may be noted.

(*i*) All the advantages listed above make it possible for the business of a sole proprietor to reach a high standard of efficiency, but everything depends upon the ability, skill and energy of the man in control. The founder of the business may possess these qualities to a high degree, but his successor may have little business ability.

(*ii*) The continuance of the business is uncertain, for there may be no one to follow the proprietor. He may bequeath it to a successor, but capital gains tax falls heavily on businesses of this type which as a result can be seriously embarrassed.

(*iii*) Since the capital is provided by the proprietor himself, the size of the business is necessarily limited and expansion is not easy.

(*iv*) The proprietor is personally liable for any debts the firm may incur, i.e. he has no special legal status.

This form of business undertaking is suitable, therefore, for the man with a little capital of his own who wishes to set up on his own account. At one time most businesses were of this type, but the growing scale of production has made it increasingly difficult for the small man to establish himself as a manufacturer. In the retail trade, however, the typical business unit is still that of the sole proprietor, in spite of the growth of large-scale trading even in this field. Many small tradesmen – plumbers, joiners, electricians – and some professional men – architects, solicitors and accountants – run undertakings of this kind. It is also a useful and convenient form of undertaking where production is carried out on a small scale because the demand for the product is small; for example, where special lines are manufactured, where variety is preferred to the standardisation of mass production or where a high degree of craftsmanship is involved.

4   Partnerships

A partnership is legally defined by the Partnership Act 1890 as 'the relation between persons carrying on a business in common with a view to profit'. A number of people can combine together for the purpose of running a business, but the number of partners, except in the case of accountants, solicitors and stockbrokers, must not exceed twenty. The Companies Act 1967 empowered the then Board of Trade (now Department of Trade and Industry) in particular cases to raise the limit for banking partnerships to twenty.

There are two kinds of partnership: ordinary and limited. In the ordinary partnership all the partners are responsible for the debts of the firm. Under the Limited Partnership Act 1907 the responsibility of partners enjoying limited liability is restricted to the amount of capital they have invested in the business, but in such a partnership there must be at least one general partner whose liability for the debts of the firm is not limited in any way. Limited partners, because they can take no share in the management of the firm, are also called 'sleeping partners'.

The limited partnership is rarely met with, since the private company with limited liability is superior to it. It is advisable that partners should regulate their relationship by a legally executed Deed of Partnership. Limited partnerships must be registered with the Registrar of Companies.

5 Advantages and disadvantages of partnerships

(a) *Advantages*.

(i) They are easily formed.

(ii) By turning the business of a sole proprietor into a partnership the capital of the firm can be increased.

(iii) Greater specialisation in the management becomes possible, each partner making himself responsible for one department of the firm. In a small manufacturing business, for example, one partner can be in charge of the technical side and the other the commercial. In the retail trade partners often take charge of branch shops.

(iv) The introduction of a new partner with new ideas may prevent a firm from getting into a rut and so will increase its efficiency.

(b) *Disadvantages*.

(i) The partners (other than any limited partners) are individually responsible for the debts of the firm, even to the extent of their private possessions.

(ii) Any general partner can bind the other partners by his actions. It is essential, therefore, to be certain of a person's integrity and business ability before entering into partnership with him.

(iii) The success of a partnership depends in a large measure on the ability of the partners to work harmoniously together. Serious disagreement may lead to the dissolution of the partnership.

(iv) As with the sole proprietor this type of business lacks continuity of existence, since the death of a partner may bring it to an end. In any case such a contingency requires a reorganisation of the partnership.

Partnerships are to be found carrying on most activities undertaken by sole proprietors. There are many examples both in the retail and wholesale trade of firms carrying on business under such designations as Smith and Brown, Robinson & Son, Jackson Bros. They are frequently found in professional practices as the rules of professional bodies often prohibit their members from forming companies (*see* below). Often firms of accountants or solicitors have very cumbersome titles, sometimes bearing the names of as many as four or even five partners. Partnerships between doctors or dentists too are not uncommon. Though the capital of a partnership may be greater than that of a sole proprietor, it is generally too small for many kinds of manufacturing, and the partnership, therefore, is not the most suitable type of business unit for this kind of activity. Where expensive capital equipment is not required, however, and where production is for a limited market partnerships can quite well undertake some forms of manufacturing.

6   The limited company or joint stock company

The typical business unit of the present day is the limited company, of which there are two main kinds – private and public. A limited company can be defined as a group of persons associated together for the purpose of undertaking some form of business activity. Its principal characteristic, whether it be a public or a private company, is that its capital is divided into shares, which people can take up in varying amounts, the firm's profits being divided among the shareholders in proportion to the number of shares held.

Companies can be established by Royal Charter, as was the case with the Bank of England; by Acts of Parliament, as were the original railway companies; or by registration under the Companies Act 1948, as amended by the Companies Acts of 1967, 1976 and 1980. Most companies today are registered companies.

Limited liability. Both private and public joint stock companies can offer all their shareholders limited liability, that is, their liability is limited to the nominal value of the shares they hold. If the shares are fully paid up no further demands can be made upon them. When a shareholder's liability is unlimited it means that his private possessions can be seized if necessary to pay the debts of the firm. At the present day there are very few unlimited companies in existence.

The main advantage of limited liability is that it encourages people of moderate means – the main body of investors – to purchase shares in companies; without it the raising of large amounts of capital would be difficult. In a few rare cases – generally non-profit-making concerns like professional bodies – liability is limited by guarantee, each member guaranteeing to pay an agreed sum if necessary.

7   The private company and the limited company

The Companies Act 1980 fundamentally changed the classification of public and private companies. Under this Act any company has to have at least two members. There is no maximum number. A public company has to state in its Memorandum of Association that it is a public company and it must be registered as such. It can invite the public to subscribe for its shares and debentures. Private companies are not permitted to do this. Public companies have to place the words 'public limited company' or the abbreviation 'plc' or 'PLC' after their name, and they must have a minimum authorised and allotted share capital of £50,000. Whereas a private company may begin trading immediately it has registered and so has obtained its 'certificate of incorporation', a public company has to obtain a 'trading certificate' first after it has proved that it has issued its authorised minimum share capital. Before 1980 the number of shareholders in a private company was limited to fifty but with this restriction now removed they can grow and develop like public companies provided that shares are not offered to the general public (this is now a criminal offence). Non-public share offers are now available to private companies, for example through bankers or business contacts.

It is important to appreciate that the 1980 Act defines a public company so that any company which does not meet the requirements of that Act is a private company. This is the reverse of pre-1980 company legislation. The 1980 Act was passed to bring UK company law into line with that prevailing in the European Economic Community.

In 1983 there were 904,336 private companies and 6,427 public companies in England and Wales. However, in terms of capital, public companies are far more important than private companies and have been responsible for the enormous expansion of industry, trade and commerce in the present century; for example, in banking, electronics, motor vehicles, chemicals and newspapers.

8   Advantages and disadvantages of limited companies

(a) *Advantages.*

(i) They can obtain much greater amounts of capital than either sole proprietors or partnerships. This is particularly true of public companies, some of which have capital running to thousands of millions of pounds. Thus the existence of the public limited company makes possible production on a large scale.

(ii) They make it possible for small investors to become shareholders. Only in this way can very large amounts of capital be obtained.

(iii) Unlike the business of the sole proprietor and the partnership, the public company has a continuous existence which is not affected by the death of even the largest shareholder.

(iv) Legal regulations safeguard the interests of shareholders and people who deal with the company.

(v) All the members can enjoy limited liability. This is probably the most important advantage that the private company possesses over the partnership.

(vi) Greater specialisation of functions becomes possible.

(b) *Disadvantages.*

(i) Management and ownership become separated, although the largest shareholder often becomes the managing director.

(ii) The large company is an impersonal organisation, and close relations between management and employees are often difficult to sustain. It is to try to bridge this gap that large firms nowadays have a personnel department, the main function of which is to keep in touch with the employees. It takes charge of such matters as the interviewing of new applicants, the introduction of new workers to their jobs, promotion, training and welfare matters affecting the workers.

(iii) The large size of companies tends to make for bureaucratic control. The larger the firm, the more necessary are rules and regulations ('red tape') to ensure smooth working. As a result there is often less scope for employees to show initiative.

(iv) The primary concern of most of the shareholders is the amount of dividend they are to receive, and they may show little interest in any long-term policy involving some present sacrifice in the hope of a future gain. They may too show little care for the conditions under which the employees work.

(v) As the size of the firm increases so does the complexity of management, and people capable of successfully filling the highest managerial posts are few in numbers.

Many of these disadvantages arise as a result of large size and, therefore, do not apply to the same extent to the private limited company, which is often quite a small, family business since there need be no more than two shareholders, so that it is in a sense a sort of partnership with limited liability for all the partners. Many a sole proprietor has turned his business into a private company by inviting his wife or some other member of his family to join him, simply in order to secure the protection of limited liability. Disadvantages resulting from large size are not restricted to public companies, but occur too in the other kinds of large-scale organisation considered in the next chapter.

9   Management of a limited company

The capital of a limited company is provided by the shareholders, who elect the directors, usually voting according to the number of shares they hold. Thus, the greater the number of shares a person holds, the greater will be his influence on the voting at a shareholders' meeting.

The board of directors is mainly responsible for the general policy of the business. They may elect one of their number – usually one of the larger shareholders – to act as managing director, and so to be responsible for the day-to-day management of the firm, or they may appoint someone from outside as general manager to undertake these duties.

10   Other types of business unit

Building societies and friendly societies are really special forms of limited companies, controlled respectively by the Building Societies Acts and the Friendly Societies Acts, instead of by the Companies Acts. Like companies, they have to be registered and make returns to their own registrars. In the case of a building society the minimum number of shareholders is three. Friendly societies enjoy certain privileges in regard to exemption from taxation, as compared with companies, but are subject to the restriction that no shareholder can have a holding of more than £1,000. Co-operative societies are classed as friendly societies, and their organisation is discussed in Chapter 17.

Questions

1. For what types of economic activity is the sole proprietor the most suitable form of business unit?

2. Compare the partnership and the private company as forms of business unit.

3. In what ways has the introduction of limited liability assisted industrial development?

4. The typical firm today is said to be the public company. What reasons can you give for this?

5. What are the chief differences between a partnership and a limited company? (UEI)

6. How does a private limited company differ from a partnership? Why are partnerships often converted into private companies? (UEI)

7. Why do professional men often go into partnership, while manufacturing businesses generally take the form of companies? (LCCI)

8. What advantages does a private limited company possess in relation to a partnership? Are there any disadvantages? (LCCI)

9. Describe the advantages and disadvantages of the joint stock company compared with those of partnerships and sole traders. (WJEC)

10. Describe (a) the advantages and (b) any drawbacks of a sole tradership compared with other forms of business organisation. (LCCI)

11. State the meaning and importance in the formation of a company of each of the following: (a) memorandum of association; (b) articles of association; (c) certificate of incorporation; (d) trading certificate. (LCCI)

12. Describe (a) the advantages and (b) any disadvantages of a partnership compared with other forms of business ownership. (LCCI)

13. Describe the functions of the following in relation to a public company: (a) the board of directors, (b) the managing director; (c) debenture holders; (d) ordinary shareholders. (LCCI)

14. (a) Compare and contrast the organisation and structure of a private limited company with a public limited company.

(b) What justification is there for these two different types of limited liability company? (LCCI)

15. (a) Explain the term 'limited liability'.

(b) What are (i) the advantages and (ii) the disadvantages of forming a limited liability company? (LCCI)

16. (a) What is meant by 'limited liability'?

(b) Describe the methods by which a public limited company may raise capital. (LCCI)

17. The Jobba Brothers operate a timber building construction business as a partnership. Garden Buildings Ltd. is a private company also constructing and marketing timber buildings. Compare and contrast the two forms of firm in respect of their: (a) formation and organisation; (b) labour requirements; (c) methods of financing; (d) purchasing of materials; (e) marketing policies; (f) legal obligations. (RSA Inter.)

18. (a) Name *three* types of business organisation, *apart from companies*, which operate in the private sector of the economy. (3 marks)

(b) How do private and public sector businesses differ as regards ownership, financing and profit distribution?   (*6 marks*)

(*c*) Choose any *one* of the types of organisation which you have given in part (a) and state its special features.   (*5 marks*)

(*d*) If a business was a large manufacturing company, name and give the function of any *three* departments into which it might divide its internal operations.   (*6 marks*)

(RSA Elem.)

19. (*a*) Explain briefly what is meant by 'unlimited liability' in relation to a business organisation.   (*3 marks*)

(*b*) Give *three* sources, other than personal savings, from which a sole proprietor could obtain additional capital.   (*9 marks*)

(*c*) Outline *two* advantages and *two* disadvantages for a sole proprietor when he forms a business partnership with another person.   (*8 marks*)

(RSA Elem.)

5 Large-scale Business Organisation

1 The increasing size of the business unit

Firms range in size from the smallest one-man business to large limited companies. As already noted, the limited company has made possible the very large concerns of today. There are two reasons for the tendency of the business unit to expand in size. Firstly, there is the pursuit of economies of large-scale operation, for more often than not the large firm can produce more cheaply than the small firm; secondly, there is the attempt to obtain some measure of monopolistic power, that is, control of a sufficiently large share of the total output of a commodity so as to be able to raise its price by restricting output.

Where expansion has been attributable to the first motive, consumers have generally reaped the benefit, for large-scale operation has made possible the mass production of a great many manufactured articles, which as a result have been made available to consumers in large quantities at lower prices than would otherwise have been possible.

Expansion arising from the second motive is clearly contrary to the interests of consumers, since it results not only in a smaller supply being available to them but also in higher prices. The governments of both the United Kingdom and the United States are keenly alive to the danger of exploitation of consumers by monopolistic producers. In the United States anti-trust laws have been passed to try to prevent the establishment of monopolies, but although some trusts there have actually been broken up, no lasting success has been achieved, since they have been reformed in a different guise in order to keep within the law.

In the United Kingdom the Monopolies Commission, established in 1948 by the Monopolies and Restrictive Practices Act, could inquire into any industry where one firm or a combination of firms produced one-third, or more, of a commodity in order to discover whether its price was higher because its production was in the hands of a monopolist. In most cases it was found that these large firms had not seriously abused their monopolistic positions. In fact, monopolists have more often than not been particularly careful not to misuse their power, for fear of this causing the government to take action against them. In 1956 a further Act, the Restrictive Trade Practices Act, was passed to protect the interests of consumers. Then in 1965 came the Monopolies and Mergers Act under which the Department of Trade (now Department of Trade and Industry) could refer to the Monopolies Commission for its consideration any proposed merger, so that if it is regarded as being against the public interest it can be prohibited. This Act reflected the increasing need to take account of the growing importance of mergers as a source of monopoly power. There was concern at the extent of merger activity, for example in banking, which began in the early 1960s and continued into the 1970s, though at a slower rate. Between 1964 and 1980 there were over 2,000 mergers in the UK which came within the scope of the 1965 Act. Of these only about 3 per cent were referred to the Commission.

In 1973 the Fair Trading Act built on the structure created by the Acts of 1948, 1956, 1964 (the Resale Prices Act, see below) and 1965. This Act set up the Office of Fair Trading headed by a Director-General, whose duties included making references to the renamed Monopolies and Mergers Commission (though only by leave of the Secretary of State). Monopoly was redefined, now being seen as existing where there is control of one-quarter of the market. Under the 1973 Act it became possible for firms supplying services, for example hairdressers, estate agents and travel agents, to be investigated. The Competition Act 1980 further increased the powers of the Director-General, for example in the control of the nationalised industries.

Today, about 50 per cent of total UK output is produced by some 100 firms and it appears likely that this process of industrial concentration will continue in the future.

2 Methods of expansion

Expansion of the scale of production can take place in two ways – by the natural growth of the business or by two or more firms combining together (mergers). Many firms established by sole proprietors have gradually grown in size as a result of 'ploughing back profits', that is, the owners have put back into their businesses each year a large proportion of the profits. In a generation or two it is possible for a very large undertaking to be built up, and yet remain a 'one-man' business. Sometimes expansion has taken place by turning the concern into a partnership or a private limited company. Where more rapid progress has been desired the firm has been turned into a public limited company and an appeal made to the general public for subscriptions for its shares. Some businesses in their development have in fact passed through all these various stages.

Combinations between firms can be either temporary associations or permanent amalgamations. They may be voluntary associations of firms, or compulsion in some form may have been exercised to bring the combination into being.

Where all the member firms are at the same stage of production the combine is sometimes described as horizontal, e.g. a group of firms engaged in dyeing or in producing some agricultural commodity such as milk or potatoes or a combine of retail shops. The banking mergers of the late 1960s were also of this type.

Where the member firms are at different stages of production — for example, spinning, weaving and dyeing — they are said to form a vertical combination. Another example of a vertical combination is the shoe manufacturer who has his own chain of retail shops and who also does his own wholesaling.

In the case of 'lateral' mergers firms producing entirely different products combine in order to diversify their range of products as a protection against changing economic conditions; for example, Cadbury and Schweppes, Wilkinson Sword and British Match. Such mergers produce industrial 'conglomerates' so that very large companies become multi-product firms.

In the past voluntary associations were sometimes formed for limited periods of time by firms which agreed not to sell the commodities in which they dealt below certain prices. However, the Resale Prices Act 1964 (which was consolidated by the Resale Prices Act 1976) made it illegal for firms to fix minimum prices for their products. These associations were both voluntary and temporary, since on the expiry of a certain period it was possible for a firm to withdraw. The most important example of this type of combine was the cartel (*see* below).

When two or more firms arrange a merger they are seeking to bring about a permanent amalgamation, this being voluntarily undertaken by the firms concerned. Compulsory amalgamations occur when industries are nationalised, as, for example, occurred when British Rail came into existence as a result of the compulsory amalgamation of the four railway groups which previously operated in this country.

3   Cartels

This type of combine is of German origin. Cartels can take many forms, but they all possess the common feature of being associations of firms producing similar commodities, that is, they are horizontal in structure. The essential feature of a cartel is the setting up of a central selling-organisation for the marketing of the product. Usually the objective of the cartel is to keep up the price of the commodity by restricting output, and therefore the member firms agree not to exceed the production quotas assigned to them, e.g. the Organisation of Petroleum Exporting Countries (OPEC).

Since a cartel is generally a voluntary association, it is liable sooner or later to break up, for the agreement will be for only a

specified period. Conditions may change, and some firms –
especially those which regard themselves as being more efficient
than their rivals – may come to think that membership of the cartel
is a hindrance to their progress.

These difficulties can be overcome only if the cartel is legally
established and membership is made compulsory on all producers of
the commodity. The marketing boards set up in Britain for
agricultural produce are of this type. They are established only if
producers of three-quarters of the total output are agreeable, but
once a marketing board is established the other producers are
compelled to participate whether they wish it or not. Marketing
boards have been set up for a number of commodities, including
milk, potatoes and hops. The admission of new firms can then be
controlled and the output of existing firms restricted by licence, as is
done in the case of hops.

4 Mergers

Expansion of a firm by natural growth is a slow process. Expansion
can be achieved more rapidly if firms amalgamate, and this is the
method by which the giant firms of today have been created. The
most permanent type of association occurs, therefore, when a
complete fusion or merger takes place by the amalgamation of two or
more firms into a single undertaking. A merger often takes the form
of a large, powerful firm absorbing a smaller, weaker rival after a
successful 'take-over' bid. The firm taken over in this way then
becomes part of the larger company whose name it then adopts,
thereby completely losing its identity. For example, in 1969 Barclays
Bank absorbed Martins Bank in this way and Martins Bank ceased
to exist. Where the firms which have agreed to amalgamate are more
equal in size and power an entirely new company may be formed to
acquire their shares. The new company may take an entirely new
name as when a number of large chemical firms, each with its own
individual name, combined to form Imperial Chemical Industries
Ltd. Sometimes, in order to retain the goodwill attached to the old

names, the two names may be combined, as was done, for example, in the case of sugar refiners, Tate & Lyle Ltd.

In England today there are only a few large commercial banks, and these were formed by the amalgamation of hundreds of small banks. Small banks combined to form larger banks, the large banks then absorbed other smaller banks, and finally mergers took place between the large banks. In the case of the nationalised industries public corporations were established, such as the National Coal Board, to take over a large number of separate firms. The four railway companies which were merged on nationalisation to form British Rail were themselves amalgamations of large numbers of small companies, most of whose names have now been forgotten.

5   Trusts

The trust is another form of permanent combine and is of American origin. It is really nothing more than an amalgamation on an exceptionally large scale, generally vertical in structure and formed by the transfer to a body of trustees of the shares in the constituent companies, the shareholders receiving trust certificates in exchange. Although in this form it was declared illegal in the United States by the Sherman Act of 1890, the name has survived in that country for other types of large-scale organisation which just contrive to keep within the law. One of the largest existing firms of this kind is the American Iron and Steel Trust, which concerns itself not only with all branches of iron and steel production but also owns coal and iron mines and railways.

Fear of a 'money' trust in the United States led many state legislatures to prohibit large-scale banking, such as exists in Britain, but in some cases this has been circumvented by means of interlocking directorates, that is, the boards of several banks include the same group of directors, who thus ensure that a similar policy is pursued by all. Groups of industrial companies have sometimes also adopted this method of working together.

6 The holding company

This is a device of fairly recent origin for bringing a number of companies under one control. In the United States the outlawing of the trust increased the popularity of the holding company, which some writers regard as a similar type of business unit to the trust.

The holding company is a purely financial institution which employs its capital to obtain controlling interests in other firms by acquiring 51 per cent or more of their shares. The advantage of this type of organisation is that it enables a whole series of firms to pursue a similar policy, and yet at the same time the various companies can retain their original names and the goodwill attached to them. For this reason, when the nationalisation of the British iron and steel industry was contemplated a holding company was set up to control it so that the goodwill attached to the names of the old companies need not be lost, some of these companies being well known all over the world. There are many examples of holding companies in Britain, among the best known being Unilever and ICI.

Since the holding company can obtain control of its subsidiaries by holding no more than 51 per cent of their share capital, it is possible for one man or a small group to dictate policy to a vast organisation merely by having a controlling interest in the holding company itself. For example, a holding company with a capital of £200,000 may control a number of companies with more than double that amount of capital (since some of the constituent companies themselves may have subsidiaries), and the holding company itself may be in the hands of a small group who hold just over half its shares, so that holders of only £100,000 might control more than £400,000 of capital. This is a serious objection to the holding company as a form of large-scale business organisation.

7 The public corporation

At one time it was thought that, in the interests of consumers, monopolies should be operated either by municipal authorities or by the state, the former where purely local services were provided and the latter where the service was of a national character. At the present day many municipalities own and operate local passenger transport. Before the gas and electricity industries were nationalised many local authorities also had their own undertakings for the production of gas and electricity, and some owned docks and harbours. Birmingham has its own municipal savings bank and Hull its own telephone service. Profits of municipal undertakings go to the relief of local rates or towards the improvement of the service; losses are borne by the ratepayers.

During the period 1919–39 a new type of business unit came into existence – the public corporation. This was regarded as being a type of organisation suitable for businesses which it was felt should not be left to private enterprise. The usual practice was for Parliament to appoint the members of the corporation and then to grant it a charter for a limited period of time – perhaps five years – during which it was left to manage its own affairs. When its charter came up for renewal this gave Parliament an opportunity to stage a debate on the corporation's policy during the previous period. Of this type one of the oldest was the Port of London Authority (PLA), established in 1908 to be responsible for the control of the entire port of London. A somewhat similar body, the Mersey Docks and Harbour Board, which now controls the docks on both sides of the River Mersey, was established as long ago as 1857. Others were the British Broadcasting Corporation (previously the British Broadcasting Company), the London Passenger Transport Board (now London Transport) and Imperial Airways, later split into the British Overseas Airways Corporation (BOAC) and British European Airways (BEA), but again merged in 1973 to form British Airways.

The oldest public undertaking in Britain, however, is the Post Office, although until quite recently this was more directly operated as a government department, its revenue and expenditure appearing as items in the Budget. Since 1969 it has been run as a public corporation.

Public corporations are created by either Royal Charters (e.g. the BBC) or, more commonly, special Acts of Parliament, e.g. the nationalised industries.

8 Nationalised industries

In 1946 the Bank of England was nationalised. Since then a number of industries have been nationalised – coal (1947), transport (railways, canals and waterways, London transport), gas (1949), electricity (1948), the iron and steel industry (1951, denationalised 1953, renationalised 1967), and in the 1970s aircraft construction (British Aerospace) and shipbuilding (British Shipbuilders). The mid-1970s also saw the creation of the British National Oil Corporation and the British Ports Authority. In most cases large, monopolistic undertakings replaced large numbers of small firms in the transport, energy and manufacturing industries.

In addition, in the period after 1975 the National Enterprise Board (NEB) acquired on behalf of the state shares in a number of companies, these at the time generally being in financial difficulties; for example, Rolls Royce, British Leyland (BL) and Alfred Herbert.

The form of organisation of the nationalised industries differs in detail, but in each case it was put under the control of a public corporation. Thus we have the British Broadcasting Corporation, the National Coal Board, British Gas, the Central Electricity Generating Board, British Rail, Roadline, etc.

For each of the nationalised industries there is a minister in Parliament who is responsible for it — the sponsoring minister. Thus the Secretary of State for Energy speaks for coal, gas and electricity, and the Secretary of State for Transport for roads, railways and waterways.

The profits (trading surpluses) of the public corporations are devoted to the development and expansion of the service, but losses have to be borne by the taxpayer. Unlike private sector business, public corporations do not have profit as their main objective, although in recent years, particularly since 1979, profitability has been increasingly sought by the government as a measure of their efficiency, and to help reduce government expenditure.

Following the return of the Conservatives to government in 1979, policy towards the nationalised industries has changed, with the sale to the public of shares in some of the industries. For example, since 1980 shares have been sold in British Aerospace, Britoil and BP. In

1982 the National Freight Corporation returned to the private sector. The NEB has also been required to sell many of its shares in companies. This process of bringing the nationalised industries into private ownership is called 'privatisation'. This term is also used to describe all those schemes which aim to reduce the size of the public sector; for example, the sale of council houses, using private contractors to provide refuse collection services, and encouraging the development of private medicine and private education.

In the future it is expected that the sale of the nationalised industries, in whole or in part, will continue, e.g. British Airways, the Royal Ordnance factories, British Shipbuilders and the British Steel Corporation. Meanwhile the nationalised industries are an important part of the UK economy, producing 10 per cent of national income, employing over 2 million people (nearly 10 per cent of the working population), owning some 20 per cent of the country's capital stock and responsible for nearly 20 per cent of the country's annual investment.

Questions

1. Name the chief types of organisation which can be adopted when production is carried out on a large scale.

2. What have been the main reasons for the increasing size of the business unit?

3. Distinguish between vertical and horizontal combines.

4. What are the main features of a cartel?

5. Compare the trust and the holding company as types of business organisation.

6. What is a public corporation? Give a few examples.

7. Write short notes on the following (a) cartels, (b) trusts, (c) trade associations, (d) mergers; and explain under what conditions they are likely to come into existence.   (UEI)

8. Account for the continued survival of small business units in this country. Does their continued existence clash with the accepted advantages of large-scale organisation of business?   (UEI)

9. Define: (a) horizontal; (b) vertical combinations. Indicate the type of business for which each is most suitable.   (NCTEC)

10. It was at one time thought that the small business would not be able to survive the competition of the large-scale enterprise, but this has proved to be incorrect.

To what do you attribute the continuance of the small business and what do you consider to be the most favourable conditions? (LCCI)

11. How do you account for the emergence of special organisations for the supply of gas and electricity? How do they differ from public limited companies in respect of ownership and control? (GCE Camb.)

12. How does a nationalised industry differ from a private enterprise business? (NCTEC)

13. Compare a public corporation with a public limited company with regard to: (a) ownership; (b) control; (c) capital; (d) disposal of profits.

(LCCI)

14. State how each of the following might distribute profits or deal with losses: (a) a sole trader; (b) a public limited company; (c) a public corporation.

(LCCI)

15. (a) Describe the distinctive characteristics of a public corporation.

(b) What are the advantages and disadvantages of this form of enterprise?

(LCCI)

16. State-owned corporations play a major role within many mixed economies. Outline the main characteristics of this type of organisation giving consideration to organisation and control, finance, economic importance and consumer protection. (RSA Inter.)

6 Transport and Communications

1 Importance of transport

Improvements in the means of transport made possible the present complex system of production, with localisation of industry and specialisation of production, both on a national and on an international basis. The vast industrial development of the past two centuries has also of itself stimulated still further improvements in transport and communication. Industrial development and transport improvement reacted on each other. The greater the degree of specialisation achieved in industry, the more important transport became. Transport has been called an ancillary of commerce, but it is really much more than that, for without an efficient transport system commerce would be of very small proportions.

Transport development received its first great impetus in the late eighteenth and early nineteenth centuries, when in turn came the building of roads, canals and railways. The nineteenth century saw the steam engine very nearly reach perfection both in steamships and in railways. In Britain that century also saw the decline of the canals and of road transport, but its closing years heralded another period of rapid development which gave us electric traction and the internal-combustion engine, as a result of which there came the twentieth-century revolution in transport with the revival of road transport and the development of travel by air.

Improved means of transport have brought regions previously

difficult of access into easy communication with one another and the rest of the world. Down to the middle of the nineteenth century only those parts of the interiors of great continental land-masses which could be reached by river were open to commerce. The construction of roads and canals widened the areas available to trade, but it was the coming of the railway that opened up the interiors of the continents. The economic development of the newer countries – the United States, Canada, Argentina, etc. – followed upon the introduction of railways. Before railways were built the only means of transport for heavy, bulky goods was the ship, with the result that most trade in those days was of a coastal character. The railway made it possible to carry great loads of heavy, bulky goods to and from places many hundreds of miles from the sea or navigable rivers.

The introduction of a new means of transport has rarely completely ousted the forms of transport previously used. Canals and roads supplemented, but did not completely replace, the use of rivers. The introduction of the railway appeared at one time to have brought road transport – except for short-distance distribution from the stations – completely to an end. The revival of travel by road, both for passengers and goods, began between the two world wars, and the expansion of road transport still continues, though at a much reduced rate compared to the 1960s and 1970s.

At the present day, therefore, the trader has a choice of many different forms of transport for his goods – by sea, inland waterway (river or canal), railway, road or air. The reasons why these various modes of transport have continued to exist side by side with the newer forms is that each has its own peculiar advantages and disadvantages. In some cases road transport is to be preferred to rail; in others the railway is superior to road haulage. In some circumstances goods may be sent by coastal steamer rather than by railway; for other goods the railway may be more suitable. Thus the trader can take his choice. It is necessary for the student of commerce to know the reasons for one mode of transport being preferred to another.

It is important to appreciate the importance of transport and communications in commerce. This is reflected in the billions of pounds spent in both the public and private sectors of the economy;

for example, the development of the motorway system and the container ports, and investment in airports and, increasingly in recent years, in telecommunications. All of these developments have speeded up the movement of goods, money, people, information and so on, and reflect the increasing importance of time in commerce – 'time is money'.

2   Carriage of goods in the United Kingdom: by rail

Britain, as might be expected of the pioneer of railway construction, has an intricate network of lines, with at one time a total length of nearly 32,000 km. There were few places in this country very far from a railway station. Since the British railway system had its origin in a large number of small companies, it did not come into being as a result of careful planning, as did, for example, the French system. Parliament's fear that a railway might secure a monopoly led to the encouragement of the building of competitive lines, with the result that there are often two or more routes between the more important towns and cities of this country, a feature retained by the Act of 1921, which amalgamated the railways into four groups. In 1947 the railways were nationalised. Before this event took place business firms had been allowed to use their own railway wagons, an interesting survival of the idea once prevalent that a railway company should not have a monopoly of traffic even over its own lines.

Many railway branch lines and small stations were closed during the 1930s; many more have been closed in recent years. Not only have the railways now to compete with public road transport but also with the private car and the aeroplane. The Beeching Report, published in 1963 after a detailed examination of the railways by Dr (later Lord) Beeching, made recommendations for the reorganisation of the railways to suit present-day needs. The Report recommended the closing of more branch lines, the abolition of many stopping trains and the eventual concentration on the provision of fast inter-city services and on some routes high speed trains for passengers and fast freightliner trains for goods on a limited number of main lines. As a result total railway route mileage was reduced by over a third by 1970. Under the Transport Act 1968 lines regarded as 'socially necessary' are subsidised by the state. This Act also set up the National Freight Corporation to establish an integrated road/rail system for goods traffic. In 1982 the NFC was sold to private sector firms for £5 million, so that it is now owned by several companies which are responsible for moving a large proportion of Britain's road freight.

For long distances the railway is speedier than other modes of transport capable of dealing with heavy loads. The fact that the economical working unit is a complete trainload means that time is taken in the marshalling of wagons, and this considerably delays the delivery of goods despatched over short distances. Provided they are not too heavy or too bulky, goods can be carried by passenger train, the charge being higher than for carriage by freight train. British Rail operates an express freightliner service with delivery of goods often guaranteed for the day following their despatch. Special containerised trains move between several terminals throughout the UK, particularly those at the ports, so facilitating the movement of imports and exports. From these terminals road vehicles then deliver the loads to their destinations.

At present there are about 20,000 km of rail. In 1981, 155 million tonnes of freight were transported by rail, compared to 198 million tonnes in 1971 – a substantial fall.

Other services provided by British Rail include the following.

(*a*) *Speedlink*. This is concerned with the movement of freight in wagon-load or lorry-load quantities.

(*a*) *Red Star*. This guarantees the delivery of small parcels to the main stations within twenty-four hours.

(*c*) *Movement of mail*. The Post Office sends the Royal Mail through British Rail's overnight trains with sorting carried out *en route*, or by ordinary trains.

3   Carriage of goods in the United Kingdom: by road

The chief competitor of the railway at the present time is road transport. The expansion of the railways in the second half of the nineteenth century appeared at the time to have put an end to transport by road. As each new stretch of line was opened the coach and goods services over that route were driven off the roads. In the last years of the century the railways found a new competitor for the suburban passenger traffic of the large cities in the street tramway – horsedrawn, steam-driven or electrically propelled – but it was not until the petrol engine had reached a reliable degree of efficiency that road transport began seriously to compete against the railways.

During the years 1919–39 expansion of road services was rapid, and by the end of that period buses were to be found operating both local and long-distance services. At the same time there was a corresponding development of road haulage for goods. At first most road haulage firms were small, and although a number of large companies came into being, on the nationalisation of transport in 1947 there were over 20,000 separate firms with an average of fewer than three vehicles each. After nationalisation they were organised in groups, each of which operated about 150 vehicles. When road transport was denationalised in 1953 these larger units were generally retained, some continuing to be operated by British Road Services (now Roadline). Road transport was renationalised by the Transport Act 1968 which set up the National Freight Corporation to take over road haulage and the National Bus Company to take over road passenger transport. The expansion of road transport still continues, the number of motor vehicles on the roads in this country increasing from 3.5 million in 1949 to over 19 million in 1981. Of this number some 15 million were private cars (12 million in 1971). Recently, however, there has been some reduction in road freight movement, as shown in the table on p. 63. In 1982 the National Freight Corporation was sold by the Conservative government as part of its privatisation programme. Today in England and Wales the National Bus Company operates through a number of subsidiaries which are locally based. It has several long-distance coach services and over 22,000 buses and coaches in operation. In Scotland the main bus services in rural areas are operated by the Scottish Transport Group.

Advantages of road transport

(a) Both for passengers and goods, road transport is generally cheaper than the railway. The relative cheapness of road haulage is most pronounced for more expensive goods. Indeed, it has long been a complaint of the railways that road operators compete unfairly against them, since they tend to carry mostly the more expensive goods. Nor were road operators compelled to publish their charges, which quite often were decided by individual bargaining. It is still generally cheaper for bulky commodities like coal to be sent by railway than by road, although with the use of larger wagons by the road operators the railways have been losing even some of this business.

(b) Road haulage can provide a door-to-door service. Goods are generally loaded on to the wagons at the sender's premises and not unloaded until they reach their destination. When goods are sent by railway they have to be collected by road from the sender, unloaded at the goods station and reloaded on to the railway wagons, this process having to be reversed when the goods arrive at the town to which they have been consigned. Not only does it save time when goods are sent by road, but in addition they do not need to be so carefully packed. The railways have tried to get over this difficulty by operating freightliner trains and by the use of road-rail containers which can be carried either by their road vehicles or by train, and thereby obviate the necessity for unloading and reloading at the stations.

(a) For short and medium distances road haulage is generally speedier than the railway, but for longer distances the railway has the advantage.

Types of road transport. The merchant or manufacturer who has a consignment of goods ready for despatch has open to him a choice between a number of different methods of sending it by road, as follows.

(a) Goods which have to be sent to distant destinations will be moved by long-distance road haulage companies. These companies are found in the public sector (British Road Services) or in the private sector, for example firms operating for large companies and concentrating on bulk deliveries. British road haulage firms, together with similar firms overseas, have produced a set of international rules, the TIR (*Transports Internationale Routiers*) rules, relating to, for example vehicle roadworthiness and guarantees to customs.

(b) For a shorter distance a local carrier may be employed, for example between market towns and the surrounding countryside.

(c) If the extent of his business warrants it he can operate his own delivery vans, but in that case he must carry only his own goods, and not act as carrier for other firms. Many manufacturers of branded goods undertake the delivery of their own products to retailers. The number of retailers operating their own delivery vans has been steadily increasing in this country in recent years, and during the past ten years their number has doubled, so that now there are well over 1,200,000 of them on the roads.

(d) Small parcels can often be sent by bus. This is a particularly useful service in rural areas, where a van might have to make a very long journey to deliver one small packet.

There are also parcels delivery companies which collect goods by road from the senders and then make them up into large consignments for conveyance by rail, with the result that they are often able to quote lower rates than the railway itself. The Post Office too operates a parcels-post service and British Rail a Red Star parcels service.

The table opposite indicates the importance of the road system in the movement of goods and people, and shows the changes since 1971.

The growth of motor transport in the present century has been reflected in the increasing length of the road system. This continued to develop in the 1970s, especially the motorway system, as shown in the table below.

4   Carriage of goods in the United Kingdom: by inland waterway

In the days when sea-going ships were small many towns at quite considerable distances from the sea were seaports – for example,

	Total			Road		
	1971	1977	1981	1971	1977	1981
Tonne kilometres (thousand million)	132.8	149.0	148.3	85.9	98.0	94.4
Million tonnes	1,882	1,723	1,565	1,582	1,422	1,270
Passenger miles (thousand million)	423.4	465.7	502.3	386.0	430.0	464.8

Source: *Annual Abstract of Statistics*, HMSO 1983.

	1971 km	1977 km	1981 km
Total	324,659	355,124	341,987
Motorway	1,270	2,275	2,833
Trunk road	13,427	13,035	12,431
Principal	32,702	33,508	34,434
Other	277,260	286,306	292,289

Source: *Annual Abstract of Statistics*, HMSO 1983.

places like Lincoln and York. Rivers essentially provide a means of inland transport, and indeed were the earliest form. In the eighteenth century the rivers came to be supplemented by canals, most of which were constructed as links between the various river systems. Of this kind were the Trent and Mersey Canal, the Forth and Clyde Canal, and the Grand Union Canal which connects the Trent with the Thames. Canals also link the rivers Severn, Thames, Trent and Mersey with Birmingham. Britain has a total length of about 4,000 km of inland waterways.

Carriage by water – sea, river or canal – is cheaper than by any other means, but it is interesting to note that at the time when the canals were built they actually provided a speedier means of inland transport than did the roads, which were of such poor quality that they were often quite impassable in winter for long periods. In hilly districts the construction of canals is made very expensive because of the necessity of building a great number of locks, passage through which also makes transport by canal very slow in such areas. None of the trans-Pennine canals justified its construction, partly for this reason, but also because they were quickly superseded by the railways. The higher portions of some of them are now closed, but even where they are still open, they carry little traffic.

The Manchester Ship Canal, however, is a different category, since it was built to accommodate large sea-going vessels of up to 15,000 tonnes in order to make Manchester into a seaport in the late nineteenth century.

The construction of railways ruined many canals, some of which have carried little traffic for over a hundred years. On the other hand, there are some rivers and canals in this country which continue to carry a considerable amount of merchandise. Among these is the river system of West Yorkshire, which drains into the river Humber, together with the canals linking it to the industrial centres higher up the valleys beyond the limit of navigability of the rivers, e.g. the Aire, the Calder, and the Trent. Large quantities of coal are transported by this great waterway system to Goole and Hull, grain being carried in the other direction. The Act which nationalised the transport of this country put the canals and navigable rivers under the control of the British Waterways Board. About 650 km of the Board's waterways are in commercial use today. Nearly 1,000 km of canals are owned by other bodies. The amount of traffic along Britain's inland waterways has been fairly steady for several years now at about 5–6 million tonnes a year.

Inland waterways have several advantages, for example they reach industrial areas not on a major river, and being energy-efficient they are a very cheap form of transport. They are suitable for the carriage of relatively cheap goods of a bulky kind – coal, coke, raw materials for the chemical industry, petroleum, etc. – where fast delivery is of little importance. They are also specially useful for fragile articles, and so are still much used for the movement of china and pottery from Stoke-on-Trent and district.

Perhaps the chief drawback from which British canals suffer is to be found in the system itself. The declining volume of goods carried by the canals during the past sixty years encouraged the belief that the canals generally were out of date, and the canal companies felt no stimulus to improve the system. Until their nationalisation, about half the British canals were owned by the railways, the rest being controlled by independent companies. Another great drawback to the canals is their lack of uniformity of depth and width and the size of locks, so that long-distance through traffic is not always possible. At the present day speedy delivery is generally an important consideration, and slowness is another disadvantage from which canals suffer.

There is a growing use of the canals again for recreational and leisure purposes, e.g. holidays.

5 Carriage of goods in the United Kingdom: by coastal shipping

Quite a considerable amount of internal trade in this country is carried by ships which ply between the country's many ports. For example, towns along the south coast of England have always obtained coal by sea from South Wales, and the usual route by which coal is brought to London is by sea from the ports of South Shields, Sunderland and West Hartlepool. Large quantities of manufactured goods and foodstuffs are also carried from one part of the country to another in this way. The attraction of this method of transport is its cheapness.

There has been a steady growth of freight carried in this way in the UK. In 1971, 47 million tonnes were transported by coastal shipping, by 1981 the tonnage had risen to 60 million tonnes.

6 Carriage of goods in foreign trade: by sea

Although year by year the number of passengers and the quantity of goods carried by air continue to increase, ocean-going ships still remain the most important means by which Britain's imports reach these shores and by which its exports are carried to other lands.

Before 1914 Britain, with more shipping than all the other countries of the world together, was the chief ocean-carrier in the world. By 1984 less than 8 per cent of the world's shipping operated under the British flag. In 1971 Britain's merchant navy consisted of 1,875 ships of over 500 gross tonnes, with a gross tonnage of 25,117,000 tonnes. By 1981 the fleet had fallen to 1,118 ships with a gross tonnage of 22,117,000 ships.

Ocean-going ships for the carriage of cargo are of the following four kinds.

(a) *Tramp steamers*. So called because they do not operate over regular routes, but instead pick up cargo at any port at which they may call and carry it where required. The Baltic Exchange (*see* Chapter 15) in London exists partly for the purpose of chartering tramp steamers, providing facilities for the owners to meet importers and exporters. Terms are determined by individual bargaining, and thus fluctuate with changes in the demand for ships and the available supply. An agreement, known as *Charter Party*, is then signed. This gives the ship's destination, details of the cargo and the freight charge agreed upon. Lloyd's Register of British and Foreign Shipping enables an exporter to know something of the ship he is chartering. In 1981 Britain had 226 tramps with a gross tonnage of 470,000 tonnes.

(b) *Cargo liners*, which ply over regular routes according to a pre-arranged time-table, whether fully loaded or not, provide an alternative to tramp steamers. Liner companies operating in the same parts of the world have formed themselves into shipping conferences to fix freight rates which all members agree to charge. In this way rate-cutting is avoided. Thus, the freight charges for transport by cargo liner, unlike those for tramp steamers, are known in advance. In the 1970s Britain's cargo liners fell sharply from 663 ships to 248 ships.

(c) *Oil tankers*. In 1971 Britain had 496 tankers with a gross tonnage of over 13 milion tonnes. During the 1970s Britain's tanker fleet steadily decreased, so that by 1981 the fleet consisted of 376 ships with a gross tonnage of 11,870,000 tonnes. The tankers are owned or chartered by the large oil companies such as British Petroleum.

(d) *Bulk carriers*. These are specialised ships built for carrying a particular type of cargo, for example iron-ore. In the 1970s Britain's bulk carrier fleet fell from 271 ships (gross tonnage 8,181,000 tonnes) to 174 ships (5,985,000 tonnes).

Cargo space in these various vessels can be bought on the Baltic Exchange in London (*see* Chapter 15).

7 Carriage of goods in foreign trade: by air

The first regular air service was that between London and Paris, inaugurated in 1919. Since then air services have been developed between all the large cities of the world, and there are now few parts of the world which cannot easily be reached by air from London. There are also a number of internal routes, as, for example, between London and Glasgow, and between Manchester, Birmingham and London, as well as links between the mainland and the outlying islands – the Shetlands, the Hebrides and the Isle of Man.

The supreme advantage of air travel is its speed, and so it is a particularly useful means of transport for passengers and mail. During the years 1968–76 the number of passengers carried by British airlines almost doubled and the amount of mail more than doubled. Over 43 million passengers were carried in 1981. A journey by air from London to Zurich occupies less than one and a half hours, while Rome can now be reached in two hours and New York in only five hours from London – even less with Concorde. Since 1972 more people have crossed the Atlantic by air than have travelled by sea. For the carriage of goods, however, air transport still suffers the disadvantage of being able to take only loads of limited weight. Since, therefore, carriage by air is relatively expensive only fairly valuable goods such as furs, expensive machinery, and diamonds can be sent in this way. Nevertheless, both British Airways and foreign airlines have greatly increased the number and frequency of their freight service. More than half the freight carried by British airlines passes through London (Heathrow) airport. Other airports include: Gatwick (south of London), Luton, Stansted, Ringway (Manchester), Liverpool, Birmingham, Leeds/ Bradford, Abbotsinch (Glasgow) and Aldergrove (Belfast).

One should remember the importance of air transport in the movement of letters, packages and parcels, i.e. communications. As will be noted below, speedy communications within and between countries is essential and this has been an important reason for the rapid development of air freight. The only alternative to air transport between countries on different continents is sea transport and this is far too slow for many present-day commercial activities. About 20 per cent of Britain's foreign trade is now carried by air.

8   Carriage of goods in the United Kingdom: by pipeline

In the UK there has been a steady increase in the use of pipelines for the transportation of liquids and gases. For example, a large amount of North Sea oil is brought to the mainland by submarine pipelines (over 1,200 km) for processing, then sent on by another set of pipelines to major consuming centres. North Sea gas is similarly brought to the UK mainland and distributed throughout Britain. In 1971 UK pipelines transported 49 million tonnes of oil, water, milk, coal (in slurry form) and so on. By 1981 the figure had risen to 75 million tonnes. Construction costs are great but the savings on (say) road transport costs make this a very economical form of transport, the use of which is bound to increase in the future in the UK and elsewhere.

9   Communications

In 1981 non-postal communications within Britain and between Britain and overseas countries became the responsibility of the British Telecommunications Authority. Responsibility for the postal communications remained in the hands of the Post Office, which, under the Post Office Act 1969, was given a monopoly over the collection and delivery of letters and packets in the UK and for overseas delivery, but not over the collection and delivery of parcels. Hence the latter can be handled by British Rail, etc.

10 The Post Office

Side by side with the speeding up of transport has gone an even greater acceleration of the means for transmitting information or instructions – or even payment – from one person or firm to another. The first postal service in England was established as long ago as 1635, and in 1710 a post office was opened in London. At first the mail was carried by postboys who travelled on horseback, later by stagecoach and at the present day by railway, motor van, ocean liner or air. In 1968 a two-tier postal service was introduced, a higher rate being charged for letters sent first-class.

There are two types of letter (packets, postcards, etc.).

(a) *Inland letters*. These can be sent through the *ordinary post* or through one of the Post Office's other services outlined below.

(b) *Overseas letters*. These are sent by air if they are addressed to countries in Western Europe, for example France. Letters to other countries may be sent by air or by surface mail depending on the amount paid in postage.

The invention late last century of the telegraph and the submarine cable, and this century of wireless telegraphy and telephony, has made direct communication possible between people who may be separated from one another by thousands of miles of land and sea, or perhaps working only in different departments of the same firm. On many telephone exchanges in Britain direct dialling of the number required was introduced in the 1930s. This has now been extended to enable callers to dial numbers throughout the country and in some cases to towns abroad.

In the case of telemessages and overseas telegrams the cost is based on the number of words in the message and the distance, and to reduce the cost of this method of communication recognised codes are used to abbreviate messages, especially for the more usual and often rather cumbersome commercial terms. Similarly, on payment of a fee to the Post Office, an abbreviated telegraphic address can be used. To speed up delivery telemessages and overseas telegrams can be addressed to telephone numbers, the message then being telephoned to that number. It is also possible to send radio-telegrams to ships at sea. The telex system enables longer messages than could be conveniently sent by telegram to be teleprinted at the receiver's end.

In addition to the ordinary postal service, the Post Office provides a variety of other services of a communications nature, including the following.

(a) *Express letters*. For a small extra charge a letter can be sent express, that is, it will be despatched by the next mail without having to wait to be sorted, and at its destination it will be sent out by the next delivery, the receiver signing a receipt for it. Payment of a late fee enables a letter to be posted at a head post office after the ordinary time of collection. It is also possible in cases of emergency, for a special charge, to have a letter specially sent by railway or delivered by special messenger.

There is also an international express air mail service called *Swiftair*. Here letters are handed in at post offices and for an extra charge they are sent on by the earliest available flight to an overseas address. This service covers most countries.

(b) *Business reply service*. This is a device by which a businessman can send out a prepaid card for a reply, postage being payable only if the card is actually posted. A licence has to be obtained before the service can be used, and the cards or envelopes must bear a special standard design, including the licence number of the firm concerned. The Post Office keeps count of the postage due, and payment is made periodically, a deposit being required in advance.

(c) *Cash on delivery (COD)*. This enables a purchase to be made by post without payment in advance, the purchaser paying the postman when he delivers the parcel if the amount does not exceed £50. If the amount exceeds £50, the parcel or packet must be collected from the Post Office. The sender (who pays the fee for this service) receives his money by a crossed warrant payable at a specified post office or through his bank. All items sent this way have to be sent by registered post (packages) or compensation fee post (parcels, *see* below) and their value must not exceed £100.

(*d*) *Registration of letters.* For a small extra charge a letter can be sent registered, in which case the Post Office will pay compensation if loss is sustained. To enable a claim to be made if this should occur, the receipt supplied by the Post Office when the letter is posted should be retained. The Post Office supplies special envelopes, the use of which is essential if money is to be enclosed in the packet. Parcels cannot be sent by registered post. Instead, they can be sent by the Compensation Fee Service for an extra charge. Registered items can only be sent through the first-class postal service.

(*e*) *Recorded delivery.* This service is a cheaper alternative to registration, but is applicable only to letters. As with registered letters, a receipt of posting is obtained and delivery is recorded by the Post Office. For a few items sent this way, compensation of up to £18 may be paid if lost. It is often used when sending documents through the post. A recorded delivery item can be sent by first- or second-class mail.

(*f*) *Franking.* To save time spent on affixing stamps to letters, a franking machine can be obtained. This prints a stamp and also, if the firm desires, an advertisement. The machine registers the number of times it is used, and the meter can be set by an official of the Post Office to print a required number, for which payment has to be made in advance. After printing this number the machine locks itself, and cannot be used again until it has been reset. Where a firm has not sufficient business to warrant the use of a franking machine, the Post Office itself will frank a batch of letters if the postage on them exceeds a certain amount. If a firm has to send a very large number of letters, as might happen if it was sending out circulars to its customers, the Post Office will collect them from the firm if the number exceeds a certain level or if the postage is in excess of a certain amount.

(*g*) *Airway letters.* The Post Office together with British Airways operate the airway letters service on a number of inland routes. On payment of a fee, first-class letters can be handed in at airport terminals and will be sent on to the airport nearest the addressee using the next available flight. The letter may be either collected at the airport or posted on to the addressee.

(h) *Freepost*. Organisations pay the Post Office a deposit and, after having obtained its permission, obtain a special address to which correspondence concerning (say) an advertisement will be sent. People responding to the advertisement do not pay any postage. This service is very popular with mail-order firms, for example as seen in Sunday newspaper supplements and women's magazines.

(i) *Datapost*. This is an overnight door-to-door collection and delivery service. It is available on a contractual basis and is used for the speedy movement of items within the UK or to a number of cities overseas. The items moved by Datapost include those with a high unit value, for example computer tapes and medical samples.

11   The British Telecommunications Authority (British Telecom)

This provides rapid communications with overseas countries through a network of cable, satellite and radio links. These links have become of ever-increasing importance to commercial activities in recent years. Some of the Authority's main services are described below.

(a) *The telephone system*. Except for the telephone services of the city of Hull, the Channel Islands and a few private lines, the Authority provides a telephone service to some 25 million home subscribers, who are, generally speaking, connected to automatic exchanges and who are able to dial direct through the Subscriber Trunk Dial (STD) network. It also provides the continental and international telephone services, whereby it is possible to telephone directly overseas (the Direct Dialling System) or through an operator at the International Exchange in London. To this end, the UK is involved in the operation of *Intelstat*, a space communications satellite system. Finally, British Telecom provides the coastal radio system which maintains radio-telephone and telex links with ships and North Sea oil and gas rigs.

(b) *Telex*. By means of telex, once a person has dialled another party, the conversation is automatically recorded on tape by a form of typewriter known as a teleprinter at both ends of the conversation. As it is not necessary for the party being contacted to be present at the teleprinter, somebody in (say) London can communicate in the morning with a party in another country where it is night, for example Tokyo. The overseas party can then deal with the enquiry first thing the following morning. In this way, telex allows some 100,000 UK subscribers and over 850,000 subscribers overseas, most of whom have important international connections, to communicate with each other with a minimum of delay, for example the BBC, Reuters, multinational companies, etc. Ships at sea can be connected to the inland telex service through a radio teleprinter service.

(c) *Radio and TV services*. These take several forms, for example wavebands are provided for emergency services, maintaining links with North Sea rigs, etc., and *Confravision*, by linking people in several centres together through sight and sound as if they were face to face, allows businessmen to hold meetings with several participants in different parts of Britain simultaneously.

(d) *Datel*. This is a digital data transmission service concerned with communicating coded information, for example invoices or cheques. The information is sent by a company through its transmitter, which is linked to the telex or telephone systems, and so to its head office or to a computer centre. In this way, firms are able to maintain up-to-the-minute records of sales, stock levels, etc.

(e) *Other services*. These include telemessages, overseas telegrams, phototelegraphs, Postfax, Ceefax, Oracle and Prestel (i.e. transmission of computerised information on to modified television sets using the telephone system, for example travel information). Bureaufax and Intelpost allow documents and so on to be communicated from London to overseas countries using satellites. Satellite communication systems such as those provided by the Goonhilly communication station in Cornwall link the UK's and overseas countries' telephone and television networks with each other via satellites.

Communications services are subject to constant change and

improvement as a result of rapid technological advances in the fields of micro-electronics, information technology, telecommunications and so on. The cumulative effect of all these developments in communications has been to affect the pace of all types of commercial activity profoundly. This pace can be expected to quicken in the years ahead as further technological progress is made.

Questions

1. Assess the importance of transport to commerce.

2. Why has the introduction of a new mode of transport rarely completely ousted the means of transport previously employed?

3. Compare and contrast the railway and road haulage as means of transport for goods in a country such as Britain.

4. What would be the factors to be taken into account when considering the means of transport to be employed by: (*a*) a manufacturer; (*b*) a wholesaler; (*c*) a retailer?

5. In the case of air transport account for the slower expansion of freight traffic as compared with passenger traffic.

6. Distinguish carefully between a Charter Party and a Bill of Lading.

7. In connection with the transport of goods by sea, what is: (*a*) a dock warrant; (*b*) a delivery order; (*c*) a 'clean' bill of lading?   (LCCI)

8. Explain carefully the factors determining the choice of different forms of transport by manufacturers and traders.   (WJEC)

9. Describe the facilities for rapid and accurate transmission of commercial information provided by the Post Office and Cable Companies.
(GCE Camb)

10. In what circumstances might it be preferable to transport goods from Liverpool to London by: (*a*) coastal steamer; (*b*) passenger train; (*c*) goods train; (*d*) road? In each case give examples of the type of goods you have in mind.   (GCE Cambs)

11. Describe the main changes that have occurred in British rail services during the past ten years and comment on the further proposed changes with reference to their probable effect on the commercial life of different parts of the country.   (GCE JMB)

12. Account for the increase in the use of containers for the carriage of goods by rail and sea. What special problems have arisen as a result of their use?   (NCTEC)

13. List the main forms of transport used in the home trade.

Explain the importance of good transport systems to the trade and industry of a country. (NCTEC)

14. Give examples of goods usually sent by: (*a*) cargo liner; (*b*) tramp steamer; (*c*) tanker; (*d*) coaster.

Describe fully the characteristics of one of these forms of transport.

(RSA)

15. How does the British Rail freightliner service compare with available road transport services? What kind of traffic is likely to use freightliners, now or in the future? (RSA)

16. (*a*) Describe the advantages of road transport using these headings: (*i*) flexibility; (*ii*) economy.

(*b*) Outline *one* important disadvantage of road transport. (LCCI)

17. (*a*) Outline the main forms of sea transport and their particular uses.

(*b*) How can a shipper hire cargo space? (LCCI)

18. (*a*) What factors contribute to the efficiency of a transport system?

(*b*) How has containerisation contributed to the efficiency of transport?

(LCCI)

19. (*a*) Describe the services offered by each of the following forms of ocean transport: (*i*) cargo ship; (*ii*) bulk carrier; (*iii*) tramp steamer.

(*b*) State briefly how (*i*) the Baltic Exchange and (*ii*) Lloyd's, are associated with ocean transport. (LCCI)

20. *Either*

(*a*) Account for the fact that canal transport has declined in recent years but has not fallen completely into disuse.

Or

(*b*) Account for the increasing popularity of transporting goods by air.

(LCCI)

21. What are the relative advantages and disadvantages of (*a*) air; (*b*) rail; and (*c*) road transport to a manufacturer for the transit of goods? (LCCI)

22. Describe, with examples, the advantages and disadvantages of transporting goods by air. (LCCI)

23. In relation to your own country, describe the main methods of transporting goods and assess the importance of each method. (LCCI)

24. What factors should a manufacturer take into account when choosing a method of transporting goods overseas? (LCCI)

25. (*a*) Explain why a manufacturer of heavy drilling machinery is likely to deal directly with his customers. (*4 marks*)

(*b*) What services is a wholesaler likely to provide to a manufacturer requiring regular supplies of raw materials such as iron ore or salt?

(*4 marks*)

(*c*) Explain *four* important considerations a large-scale manufacturer of fragile china might take into account when deciding whether to purchase his own fleet of vehicles or to use carriers in order to transport his goods in the home market. (*4 marks*)

(*d*) Explain the main considerations a manufacturer would take into account when deciding to transport his goods overseas by (*i*) tramp ship and (*ii*) cargo liner. (*4 marks*)

(*e*) Give *one* example of a government agency which advises manufacturers on the export of goods and explain how it collects and imparts its information. (*4 marks*)

(RSA Inter.)

26. Explain how technological developments in sea transport, such as the introduction of container ships and roll-on/roll-off ferries, have influenced development in:

(*a*) the size, design, and use of ships; (*b*) the use and modification of ports and port facilities; (*c*) the handling of goods carried by sea transport; (*d*) road and rail freight services to and from ports. (RSA Inter.)

27. Woodside Double Glazing PLC manufacture windows and doors which have double glazing fitted in their factory. These are sold to fifty do-it-yourself stores in the local region, which has a good road and rail network.

(*a*) List *three* main factors which should be considered by the company in deciding which method of transport to use to deliver their products to do-it-yourself stores. (*3 marks*)

(*b*) Compare, using the factors you have listed, *two* different forms of transport Woodside could use and suggest the most suitable. (*8 marks*)

(*c*) The company wishes to buy new equipment costing £100,000 because of increased demand for their products. Suggest and describe *three* sources of finance for this additional capital which could be used by the company.

(*9 marks*)

(RSA Elem.)

Part Two
Financial Aspects of Commerce

7 Sources of Business Capital

1 The capital of a sole proprietor

The first questions to be answered by anyone who contemplates setting up in business for himself are: (*a*) how much capital shall I require? and (*b*) how can I obtain this capital?

Opportunities for establishing oneself as a sole proprietor have tended to become fewer as the scale of production has increased. The amount of initial capital required in most kinds of manufacturing business at the present day is generally greater than one man by himself can supply. The retail trade probably offers most scope for the man with a little capital who wishes to set up in business on his own account.

Let us, therefore, consider the case of Jack Robinson, who began his career as an errand-boy at the Northampton branch of Multiple Grocers PLC, a firm of grocers with branches in the East Midlands. Later he took his place behind the counter as an assistant, and after some years in this capacity he became manager of the company's branch at Peterborough. In the hope of one day opening his own shop he saved a little of his income each year, and, helped perhaps by a legacy from a maiden aunt, he eventually finds himself with a sum of money in the bank which he regards as sufficient for his purpose. All the time that he has been working for Multiple Grocers PLC he has been gaining experience of the line of business which he proposes to enter and learning something of the problems he himself is likely to have to face in the future. Accumulating capital by personal saving is one method of raising the capital of a business.

Robinson may, however, find saving too slow a process and, being impatient to make a start, considers what other possibilities there are of increasing his capital. Two courses are open to him.

(*a*) He may be able to borrow in one of the following ways.

(*i*) Some friend or relative may be willing to lend him a sum of money.

(*ii*) He can approach his banker and ask him for a loan. Banks frequently lend to retailers, but not generally to those who have not yet commenced business.

(*iii*) If he intends to buy his shop premises he may be able to borrow part of the purchase price from a building society.

(*b*) He may be able to obtain credit from his wholesaler. If he can obtain stock on credit this is really equivalent to obtaining a loan from the wholesaler. As a newcomer to the trade, however, he has yet to prove his ability to make a success of his business, and so he is likely to find that wholesalers will be reluctant to grant him much, if any, credit at first.

It is clear, therefore, that the man who is about to set up for himself will at first have to rely very largely on his own resources for raising capital, and indeed he will be well advised to do so. Once he has successfully established himself, these other opportunities will then be open to him for obtaining the additional capital which the expansion of his business requires. Many large concerns have had small beginnings, and have developed into larger ones because the sole proprietor has put back into the business as much as possible of the profit each year, thereby increasing his capital out of savings.

Drawbacks to borrowing. If Robinson does succeed in borrowing some of his capital or in obtaining credit from his wholesaler he handicaps himself from the start. Interest has to be paid on loans from banks and building societies, and the loans themselves eventually have to be repaid. If he obtains goods on credit it means that he will have to pay more for them than he otherwise would, for by delaying payment he will lose cash discount, and so his profit margin will be reduced. He will therefore find it more difficult to pay his way if he borrows or accepts credit. One-third of the failures in business are due to lack of sufficient capital.

2   Real capital and money capital

So far we have used the term capital to mean money, for clearly it is money that people save, just as it is money that is borrowed from banks. But it is not really money that Robinson requires: he wants money only so that he can obtain the real capital of his business – the premises, fittings, stock, etc. Suppose that at the moment when he decides that he has sufficient capital to be able to set up in business for himself he has £40,000 in the bank. Suppose now that he accepts an offer of shop premises at £50,000 and that a building society is prepared to lend him £35,000 against a mortgage on the premises. He will therefore have to pay from his savings a further £15,000 for the premises. Fittings may cost him £7,000 and stock £14,000. This will leave him with £4,000 in the bank. It is important that he should keep some cash in reserve to cover any unexpected expenditure. Insufficient reserves are one of the most frequent causes of the failure of people running small businesses. Now that Robinson has only £4,000 in the bank when previously he had £40,000 does this mean that he has less capital than he had before? Clearly what has happened is that the form of his capital has changed: it now consists of a shop, fittings and stock, together with only a small amount of 'liquid' capital, that is, cash, whereas previously it consisted entirely of money.

3   Capital owned and capital employed

At the end of the year Robinson will draw up a balance sheet, which might read as follows.

The item capital in the balance sheet shows the capital owned by Robinson, this being the excess of his assets over his liabilities. When he commenced business the capital he owned amounted to £40,000, so that during the year he has increased the capital he owns by £8,000. He has also reduced his loan by £1,500, but on 31st December he had unpaid bills amounting to £2,500. On the assets side he has increased his stock and cash in hand, and £600 is owing to him by his customers. The capital he employs is greater than the

J. Robinson's Balance Sheet at December 31st 19—.

Liabilities	£	Assets	£
Sundry creditors	2,500.00	Premises	50,000.00
Loan	35,500.00	Fittings	7,000.00
Capital	48,000.00	Stock	18,600.00
		Sundry debtors	600.00
		Cash in hand and at bank	7,800.00
	£84,000.00		£84,000.00

capital he owns, since it includes all his assets (except debts owing to him), that is, £83,400, an increase of £8,400 over the amount he employed at the start. The greater the sum borrowed, the greater will be the excess of capital employed over capital owned.

4   Fixed and circulating capital

It is important to distinguish between the fixed and the circulating capital of a business.

(a) *Fixed capital.* As we have just seen, the assets of a firm comprise the capital employed by it. Some of these are of a durable character, like the premises, fixtures and fittings, which are used in the business over a considerable period, having to be replaced only at long intervals. These things form the fixed capital, the essential feature of which is that it is used over a period of time. In a manufacturing business the factory premises and machinery are fixed capital. The fact that buildings are fixed in situation has nothing to do with their being fixed capital. Time, and not fixity of situation, is the deciding factor. If the firm owns and runs a delivery van this would form part of its fixed capital, and obviously this would be of no service if it was incapable of movement!

(b) *Circulating capital.* This has been defined as capital used only once in the course of business. The retailer's stock forms part of his circulating capital, since once having sold it he has no further interest in it. To the manufacturer raw materials serve the single purpose of being turned into finished products, and so are circulating capital. Having sold some of his stock, the retailer uses some of the money he has received in exchange to replenish it. Similarly, the manufacturer sells his finished goods and buys more raw material. Thus circulating capital is constantly changing its composition. The retailer's circulating capital consists mostly of stock and cash in hand; whenever he sells anything his cash increases and his stock declines; when he renews his stock the form of his circulating capital again changes, stock increasing and cash decreasing. So this kind of capital circulates, and so justifies its name. Circulating capital is required to finance production, the holding of goods and their movement.

Fixed capital changes its form more slowly, but things like shop fittings, delivery vans and machinery wear out or become out of date, and have to be replaced. Premises, too, have to be kept in repair. Thus the distinction between these two kinds of capital is simply a question of time.

Because of the different lengths of life or different kinds of capital, the sources from which they are obtained also differ. If a loan is made to a firm for the purchase of fixed capital the loan is required for a long period of time; a loan for the purchase of stock or raw materials, on the other hand, can be for quite a short period, since the retailer or manufacturer expects to turn these things again into cash very soon. The sole proprietor may have to provide both kinds of capital out of his own savings, although, as we have seen, a building society would probably be willing to assist him with the purchase of the premises, that is, with some of his fixed capital. When we come to consider the sources from which large-scale enterprise obtains its capital we shall see that the sources differ according to whether the loan is required for fixed or for circulating capital.

5　The capital of a partnership

A business may start as a partnership, or a business originally established by a sole proprietor may develop into one. As we saw in Chapter 4, there may be as few as two partners or up to twenty when the business is concerned with trade or manufacturing. One of the main advantages of a partnership is that it can usually raise more capital than can a sole proprietor, but both kinds of business obtain their capital in a similar kind of way – from savings. Shortage of capital is a common reason for a sole proprietor seeking a partner who can bring into the business with him some additional capital.

6　The capital of a company

Neither the sole proprietor nor the partnership can supply enough capital for large-scale enterprises. Public companies, however, can offer their shares to investors in general, and so can raise the large amounts of capital required for modern large-scale businesses. (Private companies cannot offer their shares to the public; *see* below and Chapter 4.)

Shares are usually in units of small amounts, such as 20p, 50p or £1, though other denominations, both smaller and larger, are to be found. When a company is formed it is permitted to issue shares up to a certain amount, stated in its Memorandum of Association, and known as its authorised capital. It may, however, decide to issue less than the full amount. Thus a company may have authorised capital of £300,000, only £250,000 of which has been issued. If at some future date it is decided to increase the capital of the firm the remaining £50,000 can then be issued. Sometimes, too, shares are not fully paid-up, only a fraction of the nominal value being paid for each pound share, and in such a case the company can obtain additional capital by asking the shareholders to pay the unpaid balance on each share they hold. (*See* p. 87 for effects of Companies Act 1980.)

7   Types of shares

There are two main kinds of shares – preference shares and ordinary shares. The reason for the issue of different kinds of shares is that some investors do not wish to bear as great a risk as others.

(a) *Preference shares.* These carry a fixed rate of dividend, such as 6 per cent or 8 per cent, which has to be paid in full before any dividend is paid on the ordinary shares. There is thus less risk in holding preference shares than there is in holding ordinary shares. Sometimes, as with cumulative preference shares, the holders are entitled to arrears of dividend (if any) from previous years before dividend is allotted to the ordinary shareholders. There are also participating preference shares, which entitle their owners to dividend in addition to the fixed rate if the total profit of the company exceeds an agreed amount.

(b) *Ordinary shares.* These shares do not usually bear a fixed rate of dividend, their holders taking the residue of profit after all other claims have been met. In good years the dividend may be very high; in poor years it may be very low; and in a very bad year the ordinary shareholders may receive nothing at all. The holders of ordinary shares, therefore, bear most of the risk.

Debentures. Companies sometimes borrow money from the general public by means of debentures, which carry a fixed rate of interest. These are not shares at all, for the holders are not members of the company, but its creditors, and therefore they must be paid in full the interest due to them before there is any distribution of profits among any class of shareholders. Holders of debentures thus bear less risk than any of the shareholders and so generally have a lower rate of yield than shares. In the example below debentures carry 7 per cent interest as compared with a normal rate of 8 per cent on the preference shares. Sometimes debentures are issued on the security of the firm's assets, and in that case they are known as mortgage debentures.

Let us now see how this works out in practice. Multiple Grocers PLC is a public joint-stock company with capital of £1,600,000 made up as follows.

Multiple Grocers PLC

Issued capital	£
Loan capital: 400,000 7% Debentures of £1	400,000
Share capital: 400,000 6% Preference shares of £1	400,000
1,600,000 Ordinary shares at 50p each	800,000
Total	**1,600,000**

The following table shows the amounts available to debenture holders and shareholders when different amounts of profit are made.

Year	Trading profit	Debenture holders	Preference shareholders	Ordinary shareholders
I	£156,000	£28,000 7%	£32,000 8%	£96,000 12%
II	£220,000	£28,000 7%	£32,000 8%	£160,000 20%
III	£84,000	£28,000 7%	£32,000 8%	£24,000 3%
IV	£32,000	£28,000 7%	£4,000 1%	Nil

It will be noticed that the debenture holders were paid in full in all four years, receiving the same amount in Year II, when profit was high, as in Year IV, when it was low. In Years I, II and III the preference shareholders received the full 8 per cent dividend to which they were entitled, but in Year IV they had to accept a mere 1 per cent, since profit in that year was insufficient to pay any greater amount. The ordinary shareholders received varying amounts – 20 per cent in Year II, but nothing in Year IV, when total profit was not sufficient even to pay preference shareholders in full. If the preference shares had been of the cumulative type their holders would be entitled to 7 per cent arrears in Year V in addition to the normal 8 per cent – again, of course, if profit in that year was sufficient to enable this payment to be made.

Companies can increase their capital in similar fashion to sole proprietors and partnerships by saving, that is, by putting back into the firm some of the profit. A company does not usually distribute the whole of any year's profit to the shareholders, but instead puts some of it into reserve, to be used to help the firm in bad times or to finance expansion.

So far we have assumed that a company's shares will be taken up by members of the general public. It is true that most of the shares may be held by private investors, but large blocks of shares and debentures are acquired by financial institutions such as insurance companies, investment trusts and unit trusts. Though some foreign banks purchase shares in companies, it is unusual for British banks to do so. Insurance companies have enormous funds at their disposal, and they invest largely in shares and debentures and in government stock. Investment trusts and unit trusts take up shares in a large number of companies in order to spread the risk as widely as possible. If a man with only a little capital put it all in one company he would suffer heavy loss if that company went out of business. By putting his money into a unit trust he can enjoy the same advantage as the large investor who spreads his risk over a large number of companies, so that the failure of one has little effect upon him. Whether the shares of a company are taken up by individuals or institutions, the source of the capital is the same – it comes from the savings of a large number of people. This explains how a public company can raise the huge amount of capital required for large-scale enterprise.

The Companies Act 1980 has introduced a number of important changes, some of which affect the raising of capital by companies. Many of the changes were brought in as part of a gradual process towards harmonisation of company law within the European Economic Community as a whole. The Act defines a new kind of company known as a public limited company (plc). Such a company must have at least two shareholders and it must have an issued share capital of at least £50,000, of which at least one-quarter must be paid-up. The important aspect of this from the capital raising point of view is that only companies with an issued capital of £50,000 are now permitted to raise funds by the offer of shares to the public. All companies not in this category are now regarded as private companies, which must still raise their capital privately and so they will tend to be small and, on the whole, highly localised as a result. Another disability attendant upon private companies is that, under the 1980 Act, their shares cannot be transferred to other shareholders, unlike those of public limited companies (*see* Chapter 4).

8   Fixed and circulating capital of companies

Earlier in this chapter the need to distinguish between fixed and circulating capital was stressed. In considering the sources upon which companies can draw for their supply of capital, this distinction is particularly important. As we have just seen, a firm of this kind raises its initial capital by issues of shares and debentures. The money raised in this way is used to provide the company with its fixed capital. It is because fixed capital is used over a long period that British banks are generally unwilling to supply this sort of capital to industry, for they prefer to lend for short periods. Circulating capital is constantly changing its form, starting as money and in a short time being turned into money again. Retailers and wholesalers purchase stock which they expect to sell within a short time, and so money that has been borrowed to provide this kind of capital can be repaid fairly quickly; a manufacturer has to buy raw materials and pay wages to his employees during the period of production, but eventually he sells the goods he has made, and this makes possible the repayment of any loan obtained for this purpose.

Banks, therefore, are willing to provide businesses with some of their circulating capital, for although such loans may be renewed over and over again, they can always be called in if necessary. In 1983 total advances of British banks to business reached over £56,000 million. Thus, banks are an important source of circulating capital, but some firms provide themselves with at least a portion of their circulating capital from their own reserves, thereby saving the payment of interest on loans. Rising prices in recent years have made it necessary for businesses to employ a great deal more circulating capital than formerly, and so they have found it more difficult to provide it out of their reserves.

9 Finance corporations

The Industrial and Commercial Finance corporation (ICFC) and Finance Corporation for Industry (FCI) were both established in 1945 to help provide medium-term capital for business enterprise (banks usually lend only for a short term). The main difference between the two corporations was in the amount of assistance each could offer to industry. In 1975 they were merged as Finance for Industry Ltd (FFI). The shareholders are the clearing banks (85 per cent) and the Bank of England.

A number of other financial corporations have been established since the Second World War, usually of a specialised nature to deal with a particular industry, e.g. the National Film Corporation, the Commonwealth Development Finance Company and the Industrial Reorganisation Corporation.

10 The Stock Exchange

We have said that public companies obtain capital by the issue of shares to the public. To the company which issues the shares such an issue is a permanent one. The directors of the company concerned expect to have the permanent use of the capital subscribed by purchasers of the shares when these are first issued. At this stage these are known as *new issues*. To the investor in the shares, however, the matter looks quite different. To him, the investment may appear as merely temporary and he may well require the return of his money in exchange for the shares which he holds. He cannot, however, turn to the company whose shares he holds and request the return of his investment since the money subscribed for the shares when issued is likely to have been used to purchase physical assets for the company in the form of land, buildings, factories, plant and equipment, machinery, transport and any other items of fixed capital required for the pursuit of the company's business.

The shareholder in need of cash can, however, sell his shares on a stock exchange, which is a market in which existing shares (and any other form of negotiable securities) can be transferred from one person or institution to another. The existence of highly organised markets of this type renders securities more liquid, i.e. they are more readily transformable into cash when required, and it is this fact which makes the issue of new shares by companies much easier. When a transfer of 'old' shares is made, the company of original issue has no financial interest in the transaction. It merely registers the transfer in order to keep its share registers up to date. In addition to the London Stock Exchange and its offshoots in Leeds, Manchester and Birmingham, stock exchanges are located in many of the world's leading financial centres including New York (Wall Street), Paris (the *Bourse*), Amsterdam, Brussels, Johannesburg, Melbourne, Calcutta, Tokyo and Hong Kong. The enormous range of securities in which the London Stock Exchange deals may be inspected daily in the *Financial Times*, in which they are listed along with their current prices. Most securities, however, can be classified under one of the following headings.

(*a*) The *ordinary shares* of commercial companies.

(*b*) The various types of *preference shares* of commercial companies.

(*c*) The *debenture issues* of commercial companies.

(These three types of securities were discussed in section 7 above.)

(*d*) *Government stocks or bonds*. These are government securities issued in return for loans made by the public and the banks to the state. They are listed as *British Funds* and range from terms of up to five years to over fifteen years. Examples of these are Treasury 10 per cent 1987 and Treasury 13 per cent 2000. Additionally there are some older issues which bear no date of redemption. These are known as *undated stocks*, for example the War Loan 3½ per cent. All these securities pay a fixed rate of interest to the holder equal to the face value of the security. Their collective name is *gilt-edged securities* or *gilts* and they represent a very safe form of investment since payment is guaranteed by the government. Clearly, the presence of a market in which they may be bought and sold as required greatly facilitates government borrowing.

(e) *Local authority bonds and loans.* Since the Second World War, local authorities have increasingly supplemented their rate and central government grant income by borrowing for capital expenditure on, for example the great housing development which has been undertaken all over the country. Bonds are issued to the subscribing public and guaranteed against the rating income of the corporation concerned. Examples are the Burnley 13 per cent 1987 and the Leeds 2006 13½ per cent loans.

(f) *Overseas stocks, bonds and shares.* A wide range of foreign securities is traded on the London Stock Exchange, facilitating world-wide investment by the individual investor. These include foreign government bonds, foreign commercial company shares and loans raised by foreign local authorities and municipalities.

The importance of the Stock Exchange today may be deduced from the fact that almost everyone in Britain is either directly or indirectly involved with its fortunes. This is because, although only a few million people actually hold securities directly, almost half of the population invests in building societies, savings banks, pension funds, unit trusts, investment trusts and insurance companies, and all these financial institutions employ the savings which they collect to purchase shares or other securities on the Stock Exchange. The other half of the population is made up of the families of those who put their savings into any of the above financial institutions.

Procedures. As the Stock Exchange is a highly organised and specialised market, its procedures are ruled by definite guidelines laid down by the Stock Exchange Council. There are basically two groups on the Exchange: brokers and jobbers. A member of the public cannot, therefore, enter the Exchange himself or herself but must deal through a broker or jobber who is an accredited member. The function of the broker is to buy and sell shares on behalf of his client, and to provide advice. He receives a fixed rate of commission on transactions. The broker must deal with the jobber in carrying out a commission for his client. The jobber is the wholesaler who purchases shares from brokers and sells them to other brokers. The jobber does not earn a commission on transactions like the broker. Rather, he earns a profit represented by the difference between the prices at which he buys and sells shares. This difference is known as the 'jobber's turn'. As a glance at the *Financial Times* immediately indicates, the variety of shares coming to the market is very great with the result that no one dealer can be an expert in them all. Hence jobbers specialise in a particular line of shares, for example financial institutions, oil, breweries or gilt-edged.

The price at which a share may be bought or sold varies from day to day, depending upon the demand to buy such securities and the supply available from holders of the securities who are prepared to sell them. Precisely how prices on the Stock Exchange are determined is still something of a mystery. Clearly, if a company is doing badly, i.e. its profits are falling or it is making a loss, the price of its shares will fall. Prices are, however, influenced by a host of external factors such as the general economic situation of the country, the state of the balance of payments, changes in taxation real or anticipated, variations in interest rates and political crises at home and abroad. Often the market behaves unpredictably. During 1983–84, despite widespread industrial recession, prices on the Stock Exchange attained record heights as measured by the Financial Times Index (FTI) and the new Financial Times-Stock Exchange Index (FT-SE 100 index) first introduced in February 1984.

Transactions between brokers and jobbers are carried out in a very special manner. Suppose that a member of the public wishes to sell some shares in a certain company. The broker approaches a jobber specialising in the type of shares involved. He does not say whether he is a buyer or a seller. The broker quotes two prices: a lower price at which he is prepared to buy the shares and a higher price at which he is prepared to sell. Once a deal is struck the jobber always honours the bargain made. The motto of the Stock Exchange is *Dictum Meum Pactum* (my word is my bond).

Criticisms. The position of the London Stock Exchange as one of the most hallowed institutions of the financial system has been increasingly challenged in recent years. The chief criticisms of the Exchange may be summarised as follows.

(a) Over-activity in the Stock Exchange (the market for 'old' share issues) may cause too much attention to be paid to prices there to the relative neglect of new share issues required by firms for new capital projects.

(b) Share prices do not necessarily reflect the true performance of the companies involved.

(c) Owing to their very large shareholdings, decisions by large institutions (such as pension funds and insurance companies) to buy or to sell have an increasingly powerful effect on share prices in general. Such decisions are made by a very few individuals. In addition, the number of jobbing firms has declined and, as has been seen, because jobbers tend to specialise in particular types of shares, dealings in some types of shares may be confined to a small group of jobbers. Both of these movements involve a reduction in competition on the Stock Exchange.

(d) There has been much criticism concerning the high costs of obtaining a listing of a company's shares on the Stock Exchange. Now that there is a market for unlisted securities, however, this has been to some extent alleviated.

(e) The most serious criticisms of the Stock Exchange have recently concerned its restrictive practices. The Exchange has always regulated itself through its Council but its practices have attracted the attention of the Office of Fair Trading. The objections to Stock Exchange practice concern, firstly, fixed commissions charged to clients in contrast with competitive pricing on American exchanges. Secondly, there has been criticism of the 'closed shop', i.e. restrictions on membership. Thirdly, and once again in contrast with American practice, the single capacity system, whereby jobbing and brokerage are carried out by different persons, has been criticised. In late 1983 when it appeared that the Stock Exchange would be subjected to official investigation under the Restrictive Practices legislation, the Stock Exchange reached agreement with the Department of Trade and Industry that minimum commissions would be removed by 1986, lay members would be admitted to the Stock Exchange Council and the Bank of England would be allowed to exercise a greater role in supervision. There was, however, no agreement on the still-controversial matter of the single capacity system.

Despite these difficulties the Stock Exchange will remain a vital component of our economic and commercial system, of which fact its turnover provides the clearest evidence. In 1983 this amounted to £287,586 million – a daily average over 252 business days of £1,141 million. Of this massive total the trade in the ordinary shares of commercial companies accounted for £56,131 million.

11   Investment and speculation

Many people buy stocks or shares because they are seeking an investment which will yield them an income. Others buy shares partly for this reason but also in the hope that the price of the shares will rise in the future, so that they can then be sold at a profit. Such 'capital gains' are now taxed. Both these groups of people buy shares mainly as an investment, as an alternative to putting their savings in a savings bank or a building society. Besides private investors there are also large institutional investors, such as insurance companies, which buy stocks and shares on the Stock Exchange.

In addition to investors there are speculators on the Stock Exchange. It is not always easy to distinguish between them, but, in general, speculators are more concerned with making quick profits from buying and selling again than with income from investment. Those who buy in the hope that prices will rise are known on the Stock Exchange as 'bulls', and those who sell when they anticipate that prices will fall are said to be 'bears'. Another group of speculators comprises 'stags', who subscribe to new issues in the hope of selling the shares allotted to them when dealings in them begin. Speculators are to be found on all highly organised markets and their activities are not always bad, for their expert knowledge – and without expert knowledge a man will not remain a speculator for long – is frequently used in the service of other merchants who attend these markets. The presence of speculators on the Stock Exchange is often of great service to the ordinary investor. Their presence makes it possible for others to buy or sell shares at the times most convenient to them, for speculators will usually buy or sell at any time, though, of course, only at prices agreeable to them. Without the speculator a man finding himself short of cash but possessing some shares might find it impossible to sell them at any price, simply because no other investor wished to buy just then. Speculators also tend to steady prices by buying when other people want to sell or by selling when others wish to buy. Speculation is bad only when those indulging in it deliberately try by their own activities to force prices up or down to suit their own interests.

Questions

1. How does a sole proprietor raise the capital which he requires for carrying on his business?

2. Distinguish between: (a) real capital and money capital, and (b) fixed capital and circulating capital.

3. What comprises the capital of a retailer? Distinguish between the capital he owns and the capital he employs. In what circumstances will the amount of capital employed be likely to exceed the capital owned?

4. How does a public limited company obtain: (a) its fixed capital; (b) its circulating capital?

5. For what reasons might different investors choose to invest in: (a) ordinary shares; (b) preference shares; (c) debentures?

6. In what ways may the capital employed in a business be greater than the capital invested in it by its proprietor? Are there circumstances in which the owner would be justified in further increasing the margin of capital employed over capital owned? (RSA)

7. How far does the existence of stock exchanges assist in the efficient working of the national economy? (UEI)

8. Describe the types of capital raised by a joint-stock company. How is this capital obtained? (WJEC)

9. Describe the principal classes of share and loan capital raised by public limited companies. Why is the Stock Exchange of importance to such companies? (GCE Camb.)

10. What is the business of the Stock Exchange and how is it conducted? (NCTEC)

11. Explain the functions of the Stock Exchange in the British economy.

Discuss the possible costs and benefits to the economy of the Stock Exchange. (GCE JMB Advanced Level)

12. What are the functions of stock exchanges in the commercial and economic life of a country? (LCCI)

13. (*a*) What methods are available to the following to finance expansion: (*i*) co-operative society; (*ii*) public limited company; (*iii*) sole trader?

(*b*) What constraints are there on the issue of shares to the public by these forms of business? (LCCI)

14. (*a*) What are the main functions of the Stock Exchange?

(*b*) Describe the work of (*i*) brokers and (*ii*) jobbers on the Stock Exchange. (LCCI)

15. (*a*) Describe the functions of a stock exchange.

(*b*) Explain how shares are bought and sold through a stock exchange. (LCCI)

16. (*a*) Distinguish between each of the following: (*i*) bank loan; (*ii*) debenture stock; (*iii*) overdraft.

(*b*) Under what circumstances might a business use each of these methods to raise finance? (LCCI)

17. (*a*) Distinguish between: (*i*) bonus shares; (*i*) ordinary shares; (*iii*) preference shares.

(*b*) How and why might a company raise extra capital by methods other than by the issue of shares? (LCCI)

18. A private limited company has the opportunity to expand but needs to raise additional funds amounting to approximately £100,000. Explain *four* methods by which the money may be raised, indicating the effects of each on the organisation of the company. (RSA Inter.)

8 Turnover, Cost and Profit

1 Wages and profits

A person employed by a firm – whether it be a large limited company or the business of a sole proprietor – receives wages or salary as payment for his services. His wages may be based on a time rate, that is, calculated at a certain rate for every hour he works. If, for example, the rate of pay is £1.80 an hour, and he works forty hours in one week, his wages for that period will be £72. Alternatively, he may be paid on a piece rate, in which case his wages will be calculated at a certain rate for the amount of work he does. Thus, if his work is reckoned in units and he is paid at the rate of £1 per unit, then if he accomplishes seventy-six units of work in one week his pay will be £76 for that week. If he does eighty units of work the following week his wages will then be £80.

For their services in running the risk of providing the capital the owners of a business receive payment in the form of profit. This is clearly seen if the firm is a limited company, for, as we saw in Chapter 7, the distributed profits are apportioned among the shareholders in proportion to the number of shares they hold. It is less clearly seen in the case of a sole proprietor, who may be inclined to regard the excess of his receipts over his payments as profit, although he may have devoted the whole of his time to the management of the business. Strictly, therefore, part of his earnings comprise wages – even though he pays them to himself – and only the balance should be regarded as his profit. An economist would go farther than this, and say that he should also deduct the interest which he would otherwise have received on his capital if he had invested it in (say) government stock instead of his own business.

2   The calculation of profit: gross profit

In the case of a single article, gross profit can be regarded as the difference between its cost price and its selling price. If a bookseller buys a book for £4 and sells it for £6, then his gross profit will be £2. The difference between the two prices is the retailer's mark-up. It can be calculated as a percentage of either the cost price or, as is the usual practice in retail trade, of the selling price. In the example just quoted the mark-up is 50 per cent – £2 on £4 – if calculated on cost, but only 33⅓ per cent – £2 on £6 – if calculated on selling price, that is on sales or on returns as it is sometimes called. A recent Census of Distribution showed that in certain branches of the retail trade the average mark-up was as follows:

Branch of trade	Mark-up (percentage on selling price)
Chemists, jewellers, booksellers, stationers, furniture	30
Clothing	28½
Grocers	30
Butchers	15½
Sweets, tobacco, newsagents	15

More important than the mark-up on single articles to the businessman is his gross profit for a trading period of (say) six months or a year. To calculate this he draws up a Trading Account as shown on p. 99.

This shows that when he valued his stock at his stocktaking at the end of the previous year it came to £2,160. During the six months 1st January to 30th June he purchased additional stock to the value of £21,840 after deducting the cost of any goods which had to be returned. Towards the end of June he took stock again and valued it at £3,520. During the half-year his total sales came to £31,320 again after making allowance for any goods which were returned to him. The balance, that is, the difference between the two sides of the account – £10,840 in this example – represents his trading surplus or gross profit for the period. In order to be able to draw up an accurate trading account, it is clearly necessary to take stock at regular intervals and to keep careful records of both sales and purchases.

Trading Account
For the period 1st January to 30th June, 19—:

	£		£
Jan. 1 To opening stock	2,160	June 30 By sales (less returns)	31,320
June 30 To purchases (less returns)	21,840	By closing stock	3,520
To balance (gross profit)	10,840		
	34,840		34,840

3 The calculation of profit: net profit

The trading surplus or gross profit, however, is not what a businessman is most interested in. What he wants to know is the net profit – that is, the balance after all expenses of running the business have been met. The expenses which must necessarily be incurred in carrying on a business are known as working expenses or overhead costs, or sometimes oncost. To calculate net profit he must draw up a Profit and Loss Account as shown on p. 100.

This Profit and Loss Account shows that the working expenses of the business for the half-year 1st January to 30th June came to

£6,680, and the item £10,840 gross profit on the other side of the account has been brought down from the Trading Account for the same period. The difference between these two totals (£4,160) represents the net profit for the six months. Of course, if the total expenses exceed the gross profit, the difference will then indicate a net loss.

Net profit varies between firms in the same branch of industry or distribution according to the efficiency with which the business is conducted. Between firms in different industries there exists wide variation in the amount of net profit they earn, the explanation generally being that the greater the amount of risk involved in a particular line of production, the greater will be the possibilities of making large profits, but also the greater the risk of making a loss. Gold-mining is a more risky undertaking than worsted manufacture, and so one would expect to find a much greater variation in profits between one year and another in gold-mining than in the other industry.

Profit and Loss Account

For the period 1st January to 30th June, 19—:

	£		£
June 30 To rent, rates		June 30 By gross	
and taxes	1,400	profit	10,840
To wages	3,400		
To insurance	280		
To interest			
on loan	440		
To advertising	96		
To depreciation	560		
To light and			
heat	504		
To balance			
(net profit)	4,160		
	10,840		10,840

4 Working expenses and turnover

A manager of a business will examine both the Trading Account and the Profit and Loss Account very carefully, comparing the latest returns with previous periods in order to ascertain what progress his firm is making. The working expenses will be particularly watched and analysed, and if any item shows a serious rise an explanation will be sought immediately. To enable the returns to be fairly judged, the various items of expenditure may be calculated as percentages of the turnover of the business, that is, of its total net sales. In the above example the turnover was £31,320 as shown by the item "Sales, less returns" in the Trading Account. Interest on loans at £440, therefore, formed approximately 1½ per cent of turnover, and advertising at £96 only one-third of 1 per cent.

Rate of turnover (or stockturn). The rate of turnover is the number of times the average stock is sold during a particular period – generally one year. Stockturn is probably a better term. If the average amount of stock held by a business is valued at £2,000 and the rate of turnover for the year is 12, then total sales or turnover will be £24,000. Therefore:

Value of average stock × Rate of turnover = Turnover.

If we know the value of the average stock and the turnover it is quite easy to find the rate of turnover. The calculation of the average stock, however, is not an easy matter.

Some retail businesses have a rapid rate of turnover, as, for example, greengrocers, who often replenish their stock daily. The value of the average stock of such a business will be low, but on account of the rapid rate of turnover the yearly turnover may be considerable. For example:

Average stock	£100
Rate of turnover	200
Turnover	£20,000

On the other hand, in the case of a business like that of a jeweller or furniture dealer the value of the average stock will be very great, but because the rate of turnover is slow the turnover may possibly be little less than that of the greengrocer. For example:

Average stock	£12,800
Rate of turnover	1½
Turnover	£19,200

The business with a slow rate of turnover will have to carry a much greater volume of stock than one with a rapid stockturn. Therefore we can say that the slower the rate of turnover, the greater will be the amount of capital required.

Net profit can be calculated as a percentage of either capital or turnover. It is necessary to decide which method to adopt and then keep to it, so that one year can be compared with another. Consider the following figures, which relate to the profit earned by a business in two years.

	Year I	Year II
Capital	£32,000	£32,000
Turnover	£48,000	£54,400
Net profit	£4,800	£5,120
Net profit as percentage of capital	15	16
Net profit as percentage of turnover	10	9

It will be noticed that if net profit is calculated as a percentage of capital it shows an increase of 1 per cent between Year I and Year II, but if it is calculated as a percentage of turnover it shows a fall of approximately 1 per cent for the same trading period! Which do you consider to have been the better year for this business?

5 Increasing the turnover of a business

It is clearly to the advantage of any business to increase its rate of turnover – since this will increase its turnover – always provided that this can be achieved without proportionately increasing its working expenses. Let us consider two methods by which a firm can attempt to increase its rate of turnover.

(a) *By means of an advertising campaign.* Advertising is undertaken for two purposes. It may be undertaken simply to make an announcement, and then it is known as informative advertising; or its aim may be to persuade people that the advertised commodity is better than others of a similar kind, this being known as competitive advertising. Advertising is essential if a new commodity is to be introduced to the market. Nearly half the total expenditure on advertising in Britain goes on newspaper advertising with advertising on television and outdoor hoardings coming next in order. Nearly a third of advertising, however, is in connection with trading stamps and gift coupons, free samples, catalogues and leaflets. It is sometimes argued that competitive advertising only results in goods being dearer to customers. However, if an advertising campaign widens a manufacturer's market it may result in a reduction in his other costs and so enable him to sell at lower prices, for in general it is the more efficient firms that spend most on advertising. Most people too appear to prefer to buy goods that are advertised rather than brands of which they have never heard. Expenses incurred by advertising are known as selling costs, and in the case of some branded goods they form a very high proportion of the total cost of production of the commodity – 45 per cent, for example, in the case of patent medicines.

A firm might attract more customers by making itself known to a wider circle of people by more extensive advertising, but if this should prove too costly it might result in a reduction instead of an increase in its net profit.

(b) *By cutting prices.* A second method of trying to increase the rate of turnover is by cutting prices, that is, adopting what is sometimes known as a policy of 'small profits, quick returns'. Such a policy will be successful only if the increase in the rate of turnover is sufficient to balance the smaller gross profit obtained on every article sold. Consider the following example.

From this table we see that in the first year this firm marked up its stock by 33⅓ per cent of selling price. Thus an article purchased for 60p would be sold for 90p. In that year the rate of turnover was 5,

	Year I	Year II
Average stock (at cost price)	£30,000	£30,000
Rate of turnover	5	8
Mark-up	33⅓% on returns	25% on returns
Turnover	£225,000	£320,000
Gross profit	£75,000	£80,000
Working expenses	£15,000	£16,000
NET PROFIT	£60,000	£64,000

thus giving a turnover of £225,000. Since the stock which it sold cost £150,000 (that is, £30,000 × 5), its gross profit was £75,000. After deducting working expenses of £15,000 it was left with a net profit of £60,000.

In the second year this firm reduced its mark-up from 33⅓ to 25 per cent on sales, so that the article previously priced at 90p was reduced to 80p (the mark-up of 20p being 25 per cent of its selling price). As a result, the rate of turnover increased from 5 to 8, and turnover from £225,000 to £320,000. The cost of the goods sold in the second year was £240,000 (£30,000 × 8), and so the gross profit came to £80,000. Working expenses increased slightly – from £15,000 to £16,000, but even so net profit at £64,000 was up by £4,000 compared with the previous year.

(c) *Other methods of increasing turnover.* The small retailer is unlikely to undertake much advertising, nor is he likely to be able to cut his prices as much as his large-scale competitors. He may try, however, to attract more customers, and so increase his turnover, by his skill as a salesman, his agreeable behaviour and by making his shop more attractive, both inside and out, especially by having a good window display.

6   Costs

So far we have been considering only retail businesses. It will be of interest now to see how net profit is calculated in the case of a manufacturer. The main difference is that, instead of speaking of working expenses, the manufacturer is more likely to use the term costs. Many of his costs – rent, rates, wages, etc. – are similar to those of the retailer. Whereas, however, the retailer thinks of his turnover, the manufacturer is concerned with his output.

Costs are of two kinds – fixed and variable.

(*a*) *Fixed costs*. These are costs which have to be incurred whether the output of the business is large or small, that is, they do not vary with output. Thus the average fixed cost per unit of output will generally decline as output increases, and this is one of the reasons making for economy in large-scale production. Fixed costs, therefore, include rent and rates, interest payments on loans and the cost of office administration, for a hundred small orders will give rise to as much clerical work as a hundred large ones.

(*b*) *Variable costs*. These are the costs which vary with output, often increasing or decreasing more or less proportionately as output rises or falls. Variable costs include the cost of raw materials, power for driving the machinery and wages paid to the workmen, since all these are required in greater quantities as output increases.

Prime and supplementary costs. Sometimes costs are categorised as prime and supplementary. Prime costs comprise all the variable costs just mentioned together with the cost of administration. Though the cost of administration does not vary with every change of output, it will vary if considerable changes of output occur. A large expansion of output will certainly require some enlargement of the office staff, just as a big fall in output will lead to its reduction. All the rest of the fixed costs form the supplementary costs.

The following diagram will make the distinction between the various kinds of costs clearer.

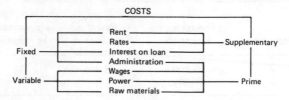

The distinction between prime and supplementary costs is of most importance in time of trade depression. Whether a firm remains in production or temporarily closes down, it will still have to meet its supplementary costs. Even though its income from the sale of its product at such a time is sufficient to cover only its prime costs, its loss will be no greater than if it closed down for a period. The advantage of remaining in production in these circumstances is that it will benefit immediately from a revival of trade. In the long run, of course, every business must cover all its costs, both supplementary and prime.

Questions

1. What do you understand by 'rate of turnover'? Show how it is calculated and of what use it may be in determining the credit-granting policy of a wholesaler. (RSA)

2. Distinguish between prime and supplementary costs and show how each enters into total costs. Your answer should be illustrated with examples. (NCTEC)

3. (a) What do you understand by rate of turnover of stock?
(b) Would you expect a fishmonger's rate of turnover of stock to be much different from that of a bookseller?
(c) If a shop has an average monthly rate of turnover of stock of 2 and an average stock valued at £1,200, what is the average yearly sales? (LCCI)

4. Explain what is meant by turnover of stock, and indicate its value to the trader as a measure of success. What steps does he normally take to increase turnover? (WJEC)

5. The following information relates to a firm for the year ended 30th June:

Department	Average stock at cost price	Rate of stockturn	Gross profit as a percentage of a turnover
X	£6,800	3.0	32
Y	£6,900	2.4	28

(*a*) Find the firm's: (*i*) turnover; (*ii*) total gross profit for the year.

(*b*) Express the total gross profit as a percentage of turnover.

(*c*) The expenses for the year, which amounted to £10,800, were allocated to the departments in proportion to rates of stockturn. Calculate the net profit of each department. (GCE Camb.)

6. (*a*) What is meant by turnover?

(*b*) The following relates to the business of a trading firm:

	Year I	Year 2
Cost price to firm of goods sold	£46,400	£57,915
Mark-up as a percentage of turnover	21%	19%
Expenses	£6,500	£5,720
Average stock on hand at cost price	£3,861	£3,408

(*i*) For each year – calculate rate of stockturn, the gross and net profits, and express the net profit as a percentage of turnover.

(*ii*) From all the information before you – after completion of (*i*) – state what conclusions you draw. (GCE Camb.)

7. What is the relationship between the rate of turnover and the amount of circulating capital required in a business? During the course of a year a businessman buys 4,000 units of a commodity at 50p each and sells them for 75p. His selling expenses are £300. The next year the cost price rises to 60p and he buys 3,960 units. If the same percentage write-up on cost price is used to fix selling price, and selling expenses fall by £10, find by how much net profit will alter. (GCE JMB)

8. If you were told that a businessman buys £5,000 worth of goods in a year and sells them for £10,000, explain what other information you would need in order to be able to calculate: (*a*) the average stock; (*b*) the percentage of net profit to turnover; (*c*) the percentage return on capital.

What would you take into account if you were asked to say whether it would pay him to reduce his selling price or not? (GCE JMB)

9. Distinguish clearly between fixed and variable costs. (LCCI)

10. What is the meaning of the term 'turnover'? What is the purpose of endeavouring to increase the rate of turnover in a retail business? By what methods can this be achieved and will such an increase always be advantageous? (NCTEC)

11. What advantages does the consumer derive from advertising by firms? Give examples. (RSA)

12. (a) What is the purpose of a balance sheet? (*4 marks*)

(b) (i) If you are examining the balance sheet of a company describe two factors which give indications as to the strength of the company. (*4 marks*)

(ii) Give two ratios that might be calculated for a company to measure the success of its operations. (*2 marks*)

(iii) What is the significance of the level of working capital to a company? (*4 marks*)

(c) Radlo Ltd. have drawn up plans for expansion and wish to raise additional finance. They require a short-term finance of £50,000 and long-term finance amounting to £250,000.

(i) Describe one source of short-term funds. (*2 marks*)

(ii) Describe two types of long-term finance. (*4 marks*)

(RSA Inter.)

13. (a) List the following as either assets or liabilities of a company as they would appear in its balance sheet: (i) issued share capital; (ii) trade debtors; (iii) trade creditors; (iv) stock; (v) debentures. (*5 marks*)

(b) Explain why, in each case, you have listed the item as an asset or a liability. (*10 marks*)

(c) Why may the issued share capital differ in value from the authorised share capital? (*5 marks*)

(RSA Elem.)

9 Making Payments in Home Trade

1 Means of payment

At the present day there are several different means by which a person in Britain can make a payment to someone. These consist of two main kinds of money and various documents which entitle their owners to specified sums, and which, therefore, can be regarded as claims to money. Money takes the form of (*a*) cash, comprising coins and Bank of England notes, and (*b*) bank deposits which, as we shall see shortly, can be transferred from one person to another by cheque. In a modern community by far the most important kind of money is the bank deposit, for most business payments nowadays are made by cheque. In Britain cash now forms only a small part of our total supply of money – in 1983 £11,527 million out of a total of £99,096 million – although for most people cash remains the normal method by which they pay for their purchases at shops, as is clearly shown by the huge withdrawals of cash which are made from the banks every December to cover Christmas shopping. Of rapidly increasing importance, however, is the use of various types of card, e.g. Access, American Express and Diners' Club. These will be examined more fully following (*see* p. 117).

Cash is provided by the state, through either the Royal Mint or the Bank of England. The Royal Mint is a government department which, under the control of its Master, the Chancellor of the Exchequer, undertakes the production of all our coins. Until 1968 it was located in London but in that year it was transferred to Llantrisant near Cardiff. The Bank of England, state-owned since its nationalisation in 1946, is responsible for the issue of Bank of England notes. Banks provide cheques for those of their customers whom they are prepared to allow to use bank deposits for making payments. The state and the banks, therefore, supply us with our money. Claims to money in the form of postal orders and money orders are provided by the Post Office, and bills of exchange can be drawn on businessmen themselves.

2   Cash

Cash, then, consists of coins and bank notes. Until the late fifteenth century only silver coins were in use in this country, the gold sovereign (£1) first being struck in the reign of Henry VII. Gold coins were withdrawn from circulation in 1915 and cupronickel replaced silver in 1946. The standard unit of currency in Britain became the pound sterling (so-called because it originally represented one pound weight of silver). When the currency was decimalised, the pound was retained as the standard unit, subdivided into 100 new pence. The coins of lowest value – 1p and 2p – are made of bronze, and the others – £1, 50p, 20p, 10p and 5p – are made of a nickel alloy. (The bronze ½p coin was abolished in 1984.) None of our present-day coins are worth as metal much more than a quarter of their face value, and for this reason they are said to be token coins.

Legal tender. This may be defined as any means of payment which a debtor can legally compel his creditor to accept in settlement of a debt. Only cash – Bank of England notes and coins – is legal tender. Since most business payments are made by cheque, it is clear, therefore, that businessmen do not generally insist upon being paid in legal tender. The former gold coins, which were worth exactly their face value, were legal tender up to any amount, but those made of other metals are only limited legal tender – 20p for bronze 1p and 2p coins; £5 for 5p and 10p nickel and £10 for 20p and 50p nickel coins; and up to any amount for the £1 nickel coin. It is not now regarded as important whether money is token or not.

Note issue. In England the only bank with the right to issue notes is the Bank of England, but several banks in Scotland, Northern Ireland and the Isle of Man enjoy limited powers of note issue. Only four denominations of notes are now printed – £50, £20, £10, and £5. Bank of England notes for £1 are still legal tender up to any amount in Great Britain and Northern Ireland, but £5 notes are legal tender only in England, and the notes of the Scottish and Northern Irish banks are legal tender only in the countries in which they are issued. Since the promise printed on Bank of England notes now simply means that, if necessary, the Bank will replace them, they are, like coins, merely tokens.

The Royal Mint manufactures all coins and then sells them to the Bank of England, which puts them into circulation as the commercial banks require them.

The Bank Charter Act of 1844 said that, except for its fiduciary issue, all Bank of England notes should be backed by an equivalent amount of gold. The fiduciary issue – that part of the note issue not backed by gold – was very small in those days, but by 1983 the whole of the note issue was fiduciary (*see* Chapter 11). The fiduciary issue can be increased – or decreased – only with the consent of Parliament. It is customary nowadays to increase the fiduciary issue temporarily at Christmas and in the summer when there is a greater demand for cash.

3 Cheques

It will be easier to understand much of the work undertaken by commercial banks if we first consider cheques and bills of exchange. A cheque can be defined as an instrument by means of which a sum of money can be transferred from the banking account of one person to that of another. It is an order made by the debtor (the drawer of the cheque) to pay to the person named on the cheque (the payee) a stated sum of money. For example, suppose that Tom Brown, who

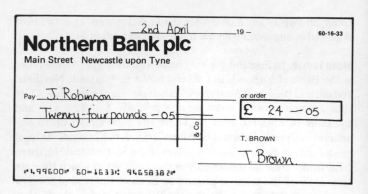

has an account with the Newcastle upon Tyne branch of the Northern Bank, owes £24.05 to Jack Robinson, who banks with the Midland at Leicester. If Brown has a cheque book he can pay by cheque. He should complete his cheque in the form shown on the specimen given above. This is as recommended by the British Bankers' Association.

The series of numbers on the bottom of the cheque enable it to be sorted by electronic means and dealt with by computer. The first number is the serial number of the cheque, the second is the code number of the branch of the bank and the third is the drawer's account number. Most British banks now have their customers' names printed on their cheques.

Brown sends this cheque by post to Robinson, who takes it to the Leicester branch of the Midland Bank and pays it into his account there. The Midland Bank then has to collect the sum of £24.05 from the Northern Bank. How this will be done will be considered shortly.

The cheque itself, however, is not money, but simply a means of transferring a sum of money in the form of a bank deposit, and therefore Robinson cannot be legally compelled to take Brown's cheque. Since a cheque is only an instrument by which the transfer of a bank deposit is effected, its value depends upon whether Brown really has £24.05 to his credit when the cheque is eventually presented at the Newcastle branch of the Northern Bank. If Brown

proves to have less than this sum in his account the bank may refuse
it, mark it 'Refer to drawer' and return it to Robinson, who then
becomes the possessor of a worthless piece of paper. When this
happens the cheque is said to be dishonoured. It is clearly risky,
therefore, to accept a cheque from a complete stranger who might be
difficult to trace if his cheque was dishonoured.

4 Order and bearer cheques

It will be noticed that on the above cheque there occurs the phrase:
'Pay J. Robinson or order'. The significance of the word 'order' is
that it makes it necessary for the payee – J. Robinson in our example
– to endorse the cheque by signing his name on the back of it unless
he is paying it into his account. Some cheques are made payable to
'Bearer', and these do not require to be endorsed. The Cheques Act
1957 requires an 'order' cheque to be endorsed only if the payee is to
receive cash in exchange for it or if he intends to transfer it to
someone else. Unless a special request to the contrary has been made
by the payee, an order cheque should always be used if it is to be sent
by post. An attempt by an unauthorised person to obtain payment of
an order cheque would require him to add the crime of forgery to his
other misdemeanour.

5 Open and crossed cheques

Another point to notice is that the specimen cheque is crossed:

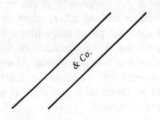

The effect of crossing a cheque is to make it necessary to pay it into a banking account, thus providing greater safety if it is sent through the post. In fact, all cheques sent by post should be crossed.

An open or uncrossed cheque, on the other hand, can be cashed by the payee, but only at the bank and branch named on it. Thus an open bearer cheque is no safer than a bank note, for anyone can cash it without formality at this one particular bank. When salaries are paid by cheque it is usual to leave them open, so that the recipients who have been paid in this way can, if they so wish, go along to the bank on which the cheque has been drawn and obtain cash for it. Some of them may not have banking accounts, and so payment by crossed cheque would cause them considerable inconvenience.

Types of crossing. To cross a cheque all that is necessary is to draw two parallel lines across the face of it, though it is usual though not essential to insert '& Co.' between the lines. Other crossings include:

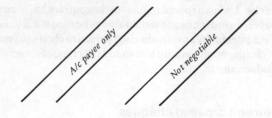

If a cheque is crossed 'A/c payee only' it can be paid only into the payee's banking account and no other, whereas in the case of the cheque crossed '& Co.' the payee can endorse it (if it is an order cheque) and himself use it in payment to someone else. The significance of the crossing 'Not negotiable' is considered below. All these are known as general crossings. A further precautionary measure which can be taken with a cheque is to give it a special crossing such as the following:

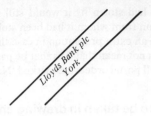

Lloyds Bank plc
York

In this case the cheque can be presented only at the branch and bank named between the lines of the crossing. Sometimes the crossing is printed, but the drawer himself may wish to withdraw cash from his account. If so he must write on it the words 'pay cash', adding his signature, and it then becomes an open cheque. The banks not unnaturally frown upon this practice, and permit it only when the cheque is made payable by the drawer to 'Self' or some other person who is well known at the bank.

Negotiability of cheques. A document is said to be negotiable if its ownership is transferable. The payee of an order cheque, as we have seen, can pass it on to someone else by endorsing it. In the case of a bearer cheque it is sufficient, just as it is with a Bank of England note, to hand it over without formality of any kind to another person. Thus an open bearer cheque is no safer than a bank note, and therefore should not be sent by post. If the creditor is willing, a debtor can pay him by means of a cheque made payable to someone else, provided, of course, that if it is an order cheque it has previously been endorsed by the payee. Thus a payee who had no banking account would have to find someone who was willing to put it through his own account. Thus, a cheque is a negotiable instrument.

The insertion of the phrase 'Not negotiable' in the crossing rather surprisingly does not of itself deprive a cheque of its negotiability, though it seriously restricts it. If it is desired that it shall be paid directly into the payee's account it should be crossed 'Account payee only' or 'A/c payee only'. If it is crossed 'Not negotiable' it means that the owner of the cheque is given no better legal right to it than the person from whom he received it. Thus if it had been received

from a person who had stolen it, it would still remain the legal
property of the person from whom it had been stolen. This form of
crossing is therefore an extra precaution in case the cheque should
be stolen, but it does not mean that it cannot be passed on from one
person to another. All postal orders are marked 'Not negotiable'.

6   Precautions to be taken in drawing cheques

The cheque can be a very useful, convenient and safe means of
payment if all possible precautions are taken to prevent its loss or
misuse. The following points should be noted.

(*a*) Care should be taken by the drawer when filling in the amount
both in words and in figures to see that no space is left in which an
additional word or figure could be inserted by some other person.
The usual practice, therefore, is to fill out any blanks with lines
which almost touch the words and figures. (Compare the specimen
cheque shown on p. 112). Some firms employ a special machine
which cuts the words and figures into the paper in order to make
alteration impossible.

(*b*) As a further precaution to supplement (*a*) the words 'Under
ten pounds' can be written on the cheque if it is for an amount less
than that.

(*c*) For reasons already given a crossed cheque should be used
whenever possible.

(*d*) By crossing the cheque 'A/c payee only' or, if the payee's bank
is known to the drawer, by using a special crossing giving the name
of this bank, the cheque can be paid only into the bank where the
payee has his own account and where he is personally known to the
cashiers.

(*e*) On receiving a cheque the payee should present it at his bank
without delay. Since the value of a cheque depends upon the drawer
having a sufficient sum in his account to meet it, it is important for
the payee to have it cleared quickly, in case it should be dishonoured.
Neglect to pay in a cheque quickly could, in certain circumstances,
result in loss to the payee, for although at the time when the cheque
was drawn the drawer may have had a large enough balance in his

account to cover it, during the interval before its presentation this may fall below the required amount. Though legally a cheque does not become 'stale' until six years have elapsed from the date on which it was drawn, a bank may refuse a cheque not presented within six months.

(*f*) In order to prevent a cheque being presented before a certain date the drawer can post-date it, that is, date it a few days ahead of the date on which the payee receives it, for a bank will have nothing to do with a cheque until the date stated on it.

Since the value of a cheque depends on the drawer having a sufficient balance in his current account to meet it, there is an element of risk in accepting payment by cheque. Nevertheless, 90 per cent of all business payments are made by this means. Many shopkeepers, however, are unwilling to accept cheques from customers who are not known to them. To overcome this difficulty cheque cards were introduced.

Cheque cards. All the British commercial banks issue cheque cards (sometimes known as bankers' cards) which at present guarantee personal cheques up to a maximum of £50. This makes personal cheques more readily acceptable as a means of payment. The holder of a cheque card can also use it to obtain cash when he is away from home, up to £50 being obtainable at any branch of any of the clearing banks irrespective of the bank at which the holder keeps his account. On the card is a specimen signature of the holder who must sign his cheques in the presence of the payee. It is usual too to write the card number on the back of the cheque.

7 Credit cards

These first appeared in the USA over sixty years ago when they were known as 'shoppers' plates'. Initially their use was limited to a trader's own stores. Later, reciprocal agreements were reached between groups of traders so that the cards could be used in other traders' stores. A major development in the evolution of cards was the creation of Diners' Club, its cards being acceptable in numerous stores, hotels, etc. The Club undertook to settle accounts and then recover the money from the cardholder. Cardholders had to settle their accounts monthly. By the 1950s several American banks were operating card schemes where the cardholder had the option of repaying only part of the amount owed and paying interest on the balance.

In the 1950s, two companies which provided credit services in the UK joined together under the Diners' Club banner and in 1963 American Express began to issue cards in the UK.

Barclays Bank, by arrangement with the Bank of America and its BankAmerica Card Scheme, launched Barclaycard as a credit card in the UK in 1966. Today there are nearly 1 million Barclaycard holders. Lloyds, Midland, National Westminster, Williams and Glyn's and the Royal Bank of Scotland formed the Joint Credit Card Company Ltd. in 1972 to provide the joint data-processing and marketing services required to introduce a new credit card called Access. Today, Access is the joint credit card service of the banks originally involved in its creation, together with the Clydesdale Bank, the Bank of Ireland and the Northern and Ulster banks. Each of the Access banks acquires its own Access cardholders and finances the balances outstanding on its cardholder accounts, while the Joint Credit Card Company provides the central services such as marketing, promotion and accounting services.

Today, NatWest is the biggest partner in Access with about 40 per cent of the business. There are 7.2 million Access cardholders. Access is part of Master Card which is a worldwide network of 3.7 million retail outlets used by nearly 100 million cardholders.

Whereas Barclaycard is a credit card and a cheque guarantee card for Barclay customers, Access is just a credit card. Access banks' customers require a separate cheque guarantee card.

Barclaycard is a member of Visa International, which is the world's main consumer payments system owned and operated by over 1,500 banks in nearly 100 countries. Visa developed from the bank card programmes begun by the Bank of America in the 1950s, and has been created by the banks to serve the banks. The name Visa was adopted in 1977. It now provides an operating structure that supports consumer payment services worldwide. By means of a

21-member international board of directors and five autonomous regional boards the banks which own Visa make worldwide decisions, then adapt each decision to customer needs country by country and region by region (Asia-Pacific, Latin America, etc.). Thus member banks are free to design their own financial, banking and travel services to meet local needs. They are also free to price those services. Visa does not, therefore, provide financial services directly to consumers or merchants, but provides a highly sophisticated worldwide telecommunications network, sets operating standards and develops products and services so allowing the member banks to offer their 100 million customers convenient and secure means of financing their purchases in 4 million outlets scattered across 160 countries. By means of effective marketing and major investment in the very latest telecommunications technology, the Visa organisation has experienced rapid growth in recent years, so that at present its authorisation and settlement systems can handle over 1 billion transactions a year.

In the UK, as elsewhere, the number of people with credit cards is steadily increasing. In 1983 there were 850,000 new Access cardholders and 600,000 new Barclaycard holders. The use of credit cards has also risen markedly; for example, Access holders made 153 million purchases in 1983 valued at over £3 billion.

Though tokens, cheques, cards and so on have been used as substitutes for cash for a long time, the use of cards as we know them today is a fairly recent development. The rapidly increasing number of cards may be grouped into three, as follows.

(a) *Bank credit cards.* These offer the cardholder credit to a pre-set limit. The holder receives a statement each month and the account can be settled in full or in part subject to a specified monthly repayment. Interest is paid on the outstanding balance. These are called *option* cards. With these cards there is no joining or annual fee.

(b) *Travel and entertainment (T & E cards).* These offer credit for the short period between using the card, for example to pay a hotel bill, and receiving the statement — a month or two. The holder is required to settle the bill in full, otherwise a penalty will be imposed. Joining and annual fees are usually charged. As there is no extended credit on these cards they are called *monthly* or *charge* cards.

Examples of this type of card are Diners' Club (the original T & E card) and American Express (Amex).

(c) *In-store cards*. These are issued to customers by retail businesses and are only valid for use in the store issuing a particular card, for example C & A, Tesco, Etam and Chelsea Girl. Usually, the cardholder makes regular monthly payments to the retailer from whom he has received his card. As a result these cards are also called *budget* cards.

In all cases, (i) cards are issued only after the applicant's creditworthiness has been accepted as satisfactory, and (ii) they involve the idea of revolving credit whereby a cardholder can keep spending and repaying the credit to a specified limit.

8   Other means of payment provided by banks

(a) *The bank draft* is really a cheque drawn on a bank. It can be open or crossed like any other cheque. Since it is drawn on a bank, there is no risk of its being dishonoured, for the person obtaining it has already paid over to the bank the sum for which it has been drawn.

(b) *Travellers' cheques*. These are issued by banks for the convenience of customers who are going to be away from home for a period and who will have to make payments to strangers who would be unwilling to accept personal cheques. They save the traveller having to carry a large sum of cash with him on his journey. They can be cashed at any bank or used as a means of payment in hotels and many shops. They are particularly useful when travelling abroad and, moreover, they are essential when travelling to or from countries which impose restrictions on the export of their currencies.

(c) *Credit transfers*. These provide a means of payment for people with or without bank accounts. A person without a bank account completes the credit transfer form and then hands it into a bank with the cash, the bank making a small charge. The amount due is then transferred to the creditor's account. The credit transfer is also useful to the person who has a banking account, for it enables him to make a group of payments by means of a single cheque.

9 Post Office means of payment

The Post Office has provided means of payment since 1792 when the forerunner of the money order – the money-letter – was first issued. This service was provided at first by a group of post office clerks, and it was not until 1838 that the Post Office itself took over the service. The aim was to make it safer to send money from one place to another in days when the danger of highwaymen made it risky to send money by coach. Postal orders were not issued until 1881.

The Post Office provides means by which payments up to a maximum of £50 can be transmitted by post. For very small amounts stamps can be used. For sums up to £1 and in multiples of £1 up to £10 there are postal orders, and for amounts up to £50 there are money orders. On both postal orders and money orders poundage has to be paid.

Postal orders can be purchased without formality, but an application form has to be completed before a money order can be obtained. Both types of orders can be crossed, in which case, like crossed cheques, they must be paid into a banking account. They are perhaps most useful to people without banking accounts, since if they are not crossed they can be cashed at a post office. This, however, increases the risk of loss, but it can be minimised if certain precautions are taken. For example, a money order can be cashed only at a particular post office by a person able to give the name of the payee which is not stated on the order itself, this information being passed on to the paying office by the issuing office. A postal order, too, can be made payable only at a particular office.

Another useful means of payment provided by the Post Office is the telegraphic money order, by which a sum of money can quickly be made available to a person at a distance. An extra charge is made to cover the cost of the telegram, and before he receives payment the payee will have to prove that he is the person for whom the money was intended.

Following the practice of some other countries the British Post Office introduced a national giro service in 1968. A feature of a giro service is that customers' accounts are all kept at one centre – in Britain at the National Giro Centre at Bootle in Lancashire. To make use of a giro account a balance must be kept at a post office, this being similar to a bank balance. Payments between giro account holders can be made by transfers from one account to another, and other payments can be made by giro cheque. No interest is paid on giro accounts. Many people who are unaccustomed to bank cheques prefer the postal giro to opening a current account at a bank.

10   Bills of exchange

Nowadays the most usual means of payment for transactions between businessmen in this country is the cheque, but occasionally a bill of exchange may be employed, although they are much less common now than they were a hundred years ago. An inland bill of exchange takes the following form.

£560   110 New Quay Street,
                                                             Manchester M4 7XY
                                                              10th June 19—.
Three months after   date pay to me or my
order Five Hundred   and Sixty Pounds,
value received.

To J. Green,
    Marine Street,   *G. Black*
       Liverpool L2 3BJ

Accepted payable at West Coast Bank, PLC, Liverpool. J. Green.

Features of a bill of exchange

(*a*) It enables the debtor, J. Green, to obtain a period of credit – three months in the above example. If Green has used the bill for the purchase of goods it gives him the opportunity of selling them before paying for them himself. Bills can be drawn for periods other than three months, or they can be made payable 'at sight'. Except in the case of 'sight' bills, three days of grace are allowed before payment is due. Thus Green will not have to pay the £560 he owes to Black until

13th September, three days after the completion of the period for which the bill was drawn.

(*b*) Unlike a cheque, a bill of exchange is drawn by the creditor. In the case of a bill the drawer and the payee are the same person.

(*c*) After being drawn by Black the bill is of no value until it has been 'accepted' by Green, who writes a statement to this effect across it, indicating at the same time the bank at which it will be payable when due. After being accepted in this way a bill of exchange is often known as an Acceptance.

(*d*) A bill of exchange is a negotiable instrument, and so Black may not have to wait until 13th September before he receives his money. He may be able to pass it on to someone else. This practice is considered in Chapter 10.

(*e*) Since the value of a bill, like a cheque, depends upon the financial position of some person, a creditor cannot be legally compelled to take this method of payment, for, like a cheque, a bill of exchange will be dishonoured if the debtor fails to meet it when due.

Treasury bills. The specimen bill of exchange shown on p. 122 is what is known as a trade bill because it has arisen in connection with a trade transaction – the purchase by Green of a quantity of goods from Black. Sometimes a bill of exchange is a means by which one person borrows for a short period. In such a case it is known as an accommodation bill. The government regularly borrows by this method, issuing three months Treasury bills each week for the purpose. Unlike trade bills, which can be for any amount, Treasury bills are issued only in fixed amounts of £5,000 to £1 million.

11 The promissory note

This is yet another instrument by which payment can be effected. It contains the promise of one person to pay another a stated sum at some agreed future date. Except that it is drawn by the debtor, and therefore does not require acceptance, it is very similar to a bill of exchange. Promissory notes are only rarely used in business in the United Kingdom.

Questions

1. What is legal tender?

2. Write brief notes on: (*a*) token coins; (*b*) the fiduciary issue.

3. Distinguish between: (*a*) order and bearer cheques; (*b*) open and crossed cheques.

4. What precautions should be taken: (*a*) in making a payment by cheque; (*b*) in receiving payment by cheque?

5. What is a negotiable instrument?

6. What means for making payment are provided by the Post Office? In what circumstances might they be used?

7. Compare the cheque and the bill of exchange as means of payment. Account for the popularity of the cheque.

8. Describe some of the ways in which a debtor in London may discharge his indebtedness to a creditor in Newcastle upon Tyne.   (RSA)

9. Describe and distinguish between: (*a*) a bearer cheque and an order cheque; and (*b*) a three months bill of exchange and a post-dated cheque.
                                                                       (WR)

10. Compare bank notes, postal orders, money orders and cheques as means of payment for the businessman. Which is the most convenient to him and why?   (LCCI)

11. Explain the purpose of crossing a cheque. Give an example of a general and special crossing.   (LCCI)

12. What do you understand by a crossed cheque, and what is the effect of the crossing? Give examples of special and general crossings, pointing out their particular significance.   (WJEC)

13. Give an outline of the Post Office giro system, mentioning the main advantages claimed for it.   (NCTEC)

14. Distinguish between Treasury bills and bills of exchange, stating the functions and characteristics of each.   (LCCI)

15. Guardrite Insurance Co. Ltd. receives payment from its customers through the post or by customers visiting its office. In one delivery of mail to the company there were two cheques, both of which had crossings printed on them. One crossing contained the words 'A/c Payee Only'. Also in this batch of mail was a postal order for £4.80. During the same day, one customer paid the company the amount he owed by credit card, while two further customers paid their bills by cash.

(*a*) State the purpose of having a crossing on a cheque, and explain the meaning of 'A/c Payee Only'. (*6 marks*)

(*b*) Would the customer who sent the postal order have paid £4.80 for it? Give a reason for your answer. (*2 marks*)

(*c*) Explain briefly the advantages to a customer of paying his bill by credit card. (*6 marks*)

(*d*) Name and briefly describe *one* other method of making payments to the insurance company other than those mentioned above. (*6 marks*)

(RSA Elem.)

10 Banks and Banking

1 Development of banking

The first English bankers were the London goldsmiths, who in the seventeenth century began to accept deposits from merchants, the goldsmiths having accommodation for the safekeeping of money and other valuables. In time the receipts given for these deposits came to be used as means of payment, especially when the goldsmiths issued them for convenient amounts, such as £5, £10, £20, etc. These goldsmith's receipts were thus the forerunners of our paper bank notes. So long as a banker had people's confidence they would be willing to accept these notes in payment. The goldsmiths too, after a time, began to lend; at first money and then their own notes. Outside London, banking developed as a sideline to the businesses of merchants and manufacturers. As their banking activities increased merchants and goldsmiths became full-time bankers.

Until the early nineteenth century all English banks (except the Bank of England) were private banks. By 1837 one hundred joint-stock banks had been established, and in times of crisis they proved to be much stronger than the private banks.

Large-scale banking developed partly as a result of opening new branches and partly by the amalgamation of existing banks. At first amalgamations were between private and joint-stock banks or between London banks and country banks. Later large banks began to amalgamate to form even larger banks.

A further series of mergers took place during 1962–69. As a result there are now only four large commercial banks in England – Barclays, the National Westminster, the Midland and Lloyds, each with between 1,000 and 2,000 branches distributed throughout the country. Most of the Scottish banks are affiliated to one or other of these four English banks. Each of the 'Big Four' now has a hire-purchase finance company as a subsidiary. Other large English banks include Williams and Glyn's, recently merged with the Royal Bank of Scotland, Co-operative Bank and the Yorkshire Bank. Some English banks also have subsidiaries (for example Barclays International, Lloyds International) with branches abroad. Thus, the great feature of the English banking system is a small number of commercial or joint-stock banks, each with a network of branches covering the whole country.

2   Types of banks

There are several types of bank in Britain.

(*a*) *The central bank*. The Bank of England acts as the central bank for the UK. Its primary function is to carry out the country's monetary policy. Only a few old firms, mostly in the City of London, have accounts with the Bank of England, for it is not regarded as sound policy for a central bank to undertake ordinary banking business. The Bank of England has branches in only a few of the more important commercial centres, such as Leeds, Manchester, Bristol, Birmingham, Newcastle upon Tyne, Liverpool and Southampton.

(*b*) *Trustee Savings Banks (TSBs)*. Originally these were small local banks, established to encourage thrift among small savers, the first being opened in 1810. An Act of 1817 forbade their making a profit. At first the TSBs concentrated on deposit accounts: (*i*) Ordinary Department accounts bearing a moderate rate of interest; and (*ii*) Investment Department accounts with a higher rate of interest, but with withdrawals subject to notice. After 1965 the TSBs began to widen their activities, their functions gradually approaching more nearly to those of the 'Big Four' commercial banks. The number of TSBs has been considerably reduced as a result of the amalgamation of local banks to form regional banks. In consequence their number fell from seventy-three in 1973 to sixteen in 1984.

(c) *The London Clearing Banks*. These belong to the London Clearing House and the Committee of London Clearing Banks and consist of Lloyds Bank plc, Barclays Bank plc, Midland Bank plc, National Westminster Bank plc, Royal Bank of Scotland plc, and Coutts and Co. They perform the typical functions of banks discussed below and are essential to the operation of the UK payments mechanism involving payments among branches or among banks through the Bankers' Clearing House or the Bankers' Automated Clearing Services (BACS).

The London Clearing Banks are sometimes called the High Street banks to distinguish them from the remaining banks. By means of a network of thousands of branches these banks provide a comprehensive service throughout Britain.

(d) *The Scottish Clearing Banks*. Scottish banking business is concentrated in the hands of the three Scottish Clearing Banks: Clydesdale Bank plc, the Bank of Scotland and the Royal Bank of Scotland plc, all of which have connections with the London Clearing Banks. Even so, they operate as independent banks and work through some 1,400 branches in Scotland.

(e) *The Northern Ireland Banks*. These two banks, Northern Bank Ltd. and Ulster Bank Ltd. dominate banking in Ulster.

NOTE: The LCBs, Scottish and Northern Ireland banks together with the Co-operative Bank plc, the Yorkshire Bank plc and smaller banks in the Channel Islands and the Isle of Man form what are commonly called the *commercial banks*. They undertake all kinds of banking business and therefore they are the most useful banks for businessmen and other people who wish to take advantage of the many and varied services they provide.

(f) *The National Savings Bank*. This developed out of the Post Office Savings Bank. Unlike the TSB it has remained as a savings bank and is not involved in either lending to the private sector or the payments mechanism. Instead, money deposited with it is invested in government securities, i.e. it acts as an intermediary between the government and savers. The Post Office operates this bank on behalf of the Department for National Savings through some 21,000 Post Office outlets.

(g) *The National Girobank*. This was established in 1968 as part of the Post Office Corporation and operates through the 21,000 post office outlets. Initially it only accepted deposits and provided depositors with a means of settling their bills. Since it was reformed in 1976 it has developed all the usual banking services, for example cheque accounts and the provision of travellers' cheques.

(h) *The discount houses*. These occupy a central position in the complex banking system of the UK, to which they are unique. They perform a variety of functions; for example, they discount bills of exchange, help the government to raise short-term finance by 'covering the tender' for the weekly issue of Treasury bills, and participate in the operation of several financial markets, e.g. the government securities or 'gilts' market. They are of great importance in the implementation of the government's monetary policy.

(i) *The merchant banks*. These banks have a long history and have developed a wide variety of functions, although their primary role is to act as acceptance houses. Here the merchant bank 'accepts' a bill of exchange (i.e. endorses it with its name) so that it becomes a *fine bill* and therefore qualifies for discounting. The acceptance also guarantees that the bill will be paid on maturity. Hence the merchant banks are important in the finance of international trade, in which the bill of exchange remains an important means of settlement of debt. The merchant banks also lend to local authorities, manage the investment funds of charities and insurance companies, act as agents for the issues of new shares by companies, advise on overseas investments and on mergers, and undertake insurance work through their insurance broking subsidiaries. Finally they are also involved in typical banking services. In fact these banks are involved in almost every conceivable productive activity of a financial and, increasingly, non-financial nature — one even owns an oil refinery.

Primary and secondary banks. Merchant banks are an example of a 'wholesale' bank in the sense that their deposits and loans are larger than those of the commercial banks (primary banks). The wholesale banks (secondary banks) are chiefly involved in international business with their deposits and loans being mainly in foreign currencies. Unlike the primary banks they have little, if any, involvement in the payments system, being concerned largely with the process of financial intermediation, i.e. facilitating the transfer of money from borrowers to lenders. Other secondary banks include:

(a) British overseas banks which are British-owned banks with their head offices in London but conducting their banking business overseas;

(b) foreign banks which are branches of banking concerns, the main retail banking business of which is in a foreign country, for example American, Japanese, Middle East and Hong Kong banks;

(c) consortium banks which are a recent banking innovation, the shareholders of which are other banks with no one bank having a direct shareholding of more than 50 per cent, and in which at least one shareholder must be an overseas bank, for example MAIBL (Midland and International Bank) plc.

3   The Banking Act 1979

Besides the central bank/primary banks/secondary banks classification the Banking Act of 1979 divided institutions which seek deposits from the public into two: 'banks' and licensed deposit takers (LDTs). To be able to take deposits an institution has to satisfy the Bank of England that it is well managed and financially secure. If an institution meets this as well as other requirements *and* provides a number of banking services, it can use the name 'bank', i.e. it is a 'recognised' bank. Generally only a recognised bank can call itself a bank. Institutions such as the National Girobank and the TSBs are exempt from the 1979 Act and so are able to retain the use of the term 'bank' in their titles. Unless an institution is a recognised bank or an LDT it cannot seek deposits from the public (*see* Chapter II).

4   Services of banks: deposit accounts

While still at school many boys and girls open accounts with savings banks. These, as we have already seen, are banks which specialise in providing safe-keeping for people's savings, the depositors being encouraged to allow the banks to look after their money by the payment of interest. The large commercial banks also allow their customers to open deposit or savings accounts.

The holder of a deposit account is generally required to give the bank a few days' notice if he wishes to withdraw from it, but if the sum wanted is small withdrawal may be permitted without notice. Few people nowadays keep large sums of money at home, for, indeed, it is foolish to do so for two reasons: (*a*) there is the fear of loss from fire or theft; (*b*) no interest is earned on money that is hoarded. The deposit account is not suitable where frequent and regular withdrawals are to be made, but it can be useful to the businessman who dislikes keeping money lying idle but yet wishes to keep something in reserve which he can draw upon fairly easily should the necessity arise.

Accepting deposits is the oldest function of British banks, and it was just because the goldsmiths had to provide themselves with strong-rooms in which to store their valuable stock that they became the first bankers in this country. In less settled times merchants who had no safe places of their own in which to keep their money were pleased to pay the goldsmith to take care of it for them. It was only when bankers found that they could make profitable use of the money deposited with them that they began to pay interest as an inducement to people to deposit money with them. Accepting deposits remains an important function of banks. To encourage small savers some banks provide 'home safes', which are really money boxes, the keys to which are kept by the bank concerned.

Money held in deposit accounts is sometimes called *time deposits*.

5 Services of banks: current accounts

In order to be able to make payments by cheque it is necessary to open a current account. In this case no notice of withdrawals is required, and also in contrast to the deposit account, instead of interest being paid, it is usual for the bank to make a charge for its services, since the use of cheques involves the banks in a considerable amount of work. In fact, dealing with cheques occupies the time of most of the clerks employed by a commercial bank. The convenience of the cheque as a means of payment and the safety it provides when money has to be sent by post have made it the chief method of payment in business.

Before anyone is permitted by a bank to have a cheque book he will have to give as references the names of one or two people who can vouch for his integrity and standing, for it is very important to prevent cheque books falling into the hands of irresponsible or untrustworthy persons. If the customer's references are found to be satisfactory the bank will then require him to give specimens of the signature which he intends to use on his cheques so that these can be compared if necessary with those on any cheques he draws. At one time the customer would then be given a pass book, which he would have to bring to the bank from time to time to be written up. Nowadays entries are usually made by computer and most banks supply loose-leaf folders and periodically issue to their customers up-to-date statements to insert in them. This provides a record of all the payments the customer has made by cheque and also shows the sums he has deposited in this account. The bank makes no charge for the cheque book.

By enabling their customers to use cheques, banks are acting as agents for payment, for the transfer of the sum of money from the drawer's account to that of the payee is undertaken by the banks.

Every time a deposit is made with a bank a form, known as a paying-in or credit slip, has to be completed and signed by the person making the deposit, whether it is for the credit of his own account or someone else's. Details of the deposit are inserted, showing how much is in bank notes, coin, cheques, postal orders, etc. For example, if Tom Brown wishes to make a deposit to his current account at the Northern Bank he will complete a credit slip similar to the specimen shown below. This shows how much of his deposit is in the form of bank notes, coin, cheques, money or postal orders, etc. He will also complete a similar counterfoil which the cashier will stamp and initial and then return to him as a receipt.

Northern Bank plc Current Account Credit	£10 notes	15
	£5 notes	5
	£1 notes	
Cashier's Stamp & Initials Date **8th March** 19 =	50p Coins	
	Other Silver	
	Bronze coin	
	TOTAL CASH	20
	CHEQUES	£50
ACCOUNT Tom Brown		12.5
		62.50
Paid in by Tom Brown Account Number 1 2 0 0 9 5 0		£ 82.50

At agreed intervals Tom Brown will receive a statement from his bank showing a summary of his transactions since his previous statement was issued. This statement will be similar to the one shown on p. 134. It will be noticed that cheques are designated only by their serial numbers. A standing order is one where the customer has instructed his bank to make a regular payment on his behalf.

Money held on current account constitutes *sight deposits*.

6   Services of banks: loans and overdrafts

One of the most important functions of a commercial bank is the lending of money to customers. It is, too, the most profitable of banks' activities. The extent of bank lending at any given time can be seen from the item 'advances to customers' in the balance sheet of a bank. In 1983 the total for the English commercial banks was £79,027 million.

Before making a loan to anyone a bank will want to know

something of the character of the borrower and the purpose for which he wishes to borrow. The borrower will also be asked what collateral security he can give the bank, and this should be something which the bank can turn into cash should the borrower for some reason find it impossible to repay the loan. An assurance policy provides an acceptable form of collateral security, because it always has a cash value. In the case of government stock or shares or debentures of public companies this is not so, for their prices fluctuate daily on the Stock Exchange, and if any of these are taken as security for loans the bank will have to be more cautious. It will have to be even more cautious if it accepts deeds of property as collateral security, for in a trade depression – just when many businesses might find the repayment of loans difficult – the value of property, especially business premises, falls considerably, and indeed in such circumstances it might be impossible to sell a factory building. In recent years, however, property has tended to increase in value.

					Sheet No.
	Statement of Account with				18
	NORTHERN BANK PLC			Description of entries	
	Main Street Newcastle upon Tyne			DIV Dividend S.O. Standing order	
	T. Brown Esq. 101 Steel Avenue Newcastle upon Tyne			Account Number	
				1200950	

Date	Description			Payments £	Receipts £	Balances £
19—	Brought forward					178.25
1 Mar.	X.Y.Z. Co.	169	102	10.10		168.15
8 Mar.	H. Smith	169	100	6.41	82.50	250.65
16 Mar.	Black & Green	169	101	12.20		244.24
17 Mar.	New Building					232.04
28 Mar.	Society	S.O.		21.08		210.96
5 Apr.	J. Robinson	169	103	125.20		85.76
8 Apr.	H. Jones	169	104	3.25		82.51

Most of bank lending is by overdraft or loan account. Of the two the overdraft is the more popular. If a borrower obtains an overdraft for (say) £1,200 it means that for an agreed period he can draw cheques for this sum in excess of the amount actually standing to the credit of his account. If he borrows by the second method the bank will place £1,200 to the credit of his current account and at the same time open a loan account for him showing a debit of £1,200. The main difference between the two methods of borrowing from a bank is that in the case of the loan account interest on the whole sum will have to be paid for the full period of the loan, whereas with the overdraft, interest is charged only on the actual amount by which the borrower's account is overdrawn, the bank calculating the interest on a day-to-day basis. A simple example will make this clear. Suppose that on 1st March Tom Brown, whose current account on that date shows a credit balance of £100, obtains from his bank a loan of £1,200 for three months at 8 per cent interest. He then proceeds to draw cheques as follows: £700 on 31st March and £650 on 30th April. Assume that he received a cheque for £50 which he paid into his account on 30th April. If he has chosen to borrow by means of a loan account the interest payable on 31st May will be £24 – 8 per cent of £1,200 for three months.

If, however, he borrows by way of an overdraft the amount by which his account has been overdrawn will first have to be calculated.

In this case the borrower would pay £24 if he borrowed by loan account but only £12 (a gain of £12) if he obtained an overdraft. Unless the full amount of the loan is required immediately and the amount to the credit of the current account is very small, the overdraft method is clearly to be preferred. It is, too, the better method when the exact amount of the loan required is not known. When a particular sum is required for a specific purpose, the exact cost of which is known in advance, borrowing by loan account can be made.

For the individual borrower there is also the personal loan. A person wishing to purchase (say) furniture priced at £120 might be able to persuade his bank to lend him £100, repayment of the loan being made in monthly instalments over a period of twelve, eighteen or twenty-four months as agreed.

A third method by which banks lend is when they discount or

rediscount bills of exchange, that is, purchase a bill at a little less than its face value, thereby permitting the debtor to be given credit while the creditor is paid promptly, less discount.

The rate of interest charged by the bank will depend on two factors: (a) the prevailing level of short-term interest rates; (b) the creditworthiness of the borrower – a private individual generally has to pay more than a business firm, and usually the small firm pays a higher rate than the large limited company.

7   Services of banks: other services

The following are some of the more important of the other services provided by banks for their customers.

(a) *Night safes.* These make it possible for shopkeepers to deposit their takings at the bank after it has closed for the day. In the outside wall of the bank there is a metal door which can be opened only by those people who have been supplied with a key. Money to be deposited is placed in a locked wallet and then put on a shelf inside, and when the door is closed again this causes the wallet to be tipped down into the bank's safe.

(b) *Cash dispensers.* The banks have installed cash dispensers which provide customers with cash. Though essentially a labour-saving device, they are useful to customers requiring cash when the bank is closed. It is also possible to obtain credit from some of the dispensers; for example, the customer can make a withdrawal from an Access account with a Cashpoint-Access card.

(c) *Banker's drafts and travellers' cheques.* Since the value of a cheque depends upon whether the drawer has a sufficient balance in his account to meet it, in certain circumstances people may be unwilling to take personal cheques in payment. Hotels bills, for example, cannot usually be settled by cheque. To cover such cases banks issue travellers' cheques and banker's drafts. These are really cheques drawn on the banks that issue them, and so are more generally acceptable. Travellers' cheques are particularly useful to people on holiday, and save their carrying large sums in cash with them. An alternative method is to request the bank to open a credit at a bank in a specified town (it need not necessarily be a branch of the same bank) so that cheques can be cashed there.

(d) *Regular payments*. A bank will accept standing orders to make regular payments on behalf of a customer, such as insurance premiums, payments to a building society or subscriptions to clubs or societies of which he is a member. Similarly, it can be arranged for interest or dividends on a customer's investments to be paid direct into his current account. Many firms pay their employees' salaries in this way.

(e) *Safe custody*. A bank will place its strong-room at the disposal of its customers for the safe custody of valuable documents like deeds of property, insurance policies, etc.

(f) *Dealings in stock exchange securities*. Though British banks do not themselves invest in stock exchange securities – Treasury Bonds, War Loan, etc., or shares in public companies – they are prepared to buy or sell them on behalf of their customers. They will also advise them regarding suitable investments for their money.

(g) *The bank as executor or trustee*. A bank will act as executor or trustee of a will.

(h) *Provision of cash*. Large firms pay out considerable sums each week in wages to their employees. Banks will undertake to provide them with the necessary cash in the form in which they require it – bank notes or coin.

(i) *Status enquiries*. A bank will act as a reference for a customer. Since a bank in its own interests has to know something about its customers' financial standing and integrity, it is in a position to supply general information on questions of this sort. Unless required by law, a bank will not, however, disclose particulars about a customer's banking account, and so it will give information only to another bank. (*See* p. 180.)

(j) *Assistance with overseas trade*. Banks will supply exporters with general and particular information regarding foreign markets and the creditworthiness of foreign buyers (*see* Chapter 20).

(k) *Foreign exchange*. Banks undertake foreign-exchange business, that is, they will obtain foreign money for their customers. The changing of money was one of the chief functions of early banks. Only limited amounts of foreign money can be obtained, the remainder having to be taken in the form of travellers' cheques which can be cashed abroad. All the various formalities in connection with foreign exchange are undertaken by the commercial banks.

(*l*) *The financing of foreign trade.* Banks, too, have a very important part to play in the financing of foreign trade transactions. This side of a bank's work is considered in Chapter 20. Banks can also advise their customers regarding trade conditions in many foreign countries.

(*m*) *Hire-purchase.* Most of the large commercial banks have acquired controlling interests in subsidiary hire-purchase finance companies. They also lend to both hire-purchase finance houses and to retailers who finance hire-purchase directly.

(*n*) *Mortgages.* In recent years banks have begun to compete with building societies by providing mortgages for home buyers. This development marks a change from the general banking practice of lending short term only.

(*o*) *Budget accounts.* The customer pays into his budget account so much per month — about one-twelfth — of his total bills for such items as gas, electricity, rates, car insurance, etc., and then draws cheques on it to meet the various bills as and when they fall due, even though this may cause an overdraft in some months. In this manner, the disruption caused by large irregular payments can be avoided, allowing customers to plan their financial affairs in a systematic way.

(*p*) *Factoring and leasing.* Most banks are involved in both of these activities. Equipment leasing allows firms to obtain equipment cheaply and quickly, whilst factoring often helps to improve a firm's cash flow.

8   The balance sheet of a bank

The items in the balance sheet of a bank provide a summary of a bank's activities. The chief item on the liabilities side is deposits. Total sterling liabilities of the London Clearing Banks in 1983 were over £64 billion, almost 35 per cent of this sum being in current accounts and the remainder in deposit accounts. The growth in sterling bank deposits since 1960 has been as follows.

Year	£ million
1960	7,230
1965	8,344
1970	9,899
1975	22,530
1980	37,763
1981	42,246
1982	50,013
1983	60,578

Source: *Bank of England Quarterly Bulletin* (1980 onwards).

On the assets side of the balance sheet the items are arranged in order of liquidity, that is, according to the ease with which they can be turned into cash. Obviously, then, cash comes first. The combined sterling assets of the London Clearing Banks in 1983 were as follows.

Sterling assets	£ million
Notes and coin	857
Balances with the Bank of England	321
Bills	1,505
Market loans	11,639
Investments	5,339
Advances	47,358
Total sterling assets	67,019

Source: *Bank of England Quarterly Bulletin* (1980 onwards).

(*a*) *Notes and coin.* This shows the banks' cash reserves. Banks must always be able to pay cash on demand. In effect, it is till money. Since 1971 there has been no requirement to keep a specific percentage of assets in this form.

(*b*) *Balances with the Bank of England.* This consists of any money which the banks have to keep at the Bank of England as a result of the calling of Special Deposits (*see* Chapter 11), cash ratio deposits which the banks, since August 1981, have been required to maintain at 0.5 per cent of their total liabilities, and balances kept at the Bank by the remaining banks to settle inter-bank indebtedness after the clearings. The banks can, of course, make withdrawals in cash from their balances at the Bank at any time, and in fact they regularly do so shortly before Christmas and at other holiday periods when there is a greater than average demand for cash.

(c) *Bills.* This item consists of Treasury bills and commercial bills of exchange which the banks have discounted.

(d) *Market loans.* This item consists of loans to the members of the discount market, chiefly to the discount houses. These are short-term loans repayable on demand or at no more than fourteen days' notice.

(e) *Investments.* This includes all securities owned by the banks, such as British government stocks with over one year to maturity, or undated stocks, stocks and bonds issued by local authorities. Investments act as a buffer between the banks' liquid assets, for example cash, and their relatively illiquid asset, advances.

(f) *Advances.* These consist of loans and overdrafts made direct to the banks' customers in the UK public and private sectors and to overseas borrowers. They form the banks' main asset and carry a rate of interest at least 2 per cent higher than their base rates. Thus they are the banks' most profitable asset — and the least liquid. Advances are usually for short periods, for example one to two years, but with the provision of mortgages for home purchasers the banks have also begun to lend long term.

Items (c), (d), (e) and (f) represent, therefore, different forms of bank lending, whilst items (a) and (b) are, in effect, reserves.

9   The clearing of cheques

Let us now consider what happens to a cheque after it has been drawn and despatched by the debtor to his creditor.

Suppose that John Smith, who has a current account with the Northern Bank at York, wishes to make a payment of £10 to William Robinson. Smith makes out a cheque payable to William Robinson or Order, crosses it and then posts it to the payee. On receiving the cheque Robinson will take or send it to his own bank, where it will be placed to the credit of his account. This bank must now collect £10 from Smith. This process is known as clearing the cheque.

Where a cheque is cleared depends on two factors: (a) whether the drawer and payee have accounts at the same bank; (b) whether the drawer's and payee's banks are in the same town, as the following table shows.

	Bank	Town	Where cleared
(a)	Same	Same	Branch
(b)	Same	Different	Head office
(c)	Different	Same	London
(d)	Different	Different	London

(a) *Branch clearings*. The clearing of a cheque is a simple matter if both Robinson and Smith have accounts at the same branch of the Northern Bank, for in that case all that is necessary is for a clerk at that branch to debit Smith's account and credit Robinson's by £10.

(b) *Head office clearings*. If Robinson, although having an account with the Northern Bank, lives in Manchester and pays the cheque into the branch of the Northern Bank in that city the clearing of the cheque will not be quite so simple. If the head office of the Northern Bank is in London the Manchester branch will send the cheque there, along with all other cheques drawn on other branches of the bank and paid into the Manchester branch that day. At the head office in London the cheques will be sorted according to the branches on which they have been drawn and then returned to these branches. The cheque received by Robinson will therefore be sent to the York branch so that Smith's account can be debited. Not until the cheque has been returned to the drawer's bank can it be determined whether the drawer has sufficient balance in his account to meet it. If he has not the cheque will be dishonoured and returned to the payee marked 'Refer to drawer'. It is for this reason that a bank will not normally allow cash to be withdrawn against an uncleared cheque until three days have elapsed after it has been paid in.

(c) *The London Bankers' Clearing House (LBCH)*. Where the
drawer and the payee have accounts with different banks, whether
in the same town or not, the cheque will be cleared at the LBCH.
Thus, if Robinson has an account with the Cambridge branch of the
Eastern Bank he will pay in Smith's cheque there. The cheque will
then be sent to the Eastern Bank's head office in London, where all
cheques drawn on other banks will be received, sorted according to
the banks on which they have been drawn and the amounts totalled.
These totals show how much the Eastern Bank has to collect from
other banks (including £10 from the Northern Bank as a result of
Smith's cheque), and a representative of the Eastern Bank will take
the cheques along with him to the Clearing House, where he can
make exchanges with the representatives of the other banks. Since
all the banks have claims on one another, these can to some extent be
offset. The amounts due from and to each bank are calculated, and
the position on the day on which Smith's cheque was cleared may
perhaps be as follows.

Bank	Amount due to other banks	Amount due from other banks	Difference (credit +, debit −)
	£ million	£ million	£ million
Northern Bank	54	48	−6
Southern Bank	61	65	+4
Eastern Bank	45	44	−1
Western Bank	49	52	+3
	209	209	−

Each bank keeps an account with the Bank of England and a
special Clearing House Account is maintained, so that all that is
necessary is for the Northern and Eastern Banks to pay into this
account cheques for £6 million and £1 million respectively, and for
cheques for £4 million and £3 million to be paid from this account to
the Southern and Western Banks respectively. The final settlement
is thus simply a matter of book entry, and although on this particular

day cheques have been cleared to a total value of £209 million, drawn on branches of the four banks all over the country and paid into banks scattered over an equally wide area, no movement of actual cash takes place. At the LBCH the average daily clearing in 1981 was over £4,800 billion. After being cleared the cheques are then returned to the banks on which they were drawn so that the accounts of the drawers can be debited. Thus, Smith's cheque will be sent to the York branch of the Northern Bank, and his account will be debited by the £10 which the Eastern Bank credited to Robinson. If Smith so desires, his bank will return the cheque to him. This is always done if there is a printed receipt on the back of the cheque.

The present-day members of the LBCH are the Bank of England, Central Trustee Savings Bank, the Co-operative Bank, Lloyds, Barclays, Coutts, Midland, National Westminster, Royal Bank of Scotland and the National Girobank. These banks clear their cheques with one another at the LBCH. Other banks, such as the Yorkshire Bank, clear their cheques by using one or more of the members of the LBCH as their agents. In 1983 about 3,340 million payment items – 13 million per working day — passed through the LBCH.

The clearing of cheques has been greatly speeded up in recent years with the application of the latest technology. For example, with the introduction of computers it has become possible to improve the methods by which paper entries can be handled, and usually it is not necessary for there to be a piece of paper for every entry. Since 1969 the Bankers' Automated Clearing Services Ltd (BACS) has performed the same role as the Clearing House but uses magnetic tapes instead of paper as the medium for the recording of entries. It receives over 500 tapes per day from local authorities, banks, firms (salary payments), government departments, and so on. These tapes contain numerous entries which are 'read' by the computer, which sorts out the entries for each bank and writes them back on to tapes. These tapes then pass on to the banks' computer departments and the contents are applied to the accounts. Hence through BACS money is transferred between accounts without the need for any paper to change hands. The number of items processed by BACS has been steadily rising.

In February 1984 a new electronic system came into operation called the Clearing House Automated Payment System (CHAPS). The system has been developed by the English and Scottish clearing banks. These together with forty other banks which have arranged to use CHAPS are now able to provide guaranteed nationwide same-day payments. In this way, CHAPS complements the existing clearing system.

Banks using CHAPS communicate with each other using British Telecom's Packet SwitchedStream Service (PSS), common hardware, jointly developed software and complex security safeguards.

In response to recent developments in technology the members of the LBCH in 1984 began a review of the organisation and operation of the clearing system to ensure that it will be able to meet the demands which will be made upon it in the future.

Questions

1. What are the chief types of bank found in Britain? State the distinctive features of each.

2. What is meant by saying that one function of a bank is to act as 'an agent for payment'?

3. Compare the loan account and the overdraft methods of borrowing from a bank.

4. What are the chief services which a retailer or a wholesaler may expect a bank to provide for him?

5. Consider the various items in the balance sheet of a commercial bank and use them to show the main functions of this type of bank.

6. What books and documents will a retailer have in connection with his current account at a bank? State how he will use each of them.   (RSA)

7. What is the Bankers' Clearing House? Outline the way in which it works.   (RSA)

8. What services can a bank offer to a businessman? Give a short description of each.   (NCTEC)

9. To what extent does the 'credit card' system of many of the joint-stock banks replace the established cheque system?   (NCTEC)

10. What are the advantages to a businessman of having a banking account? What documents will normally pass between the customer and the bank in the course of a year's business?   (LCCI)

11. What services does the banker offer to commerce and how does the trading community benefit from these services? (WJEC)

12. Describe three forms in which loans may be made by the large commercial banks. Give four examples of the kinds of security that might be accepted against them. (GCE JMB)

13. Explain the main services rendered by the banks to businessmen.

(GCE Camb.)

14. Name the principal joint-stock banks and discuss the value of services they offer to the businessman. (RSA)

15. Outline the main methods of payment provided by the commercial banks, giving an example of the use of each method. (LCCI)

16. Distinguish between:

(a) current accounts and deposit accounts;

(b) order and bearer cheques;

(c) general and special crossings;

(d) standing orders and direct debits. (LCCI)

17. Describe how the work of a commercial bank differs from that of a merchant bank. (LCCI)

18. Describe those services offered by a commercial bank which might be useful to retailers. (LCCI)

19. (a) Describe *three* main features of a current account held at a clearing bank. (*6 marks*)

(b) How does one open such an account? (*4 marks*)

(c) What is meant by the payment of standing orders out of a current account? Give an example. (*6 marks*)

(d) Why might direct debiting be used instead of a standing order?

(*4 marks*)

(RSA Elem.)

20. (a) Give *two* sources of finance available to a company apart from banks. (*4 marks*)

(b) Explain *three* ways in which a current account at a bank is important to a company. (*6 marks*)

(c) Explain how an overdraft can be obtained on a company's current account. (*4 marks*)

(d) Give *three* ways in which a bank loan differs from an overdraft.

(*6 marks*)

(RSA Elem.)

11 The Bank of England

1 Development of the Bank of England

The Bank of England (the Bank) was founded by Royal Charter in 1694 by a group of merchants of the City of London for the purpose of lending money to King William III, who was at that time engaged in war on the continent of Europe. At earlier periods English monarchs had borrowed from the goldsmiths, but the resources of these small private bankers were insufficient to finance a costly war in the seventeenth century.

The Bank differed from other English banks in that it was a joint-stock company with limited liability. Its capital, therefore, was much larger, and this made it very much stronger than the other banks, while its name added greatly to its prestige. At first, however, its business differed from that of the other banks in only one respect – though an extremely important one – namely, that it had the government's account.

Thus, the Bank, the oldest central bank, was not specifically established as a central bank, as has been the case in many other countries. Only very gradually during the nineteenth century did it take upon itself the functions of a central bank – to exercise control over the credit policy of the commercial banks and to carry out the government's monetary policy.

2 The Bank of England as central bank

The Bank is a central bank. Its aim is not to make a profit, and the little ordinary commercial banking it now undertakes is an unimportant sideline to its main activity which is to control the other banks and carry out the government's monetary policy. Consequently, a central bank must always work closely with the government of the day and the permanent officials of the Treasury. On account of its importance to a country's economic well-being, the central bank in some countries – for example, Britain and France – has been nationalised. In other countries – for example, the United States – the central bank is outwardly independent.

Until its nationalisation in 1946 the Bank had been a joint-stock company for 252 years, but for a long time co-operation between the Bank and the Treasury had been very close. It is therefore of little moment nowadays whether a country's central bank is nationalised or not, since in either case it must work closely with its government. At the present day a central bank is regarded as essential to the smooth working of a modern financial and monetary system, and there is now no country of any economic importance which does not possess one.

3 The government's bank

As banker to the government the Bank fulfils a number of functions.

(*a*) *Lender to the government*. The Bank was founded, as we have seen, for the express purpose of lending money to the king, William III. Thus the performing of a service to the government was the earliest function of this bank. At the same time, therefore, the national debt came into existence. Although direct lending by the Bank to the government is of little importance today, the Bank still retains this function.

(*b*) *Management of the national debt*. From the day of its foundation the Bank has been responsible for the management of the national debt. The funded portion of the debt consists of various government stocks such as 2½ per cent Consols, 9 per cent Treasury Stock 1992–96, 8 per cent Treasury Stock 2002–2006 and many more. The Bank's work in connection with the national debt includes the payment to the stock-holders of the half-yearly interest on these stocks as it falls due. It will be noted that two of the stocks just quoted bear dates – for example, 9 per cent Treasury Stock 1992–96. The dates indicate the period during which the government has the option of redeeming the stock at par – not earlier than the first date, but not later than the second. Thus, if it wishes, the government can repay this particular Treasury Stock in 1992, or at any time between 1992 and 1996, but in no circumstances later than 1996. The 2½ per cent Consols are unredeemable stock, that is, the government is not bound to repay them at any time. When a stock has to be repaid the government will generally obtain the money required for this purpose by the issue of a new stock. Holders of the stock to be redeemed will be asked to accept new stock in exchange, but if they are unwilling to do so they will have to be repaid. The Bank acts as the government's agent when stocks have to be redeemed or new stocks issued.

(c) *Banker to the government.* The government keeps its account at the Bank, on the balance sheet of which it is shown as Public Deposits. Into this account is paid the revenue from all taxes – income tax, VAT, customs and excise duties, etc. At the present day the UK's revenue amounts to over £80,000 million a year. Out of this the government has to pay interest on the national debt, the cost of administration and the armed forces, its share of the cost of education and other social services and make grants to local authorities. With the increasing activity of the state in the economic life of the nation in recent times payments between the government and other people have enormously increased, and so, therefore, has the clearing of cheques between the Bank and the commercial banks. Some of these payments are in connection with transactions with farmers, doctors, dentists, etc.

4   The note issue

The Bank is now the only bank in England with the right to issue bank notes.

At one time, however, all banks wished to issue notes, since in the early days of banking the lending of their own notes was their most profitable line of business. It was not until the late eighteenth century that the use of cheques became common among businessmen – and only then in London – and made possible lending by overdraft. The Bank was then the only bank in London with the right to issue notes, but in 1884 there were seventy-two other banks which issued bank notes.

The Bank Charter Act of 1844 aimed at restricting the power of banks to issue notes because at that time a large number of banks issued them, and the over-issue of notes by some banks had resulted in many bank failures. This Act divided the work of the Bank into two departments – the Issue Department and the Banking Department. The Issue Department was to be solely responsible for the issue of bank notes; the Banking Department was to cover the other activities of the Bank. The Act also compelled the Bank to publish a weekly balance sheet, known as the Bank Return. Two of the main provisions of this Act were as follows.

(a) Apart from a small fiduciary issue, the notes issued by the Bank had to be fully backed by gold. Thus the Bank could not expand its issue of notes unless at the same time it acquired an equivalent amount of gold.

(b) No new bank was to be permitted to issue notes. If an existing bank opened a branch in London or amalgamated with another bank which had a branch in London it had to cease issuing notes, the Bank at the same time being allowed to increase its fiduciary issue by two-thirds of the amount of the lapsed issue.

In the second half of the nineteenth century there were a great many amalgamations of banks. However, the great expansion of the use of cheques led to the loss of the right of note issue not being regarded as of any consequence. After 1844 banks one by one lost their right of note issue, and when in 1921 the bank of Fox, Fowler & Co. amalgamated with a bank with a London office the Bank was left as the only bank of issue in England.

However, when gold coins were withdrawn from circulation during the First World War they were replaced by Treasury notes for £1 and 10 shillings (worth 50p) and these circulated alongside Bank notes (issued only for multiples of £5) until 1928, when their issue was taken over by the Bank, which since that date has been the sole note-issuing authority in England, although some banks in Scotland, Northern Ireland and the Isle of Man still have very limited rights of note issue.

Since 1928 the Bank has been able to increase its fiduciary issue (that part of the issue not backed by gold) only with the consent of the Treasury. Nevertheless, since then there has been a huge increase in the fiduciary issue, as the following table shows.

Note Issue 1938–83

Year	Notes backed by gold £ million	Fiduciary issue £ million	Total £ million
1938	326.00	200.00	526.00
1945	0.25	1,400.00	1,400.25
1955	0.33	1,800.00	1,800.33
1965	0.33	2,650.00	2,650.33
1970	0.33	3,300.00	3,300.33
1975	–	6,150.00	6,150.00
1978	–	8,525.00	8,525.00
1979	–	8,843.00	8,843.00
1980	–	9,651.00	9,651.00
1981	–	10,160.00	10,160.00
1982	–	10,570.00	10,570.00
1983	–	10,910.00	10,910.00

Source: *Bank of England Quarterly Bulletin* (1979 onwards)

Since 1970 no part of the note issue of the Bank has been backed by gold.

5   The bankers' bank

It has been seen how useful a current account can be to a businessman who wishes to enjoy the privilege and convenience of making payments by cheque. A current account can be equally useful to a commercial bank itself for making payments to other banks. The Bank acts as banker to the other banks, which keep their own accounts there. Thus, the Bank is said to be the bankers' bank.

The most frequent cause of one bank having to make a payment to another is in the clearing of cheques. We saw in Chapter 10 that at the Clearing House the banks, so far as is possible, offset their indebtedness to one another, so that the final settlement requires only the payment of differences. Since each of the commercial banks has an account with the Bank, the settlement of any transaction involving payment from one bank to another merely requires an addition to be made to the balance of one bank and a deduction to be made from that of another at the Bank.

In addition to drawing cheques on his account in order to make payments to others, the private individual, if he so desires, can make withdrawals in cash simply by making out a cheque payable to 'Self'. In similar fashion banks also when in need of cash can make withdrawals in that form from their accounts at the Bank. At Christmas and in the summer, when the customers of the commercial banks tend to make heavy withdrawals of cash, they themselves find it necessary to withdraw cash from the Bank. Thus, the commercial banks regard their balances at the Bank as cash, and if the student looks back at the balance sheet of a bank shown on p. 139 he will see that the first item is: coin, notes and balances at the Bank. Actually about half the total is in the form of balances at the Bank, the remainder being distributed among the many branches of the commercial banks.

The two facts, (a) that the commercial banks have accounts at the Bank, and (b) that they regard their balances there as cash, have very important consequences. It is because of these two practices that the Bank is able to control the activities of the commercial banks.

6 The money market

Unlike the market in stocks and shares (the Stock Exchange), the money market has no special building of its own in which it transacts business. The members of the money market are, however, in easy touch with one another and most are to be found in the neighbour-hood of the Bank of England.

The main business of the money market is borrowing on short term, that is, perhaps for only a day or two, but in any case for not more than a fortnight. The borrowers are bill brokers and discount houses, and they require the money for the purpose of discounting bills of exchange. Thus there are two divisions of the money market, in one of which the business is concerned with short-term loans, while in the other the commodity dealt in is the bill of exchange.

Normally, bill brokers and discount houses borrow from the commercial banks, and the extent of their borrowing at any time can be seen from the size of the item 'market loans' in the banks' balance sheets. There are three large discount companies – Alexanders, the National Discount Company and the Union Discount Company – besides a number of smaller firms which undertake discount business.

In addition to the commercial banks and discount houses in the money market, there are also merchant bankers or acceptance houses which specialise in accepting bills of exchange, for unless the acceptor of a bill is well known no one will discount it. Of the merchant bankers in London probably the best known are Rothschilds and Barings. In return for a fee an acceptance house will accept a bill, originally accepted perhaps by a foreign merchant not known in London, thereby guaranteeing that it will be met when it falls due. Such a bill can then be discounted. The acceptance houses are able to do this because they make it their business to know something of the creditworthiness of merchants in all parts of the world, employing agents abroad to keep them informed on such matters. The commercial banks, too, do some acceptance business on their own account.

At the present day about two-thirds of bills handled by the money market are trade bills, the remainder being Treasury bills, that is, bills to finance short-term government borrowing. These are three-months bills. Each week the Treasury states the amount of Treasury bills to be offered to the market on the following Friday. Firms or institutions which wish to take up Treasury bills then tender for them, the Treasury accepting the highest tenders. The discount houses are expected to 'underwrite' or to 'cover the tender', i.e. take up all bills that have not been tendered for. The commercial banks do not tender for Treasury bills, but obtain them from the discount houses, generally after the latter have held them for about a month.

7   The Bank of England and the money market

What part, then, does the Bank play in the money market? It is the 'lender of last resort', that is, it lends to the market – on its own terms, of course – when the other banks are unwilling to lend. If the commercial banks find themselves running short of cash they will call in some of their loans to the money market, the members of which will then have to seek assistance from the Bank which, however, requires a higher rate of interest than that charged by the commercial banks. The discount houses and bill brokers, therefore, will not borrow from this source if they can help it, and having borrowed, they will repay their loans as soon as they are able. Thus, on account of the existence of the money market, British commercial banks when short of cash do not borrow directly from the central bank, as is customary in some countries, but, as was shown above, they prefer to call in some of their loans to the money market, and thereby compel the members of the money market to go to the central bank. The existence of the money market as a buffer between the commercial banks and the central bank is a distinctive feature of the British banking system.

8   Responsibility for monetary policy

The most important function of the Bank is to co-operate with the government in carrying out the country's monetary policy. In the nineteenth century this was left almost entirely to the Bank of England, but in the present century it has become the joint responsibility of the government and the Bank, with the government, in fact the Treasury, having the last word.

By monetary policy is meant deciding how much money there shall be in the country. To influence the supply of money a central bank must have some means of controlling the commercial banks, and since monetary policy affects the level of employment and unemployment, a central bank must, therefore, work closely with the government. The Treasury, in consultation with the Bank, may decide that the amount of money in the country shall be reduced, in which case a policy of deflation or disinflation (popularly known as a 'credit squeeze') will be pursued; or it may be decided that the quantity of money shall be increased, and if so a policy of reflation will be adopted. Whichever policy is agreed upon, the Bank will take steps to see that it is carried out.

The greater part of the money of this country nowadays consists of bank deposits. When a commercial bank grants a loan to a businessman it thereby increases total bank deposits. To decrease the quantity of money it is necessary, therefore, to persuade the commercial banks to reduce their lending; to increase the volume of money the banks have to be encouraged to lend and businessmen to borrow. The main aim of monetary policy, at present, is to reduce the rate of inflation. In the past, it has been used to help maintain a high level of employment ('full employment'), achieve a balance of payments equilibrium and keep the exchange rate at a specific parity, e.g. at $2.80 = £1 between 1949 and 1967.

9 Instruments of monetary policy

The Bank has two traditional instruments by which it can carry out its policy of increasing or decreasing bank deposits (and thus the money supply). Firstly, it may vary the rate at which it will discount bills (its discount rate). This was known as bank rate before 1972 and as minimum lending rate between 1972 and 1981. Secondly, the Bank may engage in open-market operations. These two instruments have been supported by other economic weapons, for example tax cuts, reductions in government expenditures (fiscal policy) and, until 1982, changes in hire-purchase regulations.

The Bank's discount rate is the rate at which it will discount or, more correctly, rediscount first-class bills of exchange (eligible bills), that is, those which have been accepted by a bank (*see* Chapter

10). The importance of bank rate used to lie in the fact that all other rates of interest offered or charged by banks moved up or down with it. In 1972, an important change took place. Bank rate was abolished and minimum lending rate substituted for it at the Bank for lending to the discount market. This no longer influenced interest rates generally. The commercial banks fixed their own base rate to cover their rates on deposits and their lending rate. Other rates of interest, such as that charged by building societies on mortgages and finance houses for hire-purchase transactions, however, were influenced by changes in minimum lending rate and base rate, though not directly.

In 1981 the Bank stated that it would be no longer set a minimum lending rate though the right to reintroduce this temporarily was reserved. The rate at which the Bank, since 1981, has intervened in the discount market as 'lender of last resort' has lain within a narrow unpublished band.

Open-market operations occur when the Bank itself intervenes in the market. By purchasing government stock and paying for it with its own cheques, the Bank will find itself in debt to the other banks at the Clearing House. This is easily settled, for it merely requires the balances of the commercial banks at the Bank to be credited by the amount of these cheques. Since the commercial banks regard their balances at the Bank as cash, their total cash will increase, and at the same time the ratio between their cash and their deposits will rise. The banks will then take steps to expand their deposits in order to restore their liquidity ratio. To bring this about they will become more willing to grant loans. The reverse of this would happen if the Bank were to sell securities in the market. In this case the balances of the commercial banks at the Bank would be reduced, and this would then compel them to reduce their lending in order to reduce their deposits.

Other instruments of monetary policy employed nowadays include: (a) 'moral suasion', or requests, instructing the banks to reduce their lending; (b) Special Deposits, which the Bank may require from the commercial banks when it is thought necessary to restrict their lending, and which can be repaid when bank lending is to be encouraged.

Nowadays, monetary policy is often supplemented by tax changes (such as increasing or decreasing VAT, the rates of income tax, or duties on petrol, tobacco or alcoholic drink). The aim of tax reductions is to encourage spending and so to stimulate production and increase employment; the aim of tax increases is to reduce spending and so to check inflation.

In the past, use was also made of hire-purchase regulations governing the amount of the deposit or the length of the period of payment. However, this instrument of monetary policy was dropped in July 1982.

Since 1979 the government's major economic policy has been to reduce the rate of inflation. To do this it has attempted to control carefully the rate of growth of the money supply and this has involved attempts to stabilise government and local authority spending. This policy is known as *monetarism*.

10   The Bank of England and its supervision of banks

In the UK the role of bank supervision was informal before the 1979 Banking Act, although the Bank had powers (which were never used) to regulate the other banks under the Bank of England Act 1946.

The 1979 Act had its roots in the mid-1970s when many small banks which had developed very rapidly after 1971 collapsed owing to their failure to follow the principles of prudent banking. The threat of a major crisis of confidence in the UK banking system was averted by the Bank's 'lifeboat operation', mounted in conjunction with the commercial banks. As a result of this crisis, and also the need to harmonise the regulation of UK banking with that elsewhere in the EEC, the supervisory role of the Bank was formalised in 1979.

Under the Act the Bank was granted powers to recognise certain financial institutions as banks if they offered a full range of banking services. Institutions such as the discount houses or the acceptance houses were also recognised as banks since they provided specialist services. Other institutions not providing the required range of services became 'licensed deposit takers' (LDTs). The Bank not only deals with applications for recognition or licensing, but supervises the work of the banks and the LDTs as well.

11   Other roles of the Bank of England

(a) The Bank manages the Exchange Equalisation Account on behalf of the Treasury. This account contains all of the UK's foreign exchange reserves and is from time to time used to help stabilise the rate of exchange of sterling against other currencies.

(a) The Bank maintains relations with monetary authorities in other countries, for example the International Monetary Fund (IMF), the Bank for International Settlements (BIS), the World Bank and various EEC bodies.

(c) Until October 1979 the Bank administered the UK's complex system of foreign exchange control under the Exchange Control Act 1947.

(d) Finally the Bank collects, analyses and disseminates information, for example in the *Bank of England Quarterly Bulletin*.

12   The Bank return

Consider now the weekly return of the Bank of England. This shows separately the balance sheets of the two departments of the Bank – the Issue Department and the Banking Department – which the Bank Charter Act 1844 compelled the Bank to publish weekly. It is issued every Wednesday. Below is a simplified specimen return.

The Issue Department is solely concerned with the issue of bank notes. The Banking Department shows clearly some of the other functions of the Bank – that it is the government's bank (public deposits) and the bankers' bank (bankers' deposits) and that it lends to the money market (advances and other accounts).

1. *Issue Department as at August 1983*

Liabilities	£ million	Assets	£ million
Notes in circulation	11,436	Government securities	5,394
Notes in Banking Department	4	Other securities	6,046
Total liabilities	11,440	Total assets	11,440

2. *Banking Department as at August 1983*

Liabilities	£ million	Assets	£ million
Public deposits (government's account)	42	Government securities	466
Special deposits (none in 1983)	–	Advances and other accounts (includes money lent to the money market)	1,137
Bankers' deposits (balances of commercial banks)	615	Premises, equipment and other securities	983
Reserves and other accounts	1,918	Notes and coin (*see* Issue Department, Liabilities)	4
Capital	15		
Total liabilities	2,590	Total assets	2,590

Source: *Bank of England Quarterly Bulletin*

Questions

1. What is a central bank? Why is it so important for the central bank and the government of the country to work closely together?
2. What services does the Bank of England perform for: (*a*) the government; (*b*) the commercial banks?
3. How did the Bank of England come to be the sole bank in England with the right to issue bank notes? What is the fiduciary issue?
4. Who are the members of the money market? Describe their work.
5. How does the existence of the London money market affect the working of the English banking system?
6. 'The most important function of a central bank is the carrying out of a

country's monetary policy.' Explain this statement.

7. What was the purpose of raising or lowering the Bank of England's minimum lending rate?

8. Write explanatory notes on any three of the following terms: (a) fiduciary issue; (b) limited legal tender; (c) bank return; (d) bank advances; (e) Issue Department of the Bank of England.   (RSA)

9. Explain the importance of the Bank of England in the English financial system. In what ways does it differ from other banks in the country? (UEI)

10. Outline the main functions of the Bank of England.   (NCTEC)

11. Give some account of the organisation of the London money market.
    (LCCI)

12. What services do the various financial institutions render (a) to businessmen in this country, and (b) to businessmen abroad?   (LCCI)

13. Describe three activities undertaken by the Bank of England which are not performed by the commercial banks.   (RSA)

14. Name the two traditional methods by means of which the Bank of England can cause the expansion or contraction of credit. Show how these two methods, together with Special Deposits, are used to contract credit.
    (RSA)

15. Describe the functions of a central bank.

16. (a) Explain the term 'London money market'.

(b) Describe the work of the chief institutions of the money market.
    (LCCI)

17. (a) Discuss the role of the central bank in the economy of your country.   (8 marks)

(b) Indicate clearly the influence of the central bank's control of credit on economic activity in both the public and the private sectors.   (12 marks)
    (RSA Inter.)

12   Insurance

1   The advantages of insurance

Many risks have to be faced by people who run businesses. Some of these risks, as will be seen below, cannot be insured against. There are, however, a great many risks against which it is possible nowadays to insure.

For example, in return for a payment, known as a premium, an insurance company will undertake to compensate the person making the payment (the insured) in the event of a specified loss. Thus, if Brown is the owner of a shop with a value of £10,000 which he wishes to insure against fire he will take out a policy (the document setting out the exact terms of the agreement) with an insurance company. Brown will then have to pay a premium at regular intervals, the amount depending on the value of the property insured. If he wishes to obtain full compensation for any loss he may suffer he must insure his property for its full value. If the shop should be completely destroyed by fire he will, after due inquiries have been made, receive a sum of £10,000 as compensation. Similarly, he could insure his stock against fire or burglary.

The advantage of insurance is clear. In return for a relatively small payment Brown is relieved of worry regarding the safety of his property, for he knows that should he suffer loss he will receive compensation. How, then, does it come about that an insurance company can bear risks which people like Brown cannot bear?

2   Principles of insurance

The principle upon which insurance is based is 'the pooling of risks'. If the incidence of some particular risk can be calculated from past experience its probability can be calculated. If, for example, over a long period of time fire has destroyed business premises to the value of an average of £100,000 a year, such premises can be insured against fire if the combined payments collected from people insuring against this risk total £100,000 plus the insurance company's expenses in conducting the business. Thus, what happens is that each person insuring against a particular risk pays a relatively small contribution to a common fund or pool, from which compensation can be paid to those who suffer in that way. The same result would be achieved if a large group of businessmen made an agreeement to share any loss due to fire (or any other specified cause) among themselves. It is obviously more satisfactory to allow an independent body like an insurance company to undertake the business.

Insurance, therefore, can be effected only against those risks the probability of which can be mathematically calculated. It must be stressed that the insurance company itself is not taking any risk of loss, for, by spreading the risk over as wide a field as possible, the compensation it is called upon to pay should be well covered by the premiums it collects. Most British insurance companies have now been in existence long enough to have built up large reserves which protect them against any abnormal demands which might be made upon them. If, however, insurance companies find that they are having to pay out more in compensation for a particular risk, they will clearly have to increase their premiums. An insurance company will keep a separate fund for each branch of insurance it undertakes.

Two important principles of insurance should be noted.

(*a*) *Insurable interest.* It is illegal for persons or firms to take out insurance against risks which do not directly affect them. In general, when the insured makes a claim under an insurance policy he must first have suffered some kind of loss himself. A man can insure his own property against fire or burglary, but not the house of a friend or neighbour. The insured must have an insurable interest in what he insures.

(b) *Utmost good faith.* It is incumbent on both parties to an insurance contract – the insurance company as well as the insured – to disclose at the time the insurance is effected all relevant particulars which might materially influence the other party's willingness to make the contract. No important information must therefore be held back. This would debar a man from taking out a life assurance policy if he knew that he was suffering from an incurable disease without first informing the insurance company of the fact.

3   The scope of insurance

There are many business risks which can be insured against. A shopkeeper will usually also want to insure his shop window, if it is a large one, and companies exist which specialise in this branch of insurance. Merchants and manufacturers responsible for the despatch, by railway, road, sea or air, of large consignments of goods will insure them against damage or loss while they are in transit. If the railway carries goods at 'company's risk' – the charge for which is higher than if the goods are sent at 'owner's risk' – this means that the railway itself is accepting responsibility for the goods arriving at their destination undamaged. Letters can be sent by registered post, as we saw in Chapter 6, and in this case it is the Post Office which takes responsibility for their safe arrival. In these last two instances the railway and the Post Office respectively are really acting as insurers.

Insurance against fire dates back more than a thousand years. The first company in England to undertake fire insurance was established in London in 1680. The early insurance companies operated their own fire brigades in order to try to reduce the damage for which they would have to pay compensation.

To receive compensation in the case of fire only to the value of the premises and goods which have been destroyed may not fully indemnify a trader for his loss. As a result of the fire he may be put out of business until he has acquired new premises and stock. To cover such contingencies it is possible to insure against loss of profit as a result of fire. Those who own vehicles – motor-driven or horse-driven – ships and aircraft can insure them against damage or loss. In the case of motor vehicles the law compels the owner to insure against what is called 'third party' claims. A third party is any person, other than the insurance company and the insured, who is involved in an accident. For example, a pedestrian who has been knocked down by a motor car might put in a claim against the driver for compensation for personal injury. In this case the pedestrian is the third party.

Under the Employer's Liability Acts an employee could bring a claim for compensation against his employer if he had suffered injury at work. If the injury was serious a court of law might award compensation to the extent of thousands of pounds. This, however, is now part of the National Health Scheme, but employers must under the Employers' Liability (Compulsory Insurance) Act 1969 take out insurance policies to cover themselves against actions at common law which might be brought by an employee who suffers injury while at work and can prove that the accident was due to the employer's negligence. An individual, too, can insure himself against accidents. Many people used to insure themselves before taking a journey by train, and many still do so when they are travelling by air.

Where employees have to handle large sums of money belonging to their employers there is always the risk of loss to the employer if an employee turns dishonest. The risk, too, can be insured against, and is known as Fidelity Guarantee insurance.

Another branch of insurance which is very useful to business is cover against bad debts. All firms which sell goods on credit have to face the possibility that some of their customers will not pay what they owe. This is a relatively new form of insurance, although several attempts have been made in the past to provide this kind of cover for businessmen. It was not until the insured was asked to bear a portion of the risk himself that successful schemes were worked out and operated. It is now an expanding branch of insurance. In order to encourage the export trade, the state has undertaken insurance against the non-payment of debts by foreign import merchants. British exporters can insure against bad debts of this kind through the Export Credits Guarantee Department, which has opened offices for this purpose in a number of important cities in Britain as well as in London. The business is conducted in very much the same way as that of an insurance company, the exporter paying a premium according to the risk involved (*see* Chapter 20).

The terms of each item of insurance are set out in a policy, and it is very important, therefore, that the insured should read this carefully, as sometimes there are exceptional circumstances to which the insurance will not apply and of which the insured should be aware.

Some insurance companies undertake all kinds of insurance, although some specialise in life assurance and others in general insurance.

The volume of insurance business has increased enormously during the past fifty years or so; the total assets of insurance companies during that period have increased by ten times and their premium income by twenty times.

There are many other risks besides those mentioned above which can be insured against. A society holding an outdoor function and having to incur heavy expenses in its preparation can insure against rain on the day of the event. The organisers of agricultural shows and athletic meetings often cover themselves against possible loss in this way. In the United States it is compulsory for banks to insure their deposits up to a certain amount. This is a very valuable safeguard for small investors, who suffered heavy losses from the many American bank failures of the 1930s. If you wish, you can even insure your holiday against rain!

4 Life assurance

About one-quarter of the total of all insurance premiums is for life assurance, and some companies specialise in this type of business. This branch of insurance is generally known as assurance, since the risk differs in one important particular from those covered by insurance.

In the case of insurance a premium is paid to provide cover in the case of some eventuality such as fire taking place. If the insured suffers no loss from fire during the period for which the insurance was effected, then no payment to the insured will be due from the insurance company. In the case of life assurance, however, the eventuality – the death of the assured – is certain, the only uncertainty being as to when it will occur. The sum assured also – except for whole life policies – is certain to be paid to someone, to the assured if he lives to the end of the period of assurance or to some relative if he dies before that time. Expectation of life for men and women of different ages can be calculated with great accuracy. The amount of a life-assurance premium will depend on the sex and age of the person whose life is to be assured, the length of the period of assurance and the amount of the assurance. Nowadays, most life assurance is taken out in the form of endowment policies which combine assurance with saving. In this case the assured takes out a policy for a specified number of years. If he survives to the end of the period he receives the sum for which he assured his life together with any bonuses his policy has earned.

5   National insurance

Insurance against unemployment, sickness and old age is now undertaken in many countries by the state, and in Britain it is under the control of the Department of Health and Social Security. A very limited scheme of social insurance existed in Germany as long ago as 1884, but in the UK national insurance dates from 1908–1911, Lloyd George being mainly responsible for its introduction. Previously some of the trade unions had provided insurance against sickness and unemployment for their members. In 1929 the scheme was extended to include pensions for widows.

In 1947 a more comprehensive scheme, based largely on the Beveridge Report, and including a wide range of new benefits, was introduced. Retirement and unemployment pay were increased, and the scheme was made compulsory on all but a very few workers. In addition, however, to contributions being demanded from those entitled to draw benefit, compulsory contributions have to be made by employers, and a third contribution is made by the state, which also finds it necessary to bear most of the cost of the health service. It was the intention both of Lloyd George and Beveridge that national insurance should be operated on strict insurance principles – that is, that the amounts paid should be sufficient to cover all payments of benefit. Owing to the continued decline in the value of money since the scheme was introduced, it has been necessary to increase the benefits, especially retirement pensions. Although the contributions have also been increased, this has not been sufficient to cover the cost of benefits, and since 1964 the state has had to bear an increasing share of the cost. In 1978 a more ambitious income-related pension scheme with greatly increased contributions from both employers and employees was introduced.

6   Marine insurance

The insurance of ships and their cargoes is perhaps the oldest form of insurance, for there is evidence that it existed some 2,000 years ago. Marine insurance, as this branch of insurance is called, is undertaken by underwriters who are members of Lloyd's and by marine-insurance companies. Lloyd's underwriters are the most widely known and the most important insurers in the world. They undertake all kinds of insurance business, but they are best known for marine insurance.

The members of Lloyd's are underwriters, so called because of the custom of writing their names under any risk a portion of which they were prepared to cover. At the same time they indicated the amount of risk they were prepared to undertake. If a cargo worth £20,000 is to be insured one underwriter may be willing to cover (say) £1,000, and if so he will attach his name to this amount. Another underwriter or a syndicate (that is, a small group working together) may choose to cover £1,500. The broker who acts between the shipper and the underwriters will go from one to another until the full £20,000 has been covered. In this way the risk is spread over a number of members. A marine insurance company generally covers an entire risk itself.

Types of marine insurance. Policies can be taken out to cover: (*a*) the ship; (*b*) the cargo. They can be issued to provide cover either for a specified voyage or for a particular period of time. In order to save the time and trouble involved in taking out a separate policy of insurance for every consignment of goods that is to be despatched, some firms take out an open or floating policy providing compensation up to a stated maximum amount. All that is then necessary is that each consignment of goods should be declared to the insurers on its despatch.

7 Losses at sea

There may be total loss or partial loss.

(*a*) *Total loss.* If a ship is lost at sea, or if the cargo is completely destroyed, this is known as an actual total loss. If the cargo is so seriously damaged that it can no longer serve the purpose for which it was intended, or if the ship itself has to be abandoned, this is called a constructive total loss.

(*b*) *Partial loss.* Frequently, however, a ship or its cargo may suffer only partial damage. In this connection the term average is used in marine insurance (and in fire insurance also) to mean loss. Thus, there is general average and particular average.

General average occurs, for instance, if some of the cargo has to be jettisoned in order to secure the safety of the ship. In this case the loss is not borne only by the owners of the cargo but also by the shipowners, since the loss was incurred in order to save the ship. Similarly, if the ship has suffered damage and has to be towed into port the extra expense incurred in doing this will not fall entirely on the ship-owners but also on the owners of the cargo, since it was in their interests too for the ship to be saved from total loss.

Particular average occurs when part of the cargo or the ship suffers damage, and where the partial loss is entirely borne by either the owners of the cargo or the shipowners, as the case might be. If, for example, the ship was in collision any damage would be the responsibility of the ship-owners; on the other hand, if sea water, shipped while the vessel had been struggling through heavy seas, should damage the cargo that would be the responsibility of the owners of the cargo. Thus, a policy taken out 'with particular average' provides insurance against all risks at sea, but if it is 'free of particular average', then cover is provided only against total loss and general average.

In the case of partial loss the extent of the damage has to be assessed by an independent official, known as an average adjuster. In order to secure international uniformity in the adjustment of general average, the York–Antwerp Rules were drawn up.

8   Uncertainty

We have seen that in general only those risks the probability of which can be reasonably calculated can be insured against. The probability of many risks which the merchant and the manufacturer have to face in the course of business cannot be calculated in this way. Production is carried on in anticipation of demand, for plans have to be laid well in advance of the date on which the manufacturer expects to be able to put his product on the market. He has therefore to estimate what the demand is likely to be at some future time. The making of the decisions what to produce and how much to produce is the responsibility of the entrepreneur. The skill of the entrepreneur is shown by his ability to bear this sort of risk successfully.

For risks of this kind economists prefer to use the term uncertainty, for their probability cannot be subjected to mathematical calculation. Between the taking of the decision to produce and the marketing of the product the demand for it may change for reasons entirely outside the control of the entrepreneur. It may be due to something as irrational as a change of fashion, or it may be due to a fall in the incomes of consumers, or to a rise in the price of other goods which people feel they must buy. A fall in price during the interval of production can have serious consequences for a producer whose profit margin is narrow. Similar risks have to be taken by merchants whose main business it is to hold stocks. If prices rise they will make a greater profit than they anticipated when their purchases were made, but if prices fall their profit will be cut or they may even make a loss. It was to try to reduce risks such as these that futures markets were developed (*see* Chapter 15).

Insurance, however, has been a great boon to all engaged in business, for it has removed many risks which previously had to be borne. Nevertheless, in spite of the great widening of the field of insurance, some risks still remain which those engaged in business must themselves bear.

Questions

1. Assess the importance of insurance to: (*a*) industry; (*b*) commerce.
2. What is meant by saying that insurance is based on the principle of pooling of risks?
3. What are the chief risks which a businessman can insure against? Are there any risks against which it is not possible for him to insure?
4. Explain each of the following terms: utmost good faith; insurable interest; particular average; general average.
5. What are the advantages of insurance to the community? Explain the manner in which insurance is effected upon a motor car, stating the risks insured against. (UEI)
6. Write brief notes on: (*a*) insurable interest; (*b*) indemnity; (*c*) utmost good faith; and (*d*) underwriting. (NCTEC)
7. Make clear what is meant by particular average and general average in relation to marine insurance. (LCCI)
8. Describe, in general terms, the different kinds of insurance policies which it would be prudent for a businessman to take out. (LCCI)
9. What do you understand by the statistical basis of insurance? Show how it is related to the calculation of fire insurance premiums. (GCE Camb.)
10. Explain briefly the general principles of insurance and indicate four risks against which a trader may insure. (NCTEC)
11. Indicate the extent and nature of risks covered by insurance.
(LCCI)
12. Insurance is based upon three principles: (*a*) utmost good faith; (*b*) insurable interest; and (*c*) indemnity. Write a brief explanation of each.
(RSA)
13. Briefly describe five risks against which a businessman should insure and two risks against which he cannot insure. (RSA)
14. Insurance and dealing in 'futures' both help the businessman to avoid

risks. Explain how this happens in each case and distinguish between the kinds of risk involved.   (GCE JMB)

15. Explain how the principles of insurance apply when a person: (a) insures a shop against fire, and (b) makes a claim.   (LCCI)

16. (a) Distinguish between insurable risks and non-insurable risks.

(b) Explain what is meant by the pooling of risks.   (LCCI)

17. Describe the services offered by Lloyd's of London.   (LCCI)

18. (a) What risks, apart from fire, may be covered under a property insurance policy for a commercial firm?

(b) Why might two business firms be quoted different premiums for similar fire risks by the same insurance company?   (LCCI)

19. Describe the working of the marine insurance market at Lloyd's, using the following headings: (a) membership; (b) placing of risks.

(LCCI)

20. (a) Explain the meaning of the statement that 'insurance is a pooling of risks'.

(b) What are the essential elements in a contract of insurance?   (LCCI)

21. (a) How is an insurance policy effected?

(b) What steps are taken by an insurance company before payment of a claim?   (LCCI)

22. (a) Describe why an employer might require the following types of insurance: (i) fidelity guarantee; (ii) public liability.

(b) State three principal risks against which an employer cannot insure.

(LCCI)

23. (a) Thomas Jones PLC manufacture a wide range of engineering products which they distribute to home and overseas markets. State six major risks this company should insure against.   (3 marks)

(b) Using an appropriate example, explain why large business organisations may provide their own insurance.   (7 marks)

(c) (i) Explain how insurance may assist other business organisations by providing protection against certain kinds of loss.   (5 marks)

(ii) Explain how the insurance market can be a source of additional finance for industry.   (5 marks)

(RSA Elem.)

24. Fred Briggs has won the sum of £70,000 and has purchased a small hotel. The hotel has accommodation for twenty-five guests and has two bars and also operates a minibus for transporting the guests. Fred is concerned about his insurance. Advise him on:

(a) two types of insurance that he is legally required to hold;   (4 marks)

(b) the meaning of the term 'indemnity' which he has seen on several proposal forms;   (4 marks) (*c*) the way he can insure against the dishonesty of his employees;

(*3 marks*)

(*d*) the different service he will receive from an agent compared with a broker; (*5 marks*)

(*e*) two additional risks against which he should insure. (*4 marks*)

(RSA Inter.)

25. (*a*) Explain the principles of 'insurable interest' and 'utmost good faith' in insurance. Support your answer with examples. (*14 marks*)

(*b*) How can life assurance be of benefit to a business partnership? (*6 marks*)

(RSA Elem.)

26. Mr Driver is purchasing a fleet of lorries in order to make his own deliveries of the goods in which he deals, and he wishes to obtain vehicle insurance to cover their operation.

(*a*) How would he obtain insurance cover? (*4 marks*)

(*b*) Suggest *two* reasons why he might choose fully comprehensive cover rather than third party liability? (*6 marks*)

(*c*) What would influence the level of premium he would pay? (*6 marks*)

(*d*) State *two* reasons why the premium could rise on the renewal of the policy in the second year for the *same* vehicles. (*4 marks*)

(RSA Elem.)

27. Mr White is opening a retail business selling footwear based in the High Street of a large town, with three employees.

(*a*) Give *four* examples of risks which he could insure against and *one* example of a risk which he could not insure against. (*5 marks*)

(*b*) Explain, relating your answer in each case to Mr White's business, the insurance principles of: (*i*) insurable interest; (*ii*) indemnity; (*iii*) utmost good faith. (*5 marks each*)

(RSA Elem.)

Part Three
Distribution

13 A Commercial Transaction

1 Trade journals

In this chapter we are going to follow through a typical transaction between a retailer and a wholesaler. Let us suppose that William Murgatroyd is the sole proprietor of a boot and shoe shop situated at 27 North Street, Huddersfield. He has been in business for a number of years and for some time has been obtaining supplies from a wholesaler – in this trade known as a factor – in Leeds. Most retailers read the trade journals appropriate to their own branch of trade, and so we can assume that Murgatroyd is a regular reader of the *Shoe and Leather News*. This contains articles of interest to those engaged in the boot and shoe trade, giving information on leather production and price movements and other matters of a similar nature. In many trade journals the number of pages devoted to articles may, however, be much less than the space given up to advertisements of manufacturers and wholesalers, but a retailer like Murgatroyd will be just as keenly interested in these as he is in the rest of the paper.

2 A letter of enquiry and the reply

Let us suppose that an advertisement, inserted in the *Shoe and Leather News* by Dean & Gates PLC, a Manchester firm of boot and shoe factors, catches Murgatroyd's eye, and that he responds to their invitation to write for a catalogue. At the same time he may ask to be informed of their terms. In reply Messrs Dean & Gates PLC send Murgatroyd an illustrated catalogue which gives particulars of the boots and shoes they can supply, together with their terms of payment and delivery. Let us now consider the information which Murgatroyd has received from the boot and shoe factors. First, there is the catalogue.

(*a*) *Catalogues and price lists*. Wholesalers issue to retailers illustrated catalogues giving details of the goods they sell. The various items, besides being fully described and often represented pictorially, are numbered to facilitate reference and to make ordering easier and less liable to error. The prices of the articles may be shown or they may be given on a separate price list, which merely quotes the catalogue number of each item and its current price. Some catalogues are very expensive to produce, and the latter is one method by which the cost of reprinting for every change of price can be avoided. A second method will be considered shortly.

Sometimes a *Prices Current* is issued, and this gives the prices in force at a certain date, further inquiry of the supplier being necessary to find the actual prices ruling at the moment. Where a wholesaler states the price at which he can supply a particular order, this is known as a quotation.

(*b*) *Terms of payment*.

(*i*) The prices shown in the catalogue may be subject to *trade discount*. This is a device which is frequently used to alter prices without incurring the expense of reprinting the catalogue. No changes are made in the prices shown in the catalogue, but instead the trade discount, probably prominently displayed on the front cover, is varied. For example, if trade discount has previously been at the rate of 25 per cent, prices can be raised by lowering the rate of discount to (say) 20 per cent, or if it is desired to lower prices the trade discount can be raised to (say) $33\frac{1}{3}$ per cent.

The term trade discount is, however, sometimes used to indicate the retailer's mark-up on the goods. He may, for example, buy goods quoted by the wholesaler at £6 each, subject to a trade discount of $33\frac{1}{3}$ per cent, the retailer thus buying them at £4 each to sell again at £6. The difference between the two prices is the retailer's gross profit. (*See* p. 98.)

(*ii*) *Cash discount* is an inducement offered by the wholesaler to encourage the retailer to pay promptly. If payment is made within seven days the wholesaler may be prepared to give the retailer a cash discount of 3¾ per cent, or perhaps 2½ per cent if payment is made within one month. Before Murgatroyd places an order with Messrs Dean & Gates PLC, he will particularly want to know what are their terms of payment.

(*c*) *Terms of delivery.* The cost of the carriage of the goods from the wholesaler is generally paid by the retailer in the case of small orders, the goods then being said to be supplied Carr. Fwd. (carriage forward). Another method of indicating that the buyer has to pay carriage is to quote prices ex-works or ex-warehouse, meaning that the prices are those ruling at the works or at the warehouse. On orders above a stated amount it is usual for the wholesaler to pay carriage – an inducement to the retailer to place large orders – and in this case prices are quoted Carr. Pd. (carriage paid). Another method of quoting terms of delivery is f.o.r. (free on rail), the supplier in this case paying carriage only from his warehouse to the station in his own town, the cost of carriage by railway then being borne by the buyer. Very similar is the term f.o.b. (free on board), met with in foreign trade. It is very important for a buyer to know the terms of delivery, as in the case of some goods the cost of carriage can be very considerable.

3 The order

Having closely examined the catalogue he has received and carefully considered the terms of payment and delivery, Murgatroyd may now decide to place an order with Messrs Dean & Gates PLC. If he feels that the catalogue does not give him sufficient information about the goods he may first wish to see them. If the goods are small a traveller may be sent to call upon him and show him samples; if the goods are too large to be carried around in this way he will have to pay a visit to the wholesaler's warehouse.

Murgatroyd has to decide what quality of goods to order, and this will depend to some extent on the situation of his shop. If it is away from the town centre the district in which it is situated will be the determining factor, for in such a case he must stock the kind of goods the people in his own locality are likely to want. In the town centre he will have more choice, but it will probably be to his advantage not to have too wide a range of quality. In fact, if he decides to sell the best and most expensive quality he may find that he sells a smaller quantity if he also stocks cheaper lines, as many customers like it to be known where they do their shopping if a retailer has a reputation for stocking only the best and most expensive things.

Let us now examine Murgatroyd's order. First the student should be warned that specimens of commercial documents are of importance to him only as an indication of their possible layout. They vary in style not only between one branch of trade and another but also between one trader and another in the same branch of trade. But though they may vary in detail, the purpose and general principles underlying their use are the same in all cases. Murgatroyd's order may, therefore, take the form shown on p. 179.

The following points with regard to the order form should be noted.

(*a*) In the example shown opposite those parts which would be filled in by Murgatroyd are given in italics; the rest of the document would be printed.

(*b*) The number preceding the quantity of each item (395, 277, etc.) is the catalogue number. This acts as a safeguard when ordering.

(*c*) The description of each item is also taken from the catalogue. This is an additional safeguard to ensure that the correct articles are ordered.

(*d*) The sizes of the shoes required shown as 1/3, 2/4, 2/5, etc., indicate that one pair of size 3 is wanted, two of size 4 and two of size 5.

(*e*) The prices of the shoes ordered are given, but the total amount is not shown.

```
478                        Order                    Tel. 716300
VAT              WILLIAM MURGATROYD
Reg. No. 1763          High Class Boots and Shoes
                           27 North Street
                    HUDDERSFIELD HD1 2XM

To Messrs Dean & Gates PLC,                   5th February, 19—
    Exchange Street,
      Manchester M2 3DH

Please supply
    395     6 pairs Ladies' black glacé shoe with medium
                     heel, sizes 1/3, 2/4, 2/5, 1/6.          @ £36.00 per pair
    277    12 pairs Gents' black boxcalf shoe, sizes
                     1/5, 2/6, 4/7, 4/8, 1/9.                 @ £37.00 per pair
    281     4 pairs Gents' tan willow calf shoe, sizes
                     2/7, 2/8.                                @ £41.00 per pair
    344     6 pairs Ladies' tan willow calf shoe, one inch
                     heel, sizes 1/3, 2/4, 2/5, 1/6.          @ £33.00 per pair
                        Wm. Murgatroyd
```

4   References

Murgatroyd's order will first be dealt with by the sales department
of Messrs Dean & Gates PLC, and if this is the first order they have
received from Murgatroyd they will want to know something about
his creditworthiness before sending any goods to him which have
not previously been paid for. A letter, therefore, will probably be
sent to him at this stage, thanking him for his order, but requesting
him to give the names of one or two referees, that is, persons or firms
to whom reference can be made regarding his business character.

Trade reference. The best type of reference that Murgatroyd can
give is the name of some other wholesaler with whom he has dealt on
former occasions. For example, if he has previously done business
with the Yorkshire Shoe Company PLC of Leeds he could name this
firm as one of his referees. Messrs Dean & Gates PLC will then write
to the Yorkshire Shoe Company PLC apologising for taking up their
time and requesting them to say what they know of William
Murgatroyd, at the same time offering to do a similar service for
them if at any future time the need should arise.

Bank reference. Sometimes a trader gives the name of his banker as a reference. This, however, is not so satisfactory as a trade reference, for a banker will supply information only to another banker. Thus Murgatroyd's banker in Huddersfield will supply information about him only to Messrs Dean & Gates's banker in Manchester and not direct to the wholesaler. Nevertheless, since bankers make it their business – in their own interests – to know something of the character and standing of their customers, a general statement with regard to these points may suffice.

If neither of these methods gives Messrs Dean & Gates PLC the information they require they can employ one of the various status enquiry agents, such as Stubbs' or Kemp's, who in return for a fee will supply particulars of the firm in question.

If as a result of these enquiries Messrs Dean & Gates PLC are not satisfied that Murgatroyd is a person to whom they can grant credit, they will ask for payment to be made before the goods he has ordered are despatched to him. This will be done by sending him what is known as a pro forma invoice. If, on the other hand, the wholesaler is satisfied with the replies to his enquiries the order can now be passed on to the packing and forwarding department so that it can be dealt with. Let us suppose, then, that Messrs Dean & Gates PLC decide to proceed with the order.

5   The despatch of the goods

The sales department will be informed by the despatch department of the items in the order which can be supplied immediately. The various documents concerned with the despatch of the goods can then be drawn up. In addition to the invoice, which will be considered shortly, there are three documents associated with the despatch and delivery of goods – the advice note, the consignment note and the delivery note. It is unusual nowadays for all these documents to be used in connection with a single transaction. Sometimes the advice note is dispensed with and replaced by the invoice, and either the consignment note or the delivery note used. When considering the importance of a commercial document the student should ask himself three questions: When is it used? Why is it used? What form does it take?

(*a*) *Advice note.* When employed, this document is sent by post at the same time that the goods are despatched. Its purpose is to warn the person who is to receive the goods that they are on the way, at the same time informing him of the means of transport employed and giving details of the goods he may expect (except their prices). The advice note was of greater importance in the days when nearly all goods were sent by railway, since in those circumstances a letter was almost certain to arrive before the goods. An advice note might take the form shown below.

VAT Reg. No. 7862   Advice Note   Tel. 061-177-9042
DEAN & GATES PLC
Boot and Shoe Factors
Exchange Street
MANCHESTER M2 3DH

To W. Murgatroyd,   *10th February,* 19—
27 North Street,
Huddersfield HD1 2XM
Dear Sir,
         We have despatched to you today by British Rail (North Eastern Region), carriage paid, the following goods, ordered 5th February:

  395   *6 pairs Ladies' black glacé shoe with medium heel, sizes, 1/3,*
                2/4, 2/5, 1/6.
  277   *12 pairs Gents' black boxcalf shoe, sizes 1/5, 2/6, 4/7, 4/8, 1/9.*
  281   *4 pairs Gents' tan willow calf shoe, sizes 2/7, 2/8.*
  344   *6 pairs Ladies' tan willow calf shoe, one inch heel, sizes 1/3, 2/4,*
                2/5, 1/6.

                      Yours faithfully,
                      p.p. Dean & Gates PLC,
                      J. Smith.

(*b*) *Consignment note.* This document is supplied by the carrier, e.g. British Rail or a road-haulage firm. The sender fills in details of the goods to be despatched – the type of goods, the number of packages and their weight – together with his own name and address and that of the firm to whom the goods are being sent. It is necessary to indicate also whether the goods are being sent 'carriage paid' or 'carriage forward', so that the carrier may know to whom to charge the carriage. The consignment note is handed to the carrier when he calls for the goods and it travels with them. Upon the goods being delivered, Murgatroyd or his representative will have to sign it as proof that the carrier has delivered the goods.

(c) *Delivery note*. This document gives a list of the goods similar to that shown on the advice note. It can be placed inside the parcel or it can be sent under separate cover through the post. Its purpose is to enable the consignee to check the goods on arrival. Some firms let the invoice serve this purpose. A carrier sometimes has a delivery book, which he asks the consignee to sign as proof of delivery of the goods, and in this case it takes the place of the consignment note.

6 The invoice

Next Messrs Dean & Gates PLC will send Murgatroyd an invoice, a copy of this document being retained by their accounts department. The main purpose of the invoice is to provide a complete summary of a transaction. Thus, it gives full particulars of the goods – the quantity, their description, catalogue or price-list nunbers, sizes (if any), the price of each item, any charge that may be made for the packing-case or wrapper, and the total amount due for that particular consigment. In addition it shows the mode and terms of delivery and the terms of payment. The abbreviation 'E. & O. E.', meaning 'errors and omissions excepted', is to safeguard the seller against any possible clerical error arising from an incorrect addition or the omission of an item. The phrase 'Dr to' (debtor to) is sometimes replaced by 'Bought of', which is often more suitable, as the invoice is not usually of itself a demand for payment.

The use of the invoice, however, varies between different firms, some sending it before the goods – in which case it serves the purpose of an advice note – and others sending it after the goods have been delivered – when it might serve also as a delivery note. There are probably few documents which vary so much in appearance as the invoice, and the reason is to be sought in the great variety of

Invoice   Tel. 061-177-9042
Exchange Street
MANCHESTER M2 3DH

To W. Murgatroyd,   *14th February*, 19—
27 North Street,
Huddersfield HD1 2XM

Bought of DEAN & GATES PLC
Boot and Shoe Factors

Ref. No. 207.

				£
395	6 pairs	Ladies' black glacé shoe with medium heel, sizes 1/3, 2/4, 2/5, 1/6.	@ £36.00	216.00
277	12 pairs	Gents' black boxcalf shoe, sizes 1/5, 2/6, 4/7, 4/8, 1/9.	@ £37.00	444.00
281	4 pairs	Gents' tan willow calf shoe, sizes 2/7, 2/8.	@ £41.00	164.00
344	6 pairs	Ladies' tan willow calf shoe, one inch heel, sizes 1/3, 2/4, 2/5, 1/6	@ £33.00	198.00
				1,022.00
		Packing		7.00
				1,029.00
		VAT @ 15%		154.35
				1,183.35
		Per BR Carr. Pd. 3¾% 7 days; 2½% one month, E&OE		

goods that enter into commercial transactions. Each trader, therefore, has his invoices printed to suit the special needs of his own trade. Murgatroyd might receive an invoice similar to the one shown above.

If the retailer is to pay monthly the invoice is not a demand for payment, but simply a record of the transaction, and the retailer will file it for future reference and as a check against (*a*) the order, and (*b*) the statement which he will receive later.

7   The pro forma invoice

This document has three main uses.

(*a*) It can serve as a polite request for payment before the goods are sent when the wholesaler is unwilling to grant credit because the retailer's references have proved to be unsatisfactory. It thus saves the wholesaler the embarrassment of actually having to ask for payment in advance. Except for its title, pro forma invoice is similar in appearance to the ordinary invoice.

(*b*) Sometimes a firm will send goods for a customer's inspection, permitting him to return them within a specified period if he decides not to keep them. The pro forma invoice accompanies goods sent on approval in this way, and if the goods are retained by the customer it then serves as an ordinary invoice.

(*c*) It is used in foreign trade when goods are exported on consignment, and serves to inform the importer of the expected prices of the goods.

8   Rectification of mistakes on invoices

A mistake in the money total of an invoice cannot be corrected by an alteration of the figures by the sender, since this would also necessitate making alterations in the firm's books. Instead, either a credit note in the case of an overcharge, or a supplementary invoice (or perhaps a debit note) if there has been an undercharge, will be sent.

The credit note is generally printed in red – the particulars, too, being often also typed in the same colour – to distinguish it clearly from all other documents which pass between the wholesaler and the retailer, since it shows a sum owing to, and not by, the retailer. In addition to its use in connection with overcharges it is employed also when a retailer returns packing-cases for which he has been charged on the invoice, or if he returns goods which have reached him in a damaged condition or are not as ordered. Upon Murgatroyd's returning the packing-case in which he received the shoes he had ordered from Dean & Gates PLC he might receive a credit note in the following form.

	Credit note	Tel. 061-177-9042
	Exchange Street,	
	MANCHESTER M2 3DH	
To W. Murgatroyd,		*17th February, 19—*
27 North Street,		
Huddersfield HD1 2XM		
	Cr. by DEAN & GATES PLC	
	Boot and Shoe Factors	

	£
14th Feb., 19— By one packing-case returned 16th February	7.00

The date in the column on the extreme left is that of the invoice to which the credit note relates.

9   The statement

During the course of a month Murgatroyd may have several transactions with Dean & Gates PLC, each of which will give rise to a set of documents similar to those we have already considered. Let us suppose that in addition to the transaction recorded on the invoice dated 14th February two further consignments of goods were delivered to Murgatroyd with invoices dated respectively 21st and 27th February. Let us suppose further that Murgatroyd returned packing-cases to his wholesaler on 17th and 25th February. All these items will be recorded on the statement which Messrs Dean & Gates PLC will send him early next month.

Murgatroyd will probably be allowed until 10th March to pay the amount due if he wishes to obtain the 2½ per cent cash discount which Dean & Gates PLC allow on monthly accounts. They will complete their dealings with William Murgatroyd for the month of February by sending him a receipt for this sum.

| VAT Reg. No. 7862 | Statement | Tel. 061-177-9042 |

Exchange Street,
MANCHESTER M2 3DH

To W. Murgatroyd,   *1st March, 19—*
27 North Street,
Huddersfield HD1 2XM

In Account with DEAN & GATES PLC
Boot and Shoe Factors

2½% per month.

19—			£	£
Feb. 14	To goods		1,183.35	
Feb. 21	To goods		317.40	
Feb. 27	To goods		276.00	1,776.75
Feb. 17	By returns		24.00	
Feb. 25	By returns		14.00	38.00
				1,738.75
E & O E				

Questions

1. Distinguish between cash discount and trade discount.

2. Explain the following terms: Carr. Pd.; Carr. Fwd.; f.o.r.; E & O E.

3. What documents are used in connection with the despatch and delivery of goods? What purposes do they serve?

4. Why is a trade reference generally to be preferred to a bank reference? What other sources of information are open to a wholesaler who wishes to know of the creditworthiness of a retailer?

5. A, a retailer, who has an account with the X Wholesale Company, orders from them on January 2nd one gross of men's socks which the wholesale company have offered at £2 per dozen pairs with 5 per cent rebate off the total purchase price for orders of half a gross or more pairs of socks. The terms of business of the X Wholesale Company are that accounts are rendered on the 21st of each month, payable net at the end of the following month, or with 5 per cent cash discount at the end of the month in which they are rendered. If A pays for his purchase on 28th January, show in detail the documents relating to the whole transaction that the X Wholesale Company will send to him.

(RSA)

6. (*a*) Using the following details prepare an invoice.
Sellers – The Wholesale Book Centre, 28 College Street, Winton;
Buyers – Wilkinson Bros., 16 Gordon Place, Bradfield;
Terms of payment – Net cash in one month;
Trade discount – 25 per cent; date – 17th April.

Quantity	Title and author	Price per copy
6	'Charles Dickens' Jack Lindsay	£3.15
12	'The Life of Francis Drake' A. E. W. Mason	£5.95
18	'Thirty Years with G.B.S.' Blanche Patch	£4.20
6	'Laughter in the Next Room' Osbert Sitwell	£4.95
2	'A Sailor's Odyssey' Viscount Cunningham	£6.80
3	'The Scarlet Sword' H. E. Bates	£4.85

The charge for carriage was £2.50.

(*b*) On 27th April Wilkinson Bros. returned to the Wholesale Book Centre one copy of 'Charles Dickens' in which sixteen pages were omitted. Make out the credit note.

(*c*) Using other details chosen by yourself write out a copy of the order cheque, dated today, which was sent in payment of the amount due.   (WR)

7. A London retail store writes to a wholesaler in Birmingham for the details and prices of certain goods, which are eventually bought, delivered and paid for.

Enumerate the various commercial documents which are likely to be used in this transaction, giving a brief description of each.   (LCCI)

8. What is a pro forma invoice and in what circumstances would it be used? How does it differ from an ordinary invoice?   (WJEC)

9. (*a*) What are the functions of (*i*) an invoice, (*ii*) a credit note; (*iii*) a statement of account?

(*b*) The following transactions take place between S. Smith, wholesaler, Oxford, and R. Robinson, retailer, Abingdon.

Feb. 1 Smith sells goods to Robinson £20.

10 Robinson pays Smith by cheque on The County Bank Ltd., Abingdon, deducting 5 per cent cash discount.

21 Smith sells further goods to Robinson, £32 less 25 per cent trade discount, but Robinson returns one-quarter of these as being in excess of order.

Mar. 1 Smith posts to Robinson a statement of account.

You are required to: (*i*) draw up the statement of account; (*ii*) explain the steps by which Robinson's cheque drawn on 10th February reaches Smith's bank – The City Bank Ltd., Oxford. (GCE Camb.)

10. (*a*) Identify and describe the functions of any *three* business documents which are normally used *before* goods are despatched from the seller to the buyer. (*12 marks*)

(*b*) (*i*) Define 'trade discount' and 'cash discount'.

(*ii*) Explain why a business may allow each of these to its customers.

(*8 marks*)

(RSA Elem.)

14 The Distribution of Commodities

1 Types of commodities

There are a number of ways of classifying the commodities of commerce. One method is to base the classification on the form taken by the goods: (*a*) whether they are in the form in which consumers wish to have them; (*b*) whether they have not yet reached the final stage of production; or (*c*) whether they are not required by consumers at all. All commodities are desired for the satisfaction of the wants of consumers, but whereas some fulfil this purpose directly, others do so only in an indirect way.

When goods are in the form in which consumers want them they are known as consumers' goods, and these things satisfy consumers' wants directly. They can be further subdivided into foodstuffs and manufactured goods.

All other commodities are producers' goods, which consist of raw materials like wool and iron ore, semi-manufactured goods which have not yet reached the final stage of production, like yarn, and technical products, like machinery and industrial equipment. Means of transport are also included in this category. All these things help to satisfy consumers' wants indirectly.

Classification of commodities according to this method can be summarised as on p. 190.

Consumers purchase food and manufactured consumers' goods at retail establishments, and so all these things have to be distributed among the various types of retailers. Raw materials and technical

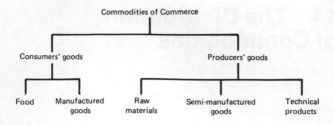

products have to be distributed from the producers to the manufacturers who require them, and semi-manufactured goods have to be
passed from the manufacturer who has carried them to their present
stage of production to the manufacturer who is to carry out the next
process. The methods by which consumers' goods are distributed
may not always be appropriate for the distribution of producers'
goods. Retailers, for example, handle only consumers' goods.

2   The wide range of consumers' goods

In its calculation of the Index of Retail Prices the Department of
Employment takes into account the prices of 350 items, including
the following foodstuffs.

> Bread, flour, self-raising flour, biscuits, cake, beef, lamb, pork,
> corned beef, sausages, bacon, ham, nine kinds of fish, fresh milk,
> butter, margarine, cooking fat, cheese, eggs, tea, granulated and
> lump sugar, potatoes, eight other vegetables, six varieties of fresh
> and dried fruits, cereals, condensed milk, cocoa, proprietary food
> drinks, jam, marmalade, tinned fruit and fish, chocolates and
> sweets, soft drinks.

Although this list includes over fifty different kinds of food, it is
by no means complete, and most students will be able to add a few
more items to it. The Index of Retail Prices also takes account of
over one hundred manufactured articles.

> Sixteen items of men's clothing, twenty-four of women's and
> twenty-three of children's, nine articles of furniture, radio sets,

bicycles, vacuum cleaners, sewing machines, electric fires, electric irons, gas fires, gas cookers, tennis rackets, gramophone records, rugs, carpets, sheets, blankets, curtains, towels, pottery, glassware, soap, polish, cleaning powders, matches, patent medicines, toothpaste, razor blades, cosmetics, newspapers, books and writing materials.

This is, of course, only a fraction of the full range of manufactured articles that are on sale to consumers, but it serves to give some indication of the enormous variety of manufactured goods available at the present day, and new articles are constantly being added.

Market research. To assist them in deciding on the size of their output and the marketing of their products, most large producers of consumers' goods undertake some market research. This involves a study of consumers' demand. Use is made of all available statistics ('desk research'), supplemented by 'field work', that is, by direct enquiries of sample groups of people in different parts of the country.

3   Factors influencing methods of distribution

The concern of commerce is then with the distribution of commodities. The method of distribution actually employed for any particular commodity depends on a number of factors including the following.

(*a*) What is the purpose for which the commodity is required? Is it, like fresh fruit, wanted in its present form by final consumers, or is it a commodity like a lathe which is required only by manufacturers or producers?

(*b*) Is it a farming product like wool or wheat; is it a commodity which has to be mined or quarried; or is it a manufactured article like calico or a bicycle?

(*c*) Is production concentrated in one or a limited number of small areas, as is the case with woollen and cotton manufacture, or is production, as with bread, widely dispersed?

(*d*) What is the structural character of the industry? Is production in the hands of a few large firms, as with matches and sewing cotton, or are there a large number of small producers, as for potatoes?

(*e*) Does the commodity require to be processed – sugar, for example, has to be refined – before it can be sold to consumers?

(*f*) Will the commodity be sold under a trade mark or brand name?

(*g*) Will it quickly deteriorate in quality if delay occurs in its distribution, as is the case with fish and fresh fruit?

(*h*) Is it home produced or is it imported from abroad? If it is imported, is it subject to customs duty?

(*i*) Is it to be exported?

It seems clear, therefore, that the method of distribution will vary considerably between one commodity and another.

4   Channels of distribution: manufactured goods

The usual route by which goods reach the consumer from the producer is by way of the wholesaler and retailer. Thus, the retailer becomes the last link in the chain of distribution, for consumers obtain most of the things they want from this source. This method of distribution is suitable for most manufactured goods produced in this country – many kinds of clothing, footwear, household goods, ironmongery, toys, electrical fittings, pottery, soap, matches, etc.

In some cases the manufacturer by-passes the wholesaler and deals direct with the retailer. As we shall see later, this generally means that the manufacturer or the retailer, in addition to performing his normal function, also undertakes the work of wholesaling, thereby incurring the expense and trouble that this involves. This occurs particularly in the case of 'branded' goods, that is, goods bearing manufacturers' trade marks. It is usual for such manufacturers to undertake their own wholesaling and supply retailers direct, since they are anxious to ensure that as many retailers as possible stock their products. Where goods are large and expensive and where the rate of turnover is slow as with furniture, they, too, may go straight from the manufacturer to the retailer.

Examples can also be quoted of manufacturers who carry out both distributive functions in addition to being producers in order to be able to sell direct to consumers. To do this they may have to open their own retail shops or set up mail-order departments. Both wholesalers and large retailers also frequently deal with consumers through the post.

Imported manufactured goods will probably pass through the hands of an import merchant on their way to regional wholesalers, who then distribute them to retailers in the usual way.

5   Channels of distribution: foodstuffs

Some producers of foodstuffs sell direct to consumers. Some farmers, for instance, take commodities like butter and eggs to small local markets. Dairymen whose farms are situated on the outskirts of large towns frequently act as milk roundsmen.

Production of many agricultural commodities, like potatoes and other vegetables, is in the hands of a large number of small producers. In such cases it is usual for merchants to buy in bulk from them and arrange for the goods to be sold at large wholesale markets, from which they go by way of another wholesaler to the retail greengrocer. With perishable foodstuffs, such as fresh fruit, special arrangements have to be made for the speedy despatch of the commodity from the growers to the local wholesale markets. Similarly, special express trains are run to take fish from the ports where the catch is landed, such as Grimsby and Hull, to markets in London, Manchester, Leeds, etc.

Many foodstuffs, however, require to be processed in some way before they are ready for eating. Wheat, after being threshed on the farms, has to be taken to the millers to be ground into flour, which is then bought by flour merchants, who distribute it among bakers and grocers. Jam manufacturers buy fruit from fruit-growers; canning factories buy fruit or vegetables from producers; after processing and probably branding, these commodities are then distributed in the same way as manufactured goods.

Foodstuffs coming from abroad pass through the hands of importers, who arrange for their sale at organised markets from which they enter the normal channels of distribution and reach the consumer by way of the wholesaler and the retailer. Imported goods are thus handled by several merchants or wholesalers. Imported foodstuffs frequently have to be processed after being sold at the produce exchanges at the ports of entry. Thus tea is blended and perhaps packaged; sugar is refined and also usually packaged nowadays; and wines are bottled after being imported in bulk.

The following diagram illustrates the main channels of distribution for consumers' goods.

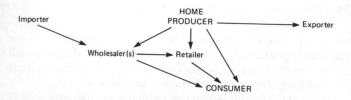

6   Channels of distribution: raw materials

Although some raw materials are produced in the United Kingdom, they form one of the main groups of British imports. If coal is included in this category it becomes the only commodity of this type which this country normally produces in sufficient quantities not only to supply its own needs but also generally to be able to make some available for export. Heavy industries are mostly situated near to coal or raw materials, since the cost of transporting such goods is heavy. Coal is both a producers' good and a consumers' good, but in either case it usually passes through a merchant on its way to the users. Home-produced minerals generally go direct from the mines to the manufacturers who require them. In some cases, however, these commodities are sent first to a market, such as the London Coal Exchange.

For imported raw materials there are organised markets, imported wool being sold at the London Wool Exchange, tin and copper at the Metal Exchange, timber at the Timber Exchange, hides and skins at the London Commercial Sales Rooms, etc.

Questions

1. What is meant by saying that certain goods satisfy consumers' wants indirectly?

2. What do we regard as the 'normal' channel of distribution? What other channels of distribution are there?

2. What factors influence the distribution of the following commodities: apples, sugar 'Thompson's Jam', looms, wireless sets?

4. Select two commodities – one a consumers' good and the other a producers' good – produced in the district in which you live and show how they are distributed from the place of production to the people who wish to make use of them.

5. In which circumstances would a manufacturer decide to sell his products directly to the ultimate consumers instead of using the customary trade channels?   (LCCI)

6. Direct selling by manufacturers to consumers is carried out in several ways. What are these ways and what advantages have they: (*a*) for the manufacturer; (*b*) for the customer?   (LCCI)

15   The Wholesale Trade

1   The retailer's sources of supply

The retailer can buy his stock from either the wholesaler or the
manufacturer. The fact that he will pay a lower price if he buys from
the manufacturer may induce a retailer to buy from this source, but
generally it is to his advantage to resist this temptation to buy more
cheaply. Manufacturers prefer to sell in large quantities, and since
most retailers' businesses are small this would mean their stocking a
large quantity of one line of goods and probably having insufficient
capital – even if they had the storage space – to buy other lines. Only
by purchasing his stock from a wholesaler can the retailer buy in
quantities to suit his turnover and obtain that variety of stock which
is so essential a feature of this branch of distribution.

Firms engaged in large-scale retail trade, such as multiple shops
and department stores, can afford to buy direct from the manufacturer, since their turnover is large enough to make it possible for
them to buy in large quantities. What actually happens, as will be
seen shortly, is that these large concerns undertake their own
wholesaling.

2   Functions of the wholesaler

The importance of the work of the wholesaler can best be judged
from a consideration of his functions as a distributor.

(a) *The breaking of bulk*. The wholesaler buys stock from the manufacturer in large quantities and sells in small quantities to the retailer. This business of 'breaking bulk' is perhaps the main function of the general wholesaler. If the manufacturer dealt directly with all his retail customers he would have to despatch a large number of very small parcels, many of which would have to travel long distances, and this would entail a great deal of trouble and expense. The more convenient situation of wholesalers reduces the number of parcels to be sent out by manufacturers, and when these have been split up by wholesalers they have to go only relatively short distances, thereby reducing transport costs, as the following diagram shows.

(a) DISTRIBUTION
THROUGH WHOLESALER

(b) OMISSION OF
WHOLESALER

R^1 TO R^{10} = RETAILERS

(b) *Warehousing*. The holding of stocks is another important function of the wholesaler. Producers prefer to dispose of their output as soon as possible, since they do not generally make provision for the storage of large quantities of stock. The production of many commodities, too, is irregular, especially farming products, many of which have only one short harvest period each year. Retailers, on the other hand, have to try to satisfy a steady demand. Someone, therefore, must accumulate large stocks when the commodity is available and release it gradually to the market as demand requires, thereby helping to make the economic system run more smoothly. This is one of the most important functions of a wholesaler. Another important economic consequence of the holding of stocks is that it tends to reduce price fluctuations.

(c) *The wholesaler as financier.* The holding of stocks costs money, but besides acting in a financial capacity in this connection, the wholesaler also helps to finance the retailer by allowing him credit, for many retailers operate on only a small amount of capital. Thus, the wholesaler who holds stocks requires much more capital than the average retailer.

(d) *The state of the market.* Through his retail customers the wholesaler is in close touch with the market, and he can, therefore, assist the manufacturer by keeping him informed of the demand for his commodity.

(e) *Expert buying and selling.* In the case of imported goods which pass through organised produce markets (*see* p. 206) expert knowledge of the commodities and their market is required as well as the ability to assess their quality. Expert buyers and sellers, therefore, are needed.

(f) *Preparation of commodity for sale.* Sometimes the wholesaler packs, grades or brands the goods he buys before passing them on to the retailer. This, however, is not strictly a wholesale function.

3 Types of wholesaler

In home trade the following four types of wholesaler can be distinguished.

(a) Some wholesalers for a period own and warehouse the goods but do not carry out any process in connection with them. Most wholesalers of manufactured goods are of this type. In the case of boots and shoes and some other commodities he is known as a factor.

(b) Other wholesalers own and warehouse the goods and in addition carry out some process – for example, the tea merchant who blends tea and puts it up in packets.

(c) Other wholesalers are responsible only for organising the distribution of a commodity – for example, motor-car distributors.

(*d*) Middlemen, like brokers and agents, work on commission, buying or selling on behalf of other wholesalers.

In foreign trade there are a great many intermediaries, many of whom never own or even handle the goods in which they deal, though others undertake the warehousing of the goods after they have been unloaded at the docks. There are importers and exporters, specialist buying and selling brokers and *del credere* agents. In return for a higher rate of commission, the *del credere* agent guarantees that payment will be made for what he sells.

4   The wholesale warehouse

Whereas the distinctive premises of the retailer are the shop, those of the wholesaler are the warehouse, since it is necessary for him to have ample storage for the large stocks which he has to carry. The retailer generally likes his shop to occupy a prominent position on an important shopping street, as he hopes to attract casual passers-by, but this is not necessary in the case of the wholesaler, most of whose orders come to him by post. Since a wholesaler's orders are usually fairly large (that is, compared with those of a retailer), and as they often come from a considerable distance, a packing and despatch department is required. He may operate his own fleet of vans for the delivery of his orders or he may use British Rail or road-haulage.

The divisions of a wholesaler's business are as follows.

(*a*) *Buying.* Since he buys in large quantities he must employ expert buyers.

(*b*) *Selling.* When the wholesaler deals in a wide variety of goods each commodity or group of commodities will form a separate department.

(*c*) *Packing and despatch.* In this section orders are made up, packed and made ready for despatch.

(*d*) *Publicity.* Advertising in the appropriate trade journals is the responsibility of the publicity division, which also undertakes the compilation and issue of catalogues.

(*e*) *Administration.* This department deals with general enquiries and all the accounting work.

5 Are there too many middlemen?

In some branches of trade a single wholesaler provides the link between the producer and the retailer; in other branches there may be two or more middlemen. There is still a popular belief that the presence of middlemen in the business of distribution merely has the effect of making goods dearer to the retailer and, therefore, also to the consumer. Since, however, there is no compulsion on the retailer to buy from a wholesaler, he clearly must do so because he believes this to be to his advantage; similarly, the manufacturer appears generally to prefer to sell to the wholesaler rather than direct to a number of small retailers. The fact that the retailer and the manufacturer both voluntarily deal with the wholesaler rather than directly with one another seems to show that they regard his services as desirable.

Where more than one middleman or wholesaler acts between the manufacturer and the retailer this can be justified only if each is performing some special function which is best left to the expert. In the case of some commodities the work of distribution is more complicated on account of irregularity of supply, as with some farming produce, or because of the large numbers of producers or a particularly large number of retailers. Where the production of an agricultural commodity is in the hands of many small producers it is clearly impossible for each to undertake the marketing of his own output. This gives an opportunity for an agent, working on commission, to arrange for the product to be collected from the growers and delivered to one of the large wholesale fruit or vegetable markets such as Nine Elms. The demand for commodities like fruit and vegetables is widespread and steady, and so between the buyers at these large markets who deal in particularly large quantities and retailers another group of smaller wholesalers is generally to be found. In such cases there may be as many as three or four more middlemen between producer and retailer, but so long as each is performing a necessary service – but only on this condition – their intervention in the business of distribution can be justified.

In foreign trade the number of middlemen will be greater than in home trade because there are more specialist functions to be performed, such as those of the exporter, the importer and the specialist buying and selling brokers.

The greater the amount of specialisation that is introduced into distribution, the greater will be the number of middlemen employed between the producer and the retailer, but this should result in a much higher standard of efficiency at each stage of the work, and in consequence a reduction and not an increase in the cost of distribution, for this has been the effect of the introduction of division of labour into other branches of production.

6   The elimination of the wholesaler

(a) *Large-scale retailers.* We have just seen that wholesaling is an essential part of the work of distribution which it is impossible to cut out. Therefore, to dispense with the wholesaler merely means that someone else – the manufacturer or the retailer – has to do his work. If a manufacturer undertakes the distribution of his commodity as far as the consumer and, in order to do so, opens his own retail shops, he will also have to undertake the function of wholesaling, as well as retailing, with all the extra cost which this involves. Such a manufacturer may, of course, try to influence consumers by claiming to supply them direct, the implication being that as a result his goods will be cheaper because the middleman has been cut out.

Multiple shops, supermarkets and hypermarkets buy direct from the manufacturers because their turnover is large enough to justify it. This means, however, that they have to undertake the warehousing of stocks and their distribution among the various branches – that is, they act as both wholesalers and retailers.

Department stores also buy direct from manufacturers, again because of their large turnover. In their case much of what they gain in this way is expended on the upkeep of their huge premises.

(b) *Manufacturers of branded goods.* The modern practice of pre-packaging goods is another factor that has contributed to the decline of the wholesaler. Very often the main motive for eliminating the wholesaler is not to cut the cost of distribution but to enable a manufacturer to ensure that his product reaches the maximum number of retail outlets. It is mainly for this reason that manufacturers of branded goods prefer, wherever possible, to distribute their commodities as far as the retailers. An independent wholesaler may not push a particular commodity so strongly as its manufacturer would like, since to him a sale of one brand may be equally as profitable as a sale of another.

The by-passing of the wholesaler by large-scale retailers and the reduction in the number of small independent shops consequent on the ending of resale price maintenance have seriously reduced the volume of business of many wholesalers. The survival of the independent retailer, therefore, is as much the concern of wholesalers as of the independent traders themselves. This has led some of them to form voluntary chains with groups of retailers for their mutual advantage. (*See* p. 246.)

7   Branded goods

During the past fifty years or so the branding of goods has become very widespread. By branding is meant the distinguishing of the commodity produced by one manufacturer from that of his competitors by some distinctive name, trade mark or label. This technique is known as *product differentiation* and the basis of it is the advertising campaign, which has the effect of familiarising consumers with the new name and, at the same time, persuading them that, for example, Jackson's Polish is different from, and superior to, all other makes of polish. If the manufacturer succeeds in these objects it gives him some of the market power of a monopolist, for he is the sole maker of Jackson's Polish and he commands a loyal consumer following to the extent that a segment of the polish market believes that there is no other polish exactly like it. Further, if the brand name is registered under the Trade Marks Act 1938, no other manufacturer may use it.

Closely associated with branding has been a huge increase in the packaging of an expanding variety of goods in distinctive packages, a development encouraged by the introduction and spread of self-service in retailing. For a long time groceries have been sold in packets, tins or jars, but nowadays fruit, vegetables and a very wide range of other commodities are sold in this way.

Branded goods have advantages and disadvantages to both retailers and consumers.

(a) *Advantages to the retailer.* Branded goods are uniformly packed, easy to handle and can be ordered from the manufacturer without previous inspection. The retailer is saved the trouble of weighing out quantities for individual customers. Less knowledge of the commodities is required, and so less skilled labour can be employed. The manufacturer also makes himself responsible for advertising these products.

(b) *Advantages to the consumer.* Definite qualities equally well packed can always be expected of particular brands, whether the consumer buys from the large store or the little shop at the corner of the street.

(c) *Disadvantages to the retailer.* In order to satisfy the whims of his customers who regard one brand of a commodity as something quite distinct from another, it is no longer sufficient for the retailer to stock (say) three qualities of tea, but a great many different brands. Before the ending of resale price maintenance (*see* below) all retailers had to sell these goods at the same price, and so it was not possible at that time for the more efficient retailer to attract custom from his competitors by cutting prices.

(d) *Disadvantages to the consumer.* Branded goods are higher in price than unbranded equivalents. Branding greatly facilitated the growth of resale price maintenance. The high costs of TV, newspaper and other forms of advertising are passed on to the consumer, and in some industries such as patent medicines and cosmetics as much as three-quarters of the total cost of production are represented by advertising and selling costs.

8 Resale price maintenance

Resale price maintenance (RPM) began in the 1890s when fierce competition in the retail trade forced firms to cut quality in order to remain in business. Some retailers persuaded manufacturers to include clauses in their contracts of sale to the effect that their goods should not be sold below a price fixed by the manufacturer. The latter in time took the initiative in this by refusing to supply retailers who attempted to sell below the manufacturer's fixed price. This was because retail price competition which forced retailers to cut prices was likely to be transmitted to manufacturers in the form of pressure to cut their own profit margins. Furthermore, fierce retail competition would force less efficient retailers out of business and so reduce the number of retail outlets for their products, and cause inconvenience to the shopper. Whereas the practice of RPM commenced in the pharmaceutical industry, by 1945 it had spread to a great variety of goods including confectionery, electrical goods, tyres, paints, sound reproduction equipment and gramophone records, tobacco and cosmetics, and many others.

After 1945, the idea of self-service retailing began to be taken up in Britain and these retailers, having cut their staffing costs considerably, were making very high profits as a result of RPM. This caused widespread public opposition to RPM and, by the 1950s, much public and academic debate on the subject. By this time also, large-scale retailers and especially the multiples were anxious to be free of RPM and take advantage of their relatively high efficiency to cut retail prices.

The first small breach in the RPM system was brought about by the Restrictive Trade Practices Act 1956. This permitted RPM between manufacturer and first buyer in the grocery trade, but prohibited it in the event of resale of the goods to a second buyer in the trade. Despite this, however, RPM remained strong in such popular fields as confectionery, tobacco, records, electrical appliances, books and many other goods.

Following the 1956 Act, the grocery trade saw a rapid growth of self-service supermarkets based on large scale, large and rapid turnover and price-cutting. Attention became focused on the remainder of the retail trades which remained subject to strict RPM. Debate once more became very fierce with the manufacturers and smaller retailers defending their position against the larger retailers and those who advocated open competition, the latter pointing to the freedom to cut prices enjoyed in Canada and the United States.

In 1964, under the pilotage of Mr Edward Heath, the Resale Prices Act was passed. This allowed a manufacturer to continue to include restrictive clauses in his contracts of sale with regard to resale prices of his goods, but the practice had to be registered with the Registrar of Restrictive Practices instituted by the 1956 Act. Several thousand registrations were made and a number actually defended in the Restrictive Practices Court, but the long-term result of the 1964 Act has been the abolition of resale price maintenance for all goods with the exception of books and certain medicines.

The effects on the retail trade of the abolition of RPM are clearly visible in our streets. With free competition many small retailers have been forced out of business. The resultant inconvenience has been borne by those to whom the street-corner shop was of greatest utility: the disabled, the aged, etc. Younger people and those with their own transport are, of course, able to shop at the new supermarkets and take advantage of lower prices. Some supermarket firms have more recently alleviated the situation of the disadvantaged shopper by providing free bus services from key points. Discount selling has become the rule in an enormous range of products, and, in the absence of RPM and with the growth of competition, the manufacturer today frequently places a 'recommended retail price' on his products as a guide to the retailer.

9 Markets and fairs

A market is where buyers and sellers meet to do business. In the narrower sense it denotes particular places where commodities are bought and sold. Up and down the country there are market towns, so called because they enjoy the privilege of holding open-air retail markets on one or two days of each week. Some towns have permanent covered retail markets. At one time the right to hold a market was granted by Royal Charter, but now local authorities have this power.

In the wider sense of the term a market signifies any area – possibly embracing the whole world – in which buyers and sellers can make contact with one another. Thus we may speak of South

America as a good market for a particular commodity when we mean that there are many people in that part of the world who are likely to buy it.

Besides the numerous local retail markets, there is a wide range of highly specialised markets dealing in specific commodities or ranges of commodities of a specific type. In some of these, such as the Foreign Exchange Market, actual physical contact between buyers and sellers is not necessary since business is carried on by telephone. The chief specialised markets are as follows.

(a) *The London Metal Exchange* where copper, tin, lead, zinc, aluminium and nickel are traded.

(b) *The London Tea Auctions* where buyers representing all the well-known British brands of tea come to bid for the supplies of tea from all the world's growers.

(c) *The London Commodity Exchange* which deals in a wide variety of the world's products, including cocoa, coffee, rubber, sugar, fishmeal, copra, pepper, spices, bristles, hair, ivory, jute and certain vegetable oils such as that of the soya bean.

(d) *The London Fur Market.*

(e) *The London Gold Bullion Market.*

(f) *The London Silver Bullion Market.*

(g) *The London Wool Futures Market* where wool for future delivery is traded.

(h) *The London Wool Exchange.*

(i) *The London Diamond Market.*

(j) *The English Grains Market* which is located in London and deals in wheat, maize, barley, etc.

(k) *The Baltic Exchange.* This is a specialised group of markets.

(i) Firstly, and most significantly in terms of the number of transactions taking place on the Exchange, there is the Freight Market. Here ships are chartered to carry cargoes. Most of the chartering is confined to tramp ships, i.e. ships let out by their owners to trade in any direction, voyage by voyage, carrying the most profitable cargo available at the time. Such ships usually carry a single commodity at a time, for example grain, coal, sugar, iron ore and sulphur. Cargo liners are also chartered at the Baltic Exchange.

These ships run a regular service on a particular route and they will often carry a mixed cargo.

The need for a central chartering exchange may be seen in the fact that there are thousands of tramp ships seeking employment and merchants and shippers all over the world seeking ships to carry their cargoes. The central organisation finds the right ship for the right cargo and *vice versa* (*See also* Chapter 6.)

(*ii*) Next there is the grain and feed trade of the UK. This is carried on by the Grain and Feed Trade Association which was formed in 1973 by the amalgamation of the London Cattle Food Trade Association and the London Corn Trade Association. The Grain and Feed Trade Association consists of three groups: shippers, manufacturers and brokers. Shippers buy goods in the country of origin and sell to the country of destination, engage the necessary freight and undertake finance and insurance. The manufacturers consist of flour millers, animal feed manufacturers and merchants, while the brokers act as intermediaries between shippers and manufacturers. Note that this market also deals in soya bean futures. The Baltic Exchange also encompasses the London Grain Futures Market. The methods of dealing in futures and hedging operations are dealt with below. The chief commodities traded here are wheat and barley. Basically, futures dealing is an extension to normal trade providing facilities for hedging and procurement of supplies.

(*iii*) Next comes the oil and oilseeds market of the Baltic Exchange. Here, under the members of the Exchange who are also members of the International Federation of Oils, Seeds and Fats Associations, the trade in oils and oilseeds is carried on. This is a trade of the greatest importance since many of the oils are of high protein value in human and animal diet, for example sunflower, fish and nut oils. In addition, many of the non-edible oils have important industrial uses, for example linseed, castor and tung oils and tallow.

(*iv*) The Baltic Exchange is also the centre for air chartering. From its beginnings in 1928 when the first charter was signed at the Exchange, there has developed the Baltic Air Market under the Baltic Air Charter Association formed in 1975. Today about 100 aircraft-operating companies are represented on the Exchange. The

Air Market consists of two groups: brokers who represent those offering business and brokers who represent those offering the services, i.e. the aircraft operators. Brokers in this market often act in both these capacities simultaneously.

(v) There are also about half a dozen firms on the Baltic Exchange who engage in the highly specialised business of the purchase and sale of ships. Today over 50 per cent of total world ship purchases and sales pass through firms which are represented on the Baltic Exchange.

(*l*) *The wholesale food (produce) markets.* Covent Garden, the famous fruit and vegetable market, is now located away from the opera house precincts, at Nine Elms, but has retained its old designation. Smithfield Meat Market is the chief centre for the wholesale trade in meat from all over the world, while the Billingsgate Market deals in fish.

(*m*) *The insurance market.* This is largely centred around Lloyd's of London. Insurance in general is dealt with in Chapter 12. Here it is noted that Lloyd's is not an insurance company but a corporation which regulates the conduct of its members who are insurance *underwriters* and which maintains a close watch over their financial standing. From its beginnings in Lloyd's coffee house in London in 1688, where informal insurance business was done in the field of marine risk, Lloyd's has grown into a highly organised insurance market with over 14,000 members grouped into some 300 syndicates which vary in size from a handful to several hundred names. Syndication developed because of the enormous expansion in the scale of business and risks covered as well as the extension of business from the 1880s into non-marine areas. The formation of syndicates was essential if potentially ruinous risks were to be spread. Lloyd's also provides a number of ancillary services. Lloyd's agents have existed since 1811. Today there are about 500 such agents all over the world who together form a worldwide shipping intelligence service. They also deal with damage claims and may in addition handle non-marine matters such as aviation damage and claims. The vast amount of intelligence collected and transmitted by the agents is processed by the Intelligence Department. Marine casualty lists are displayed in the underwriters' rooms and distributed to insurance companies, shipping companies and the news media.

(*n*) *The financial markets*. These are essentially the Stock Exchange (*see* Chapter 7), the Discount Market (*see* Chapter II) and the Foreign Exchange Market.

(*o*) *The London Oil Market*. This has obviously increased in importance since Britain itself became an important oil-producing country with the advent of North Sea oil. However, supplies from all over the world are traded in London. In the London market both spot trading and futures trading are carried out. The trade is in crude oil, gas oil and oil products such as gasoline and fuel oils.

(*p*) *Provincial markets*. By no means all the highly specialised markets are confined to London. Important stock exchange branches exist in most major cities, for example Leeds and Manchester. In Bradford the Wool Exchange deals in wool tops and noils, while Liverpool still houses its traditional market for cotton in the shape of the Liverpool Cotton Exchange.

10 Methods of doing business on commmodity markets

(*a*) *Sale by private treaty*. On the commodity markets goods are sold either by auction or by private treaty. Which method is adopted depends on whether or not the commodity can be graded. Where grading is possible it means that the commodity can be dealt in without the necessity for its actually being present at the time of the sale, since the mere mention of the grade by name is sufficient to inform an expert buyer or seller exactly of the particular quality of the commodity under consideration. In such cases the method of doing business is by private treaty, that is by individual bargaining – sometimes called 'haggling' – between buyer and seller. Two commodities, both of which are capable of being accurately graded, are cotton and wheat. In this country the grading of cotton is in the hands of the Liverpool Cotton Association, a body which represents the various branches of the trade. The cotton is graded on arrival at Liverpool, the ten different qualities being distinguished as 'good ordinary', 'strictly middling', 'fair middling', etc.

(b) *Sale by auction.* Where the commodity cannot easily be graded, business clearly cannot take place without the commodity previously being seen and tested for quality. Provision therefore has to be made for prospective buyers to sample the commodity. This is done in the case of both wool and tea. These commodities are then sold by auction. Raw wool cannot easily be graded, because there is great variation in the quality of the wool even in different parts of the same fleece. Tea is somewhat similar, different qualities being obtained from the same leaf.

Upon its arrival in this country the importer makes himself responsible for warehousing the wool or tea until the day of the sale. Both commodities are usually imported on consignment. Since, therefore, they are sold in large quantities, a slight error in the judgment of quality would be serious, and so both expert buying and selling brokers are employed. The importer issues a catalogue listing the lots that are to be offered for sale, and copies are distributed among prospective buyers. Particulars are given of the various lots and the name and address of the warehouse where the goods can be inspected. Buying brokers visit this warehouse to sample the commodity, in the case of wool the bales being cut open to allow the contents to be examined. The buyers pass round, test the quality and make notes in their catalogues to guide their bidding at the auction later. For tea the method of testing is by tasting. At an auction the various lots are sold in turn to the highest bidders. At the London Wool Exchange the buyers sit at desks, arranged in semicircular tiers facing the selling brokers. In front of each desk is a label stating the name of the firm. Tea is auctioned at the London Commercial Sales Rooms, where other commodities such as coffee and cocoa are also dealt in. Only a limited number of wool auctions are held during the year – six in the case of fine wool – but those for tea take place regularly each week.

When tea is auctioned the buyer of each lot must name the firm on whose behalf he is acting within twenty-four hours of the sale taking place. The seller supplies the buying broker with a weight note showing the amount of the commodity he has purchased, and the buying broker then informs the firm which he has been representing by means of a bought note. The release of the goods from the warehouse where they have been in store can be effected only on production of a warehouse warrant.

11   Dealing in 'futures'

We have already seen that when a commodity is capable of being graded it does not need to be seen and handled before being bought and sold. This characteristic of a graded commodity also makes possible what is known as a 'futures' market. Futures originated as contracts to deliver specified goods at some future date. The prices of goods for delivery at a certain future date will usually be different from their 'spot' prices, that is, their prices for immediate delivery.

Dealing in futures provides a means by which a merchant can cover himself against fluctuations in prices – a practice known as 'hedging'. He might, for example, buy goods for delivery in (say) three months, but on the expiry of that period he may not take delivery, instead receiving or paying the difference between the spot price and the futures price, according to whether price has risen or fallen in the interval. What he gains on one transaction he loses on the other, and the cost can be regarded as a payment for insurance against price fluctuations. Thus, futures are bought simply as a cover against price changes, and therefore are quite different from contracts for future delivery which involve the actual delivery of goods at a specified future date.

The most highly developed futures market in this country is in cotton, this commodity being capable of very accurate grading. There are also futures markets in wheat, sugar, cocoa, oil, coffee, gold and silver and base metals.

In Britain there was no futures market in wool until 1953, when a market was opened in London. The difficulty of accurately grading wool had been the chief obstacle to the opening of a futures market in that commodity in the past, although for many years such markets had existed abroad. The market does not deal in the raw materials, as is customary in other commodity markets, but in wool 'tops', a semi-manufactured product.

Some people decry futures markets on the grounds that they encourage speculation. All speculation, however, is not bad, and since operation on these markets requires expert knowledge, they could not function without the presence of speculators.

Questions

1. What are the services which the wholesaler renders to the retailer?
(RSA)

2. Argue the case for or against the elimination of the wholesaler.

3. In some cases a single wholesaler is found between the producer and the retailer; in other cases there are several middlemen. How do you account for this? Does it show that too many middlemen intervene in the work of distribution?

4. Explain what you understand by the term 'market'. Give two examples of London commodity markets with a brief description of the work of each.
(NCTEC)

5. Why are goods sold by private treaty on some markets and by auction on others?

6. What are 'futures'? What purpose do they serve?

7. Why do some independent grocers join a voluntary chain? Describe the chief activities of such a group.
(RSA)

8. (a) Describe the services which a wholesaler can render to the producer and the retailer respectively.

(b) Would the consumer necessarily benefit if the producer decided to dispense with the services of the wholesaler? Give reasons for your answer.
(WR)

9. Is the wholesale warehouse, in your opinion, gaining or losing in importance? Give reasons for your answer.
(UEI)

10. Account for the growth of the practice whereby manufacturers market their products under a trade mark or brand. What are the advantages and disadvantages of this practice to: (a) the manufacturer; (b) the consumer?
(WJEC)

11. Give five examples from different branches of commerce which illustrate how agents are used. What is: (a) brokerage; (b) *del credere* commission?
(GCE JMB)

12. What are the functions of the wholesale merchant? How far is it true to say he is being eliminated? (GCE Camb.)

13. 'Branding is effective only if supported by advertising.' Discuss this quotation and explain what is meant by branding; state what are the usual forms of advertising. (RSA)

14. Describe the services made available by wholesalers for (a) producers and (b) retailers. (LCCI)

15. What is meant by a produce exchange? Select *one* produce exchange and describe the work carried on there. (LCCI)

16. (a) What services does a wholesaler provide to: (i) the retailer; (ii) the manufacturer?

(b) Explain why some retailers have dispensed with the services of wholesalers. (LCCI)

17. 'The level of activity on the commodity exchanges showed considerable variation. The coffee market had a high level of activity in futures following a cold spell in Brazil and prices have risen by £100 per tonne. The metal market was steady with little trading. Activity in cotton was sparse and low prices reflect the state of the industry during the current recession.'

Answer the following questions relating to the above passage.

(a) What is the reason for the existence of commodity exchanges?

(2 marks)

(b) Name *three* London commodity markets. (3 marks)

(c) What are futures? Why is there such activity in the coffee market?

(5 marks)

(d) Explain the last sentence in the passage. (4 marks)

(e) Explain the functions of the Baltic Exchange. (6 marks)

(RSA Inter.)

16 The Retail Trade

1 Expansion of the retail trade

We saw in Chapter 3 that the expansion of commerce came with increasing specialisation of production. No branch of commerce has expanded to a greater extent than the retail trade during the past two hundred years. Before 1964 both the number of shops and the number of people employed in retailing increased more rapidly than the population, but since then the number of both shops and employees in retail distribution has fallen (*see* table below). This change has been brought about by a fall in the number of small, independent shops in the face of competition from large shops, and an increase in self-service.

Date	Number employed in distribution (thousands)
1950	2,571
1960	3,284
1964	3,495
1968	2,770
1972	2,641
1976	2,723
1978	2,422

In Britain today, retail distribution employs some 2.5 million workers and there is on average one shop to every 150 persons. Thus retail distribution constitutes a significant area of economic activity.

The proportion of shops to population varies greatly between one part of the country and another. The large cities which serve as regional shopping centres – originally because of their railway connections – have the greatest number of large shops. Old towns too tend to have proportionately more shops than new towns. In Manchester, for example, there is one shop for every 60 persons, but in Dagenham only one to every 200 people. A feature of modern commerce in countries such as Britain is the large number of shops.

The expansion of the retail trade is a comparatively recent development, for only two hundred years ago this country had relatively few shops. At that time there were few large towns – and shops are a characteristic feature of towns. In days when people ministered largely to their own wants there was less need of shops. For things which they could not provide for themselves there were the itinerant salesmen and annual fairs.

The tremendous industrial development of the nineteenth and twentieth centuries resulted in the growth of new towns. To factory workers shops are essential, and so the Industrial Revolution brought with it the need for more shops. Shops were necessary because those employed in factories – often the whole family – worked from early morning until late at night for six days a week, and so they had neither the time nor the opportunity to provide for their own needs. In fact, many of the early factory owners built both houses and shops as well as their factories. As the scale of production has increased, an ever-widening range of cheap commodities has become available, and with the steady rise in the standard of living, these have been brought within the reach of more and more people. As a result the number and variety of shops increased.

2 Services of the retailer

It is the function of the retailer to ensure that consumers are offered the things which they want in the form in which they want them.

Convenience of situation of the shop is a very important asset to a retailer, particularly if he is selling goods in regular demand, like foodstuffs. To meet the needs of consumers who like to be able to satisfy their wants easily and quickly and without too much trouble to themselves, shops are to be found close to most residential areas of towns.

At one time shops used to open early in the morning and stay open until late at night in some districts in order to give the consumer the maximum amount of choice with regard to the time at which to make his purchases.

The retailer, too, must sell in small quantities, since most consumers nowadays do not normally care to keep large stocks of things themselves. At one time it was customary for people to lay in stocks at the annual fair to last the whole year, and in the more remote parts of the country even today it is still necessary for them to provide themselves with sufficient to last through the winter.

The retailer should also offer his customers as great a variety of things appropriate to his particular branch of trade as his turnover will allow, to enable them to exercise their choice, for people usually prefer to be able to compare one thing with another before making a purchase. Many customers, too, like to receive the personal attention of the shopkeeper, as this makes them feel that their own particular wants are being considered. This will probably be more easily achieved by the smaller shop, run by a sole proprietor, than by the larger retail concern (especially if the latter is a supermarket or is of the self-service type), since the owner of the small business generally knows his customers individually. This makes it possible for him, if he so wishes, to allow credit to those of his customers whom he thinks that he can trust.

Another service provided by retailers is repairs, for example in the electrical and jewellery trades.

The retailer also assists the wholesaler – and through him the manufacturer – by keeping him informed, by the size and frequency of his orders, of the commodities in greatest demand.

3 Shops

The commonest form of retail outlet is the shop. The Department of Trade and Industry organises periodic counts of the number of retail shops in Britain, their financial turnover, and the number of people engaged in the various branches of retail trade. According to the latest returns, which relate to 1978, the total number of retail outlets was 350,039. This figure includes a range of shops from the very smallest front room of a house converted for retail trade to huge palatial establishments such as department stores. The number of single-outlet retailers' shops was 208,022, indicating that the small retailer retains an important place in distribution in Britain despite the growth of the large establishments such as supermarkets (*see also* Chapter 17). A further 67,933 outlets belonged to small multiple concerns, each with an average of only 2.66 shops. The remaining 74,083 outlets were under the control of 1,225 large-scale multiple concerns, each thus controlling an average of 60 outlets. This large-scale group included 10,207 co-operative retail outlets controlled by 202 societies. In 1978, the distribution of retail outlets among the various trades, along with the numbers employed in each, was as shown in the table below.

Distribution of retail outlets and employees, 1978

	Outlets	Persons engaged	Total turnover inclusive of VAT
		(thousands)	(£ million)
Grocers	45,255	182	3,340
Large general food retailers	7,034	238	6,178
Dairymen	6,759	50	1,057
Butchers	21,422	89	1,724
Fishmongers, poulterers	2,999	9	150
Greengrocers, fruiterers (including those selling fish)	14,799	55	615

Bread and flour confectioners	12,914	72	551
Off-licences	9,015	31	1,101
Confectioners, tobacconists, newsagents	49,491	253	3,668
Footwear retailers	10,961	72	921
Men's and boys' wear outfitters	10,698	54	952
Women's, girls', children's and infants' wear retailers	26,638	124	1,483
General clothing and household textiles retailers	11,966	64	1,032
Furniture retailers	18,458	94	2,167
Electrical and music goods retailers (excluding hire)	13,725	80	1,804
Television hire businesses	4,552	43	699
Hardware, china, wallpaper and paint retailers	19,623	87	1,630
Chemists	11,206	63	1,103
Photographic goods retailers	1,605	8	212
Cycle and perambulator retailers	1,619	5	70
Booksellers and stationers	4,556	29	481
Jewellers	6,583	38	664
Gifts, leisure and travel goods retailers	12,851	50	692
Florists, nurserymen and seedsmen	3,472	17	183
Non-food retailers (nes)	3,471	12	164
Large mixed businesses with food sales	10,192	413	7,964
Large mixed businesses without food sales	1,466	77	1,273
Other mixed businesses with food sales	3,649	26	436
Other mixed businesses without food sales	2,983	31	409
General mail order houses	78	54	1,745
TOTALS	350,039	2,422	44,467

Source: *Annual Abstract of Statistics*

It is difficult to classify retail shops very precisely according to the trade carried on because of the presence of so many mixed businesses. It is clear from the above table, however, that the greatest numbers of outlets are in the confectionery, tobacco and newsagency and grocery trades. Measured in terms of the numbers employed and the level of turnover, however, the highest concentration to be found in the retail trade is in the large mixed businesses which also deal in food. In general, food is the largest item of retail trade in Britain, with some 135,000 shops either partially or totally involved in its sale. Other concentrations are to be found in the women's and children's clothing trades, furniture, electrical, hardware, and chemists' sectors.

There has been a considerable increase in the number of 'self-service' shops. In such shops goods have to be clearly displayed and so arranged that customers can walk round, pick up the things they want and put them into receptacles supplied to customers for this purpose as they enter the shop. On leaving the goods are checked and paid for at the cashier's desk near the exit. Multiple shops and co-operative societies were the first to open self-service shops. An increasing number of independent retailers have followed their example. To the retailer there is a saving of labour as fewer assistants are required; to the customer there is probably a saving of time and goods may be cheaper, but clearly, as the name of the type of shop implies, there is a loss of service. The first shops of this kind were those selling groceries, but self-service shops are now found also in many other branches of retail trade. The huge expansion that has taken place in the production of packaged goods has made this development possible, for commodities that have to be weighed out by the retailer do not lend themselves to self-service trading. The large self-service shops are known as supermarkets, the exceptionally large ones being termed hypermarkets (*see* p. 244).

During the past twenty years or so, the above developments have led to very important shifts in the relative shares of retail trade held by the various forms of outlet, as shown in the following table.

	1961	1966	1971	1978
		(*thousands*)		
Independent traders	480	403	391	208
Co-operative shops	29	26	15	10
Multiple shops	67	73	67	142

4   Other forms of retailing

The shop is not absolutely essential for carrying on retail trade. Where retailing is undertaken without shops it can take many forms.

(*a*) There are street traders who set up their stalls or barrows by the side of streets in large cities. Some of them carry their wares on trays strapped round their shoulders and walk up and down the gutter trying to attract the attention of passers-by.

(*b*) Then there are itinerant salesmen who call upon their customers at their homes. These include pedlars and hawkers, the former carrying their stock-in-trade by hand, and the latter using carts or motor vehicles. Pedlars are more frequently met with in the remoter parts of the country where shops are fewer than in the towns, but hawkers remain well established in some forms of retail trade, such as greengrocery, where customers enjoy the advantage of having bulky goods brought conveniently to them. In recent years there has been a huge increase in the number of 'mobile shops' – motor vehicles designed as shops – in other branches of retail trade, especially for the sale of groceries, confectionery and meat. These are usually operated in conjunction with ordinary shops, and are very popular with co-operative societies. With the exception of a few commodities such as fish and coal, anyone who wishes to sell in this way must first obtain a certificate or licence.

(*c*) Market stall-holders are retailers who hire stalls at towns which hold markets in the open air usually on one or two days each week. These market towns serve the surrounding countryside, and since market day varies between one place and another, retailers engaged in this form of trade generally hire stalls at a number of markets, so that they can travel from one market to another and so do business every day of the week.

(d) Mail-order business is undertaken by many of the large department stores which are to be found in the larger cities (see Chapter 17). This, however, is not strictly retailing without shops, but rather putting an existing shop at the service of a wider range of customers, especially those to whom access to shops is difficult. There are other firms which make mail-order business their only form of trading, and these are often manufacturers who, because the goods they produce are fairly expensive and of limited appeal, prefer to market them in this way. There are wholesalers, too, who also engage in retail trade in the form of mail-order business. Then there are the specialist mail-order houses.

For people who live at a distance from shopping centres mail-order business is particularly attractive. This form of retailing has become increasingly popular, the volume of business having more than doubled in recent years. There are several reasons for this: (a) the wider range of goods now available by mail order; (b) the convenience of the system, especially to married couples where both husband and wife go out to work; (c) its convenience also to people living at a considerable distance from large towns; and (d) credit terms are often offered.

5 The situation of shops

The retailer can often choose between opening a shop in the centre of a town or in the suburbs; in the former case he has the further choice between the main shopping centre and a less-frequented street.

Generally he will have less competition to face if he opens his shop in the suburbs, probably lower costs in the form of rent and rates, but a smaller number of people upon whom to draw for custom. In the centre of a town he will have to pay heavily for a prominent site, especially if it is a corner at the junction of two main shopping thoroughfares, and at the same time he will have to face more competition. On the other hand, large numbers of people pass up and down the streets in town centres, and each one of these is a potential customer.

In the suburbs or less-frequented streets of the town a retailer will have to rely chiefly on regular customers, but in the main shopping centre – and the larger the city, the more important this becomes – there may be a large number of casual customers.

Whether a shop shall be in the town centre or in the suburbs depends also on its turnover. Only shops selling goods in regular demand – grocers, confectioners, greengrocers, butchers, sellers of newspapers, sweets and cigarettes, and sometimes small drapers and hardware dealers – are to be found in the suburbs. For the purchase of jewellery, furniture, books, etc., it is usually necessary to visit the town centre. For some branches of trade particular sites often have special advantages – for example, near a place of entertainment in the case of a shop selling cigarettes and sweets, or near the approach to a station in the case of a newspaper-seller. In places where redevelopment of town centres has occurred, traffic-free shopping precincts have been built, often with multi-storey car parks or roof-top car parking.

The vast increase in the number of motor cars has made shopping in town centres increasingly difficult for motorists. In the United States this has led to the development of 'drive-in' shopping areas just outside large towns. In Britain the development of out-of-town centres has been much slower due to a fear that such development would bring about the decay of the old-established central shopping areas.

A feature of many large old cities is the way in which shops in the same trade cluster together. In London, for example, many jewellers are to be found in Bond Street, and the leading tailors in the neighbourhood of Savile Row. In most towns the butchers are to be found in the same street, and in the older towns the streets are often named after particular branches of the retail trade, for the custom of siting shops in the same trade close together dates from the Middle Ages. The reason for this in those days was to prevent one trader obtaining an unfair advantage over another. Nowadays this may seem at first sight a foolish practice and serving only to intensify competition. If, however, most of the retailers already in the trade are to be found in one small district, a newcomer will find it to his advantage to set up among them, since consumers have become accustomed to doing this particular type of shopping in that neighbourhood.

6   Credit sales: between wholesaler and retailer

Retailers frequently purchase goods from wholesalers on credit, the most common period being for one month. In order to encourage retailers to pay promptly a wholesaler may offer a cash discount if payment is made within seven days; on monthly accounts he may possibly allow a smaller discount; but if payment is delayed beyond one month he will require the full amount to be paid, that is, his prices will then be net.

A retailer who can obtain goods on credit will be able to run his business with a smaller amount of capital than would otherwise be possible. Since in such circumstances the wholesaler is helping to finance the retailer, he will, on the other hand, require a much greater amount of capital.

The drawback to receiving credit is that it narrows the retailer's profit margin, since in effect he has to pay a higher price for his stock. From the point of view of the trader allowing the credit the chief danger lies in the accumulation of bad debts.

7   Credit sales: between retailer and consumer

Somewhat similar considerations confront the retailer who contemplates allowing credit to his customers. Many retailers, especially those operating on a large scale, insist upon all sales being on a cash basis. In competition with these firms others can offer their customers an extra service in the form of credit. There are two main groups of people who prefer to buy on credit: (a) those who spend their wages quickly and so find themselves temporarily short of cash between pay days; (b) those who find it more convenient – perhaps because they are paid monthly – to pay at longer intervals, probably by cheque.

Thus, by granting credit the retailer hopes to enlarge his circle of customers, and so increase his turnover. Nowadays it is not usual, however, for retailers, unlike wholesalers, to offer their customers a cash discount as an inducement to pay promptly, although at one time it was not uncommon for a small discount to be allowed on customers' monthly accounts. Indeed, those customers who pay for what they buy at the time of purchase often have to pay rather more at a shop which grants credit than they would at one where all transactions are for cash. The reason is that the retailer who grants credit usually charges slightly higher prices than other retailers in order to cover himself against bad debts. However careful he may be in his selection of customers to whom to allow credit he will find it impossible to secure payment of all his accounts. He can, of course, sue in court those customers who deliberately try to avoid payment, but this will cost him both time and money and, surprisingly perhaps, damage the goodwill of his business.

A retailer who sells on credit will require much more capital than one who sells for cash, and the granting of credit by a retailer who has insufficient capital is a proceeding fraught with great danger. More than one small retailer has found this out to his cost and has been driven out of business just because he could not secure payment of outstanding debts.

Another method by which the consumer can obtain credit from retailers is by means of credit cards which are issued by some banks and a number of credit card companies that specialize in this kind of business (*see* Chapter 9).

8　Hire-purchase

The purchase of expensive goods has always been a difficult undertaking for those people who find it hard to save the required sum in advance. Many people, it appears, find it easier to make regular payments after they have received the goods than to save in advance. It was to overcome this that the hire-purchase system was introduced. Where it operates it is usually possible to obtain the goods on the payment of a deposit, the balance being paid in regular instalments, weekly or monthly, spread perhaps over as long a period as two years.

The goods are regarded as being on hire, and therefore the property of the seller until the final instalment has been paid. Should the customer fail to keep up with his payments the seller, subject to certain restrictions, can reclaim the goods. Hire-purchase had its origin in the United States, where it is even more prevalent than in this country. In Britain it is now a recognised method of doing business wherever fairly durable, high-priced goods are dealt in. Thus, hire-purchase is well established in the sale of furniture, pianos, music centres, gas and electric cookers, washing machines, bicycles and cars. In recent years there has been a huge expansion of hire-purchase business in Britain.

At one time only the large retailers were able to offer their customers hire-purchase facilities on account of the large amount of capital required for carrying on this method of doing business. Nowadays only a few retailers finance hire-purchase transactions themselves. Most of the finance now comes from finance houses (some of which are subsidiaries of the large commercial banks) which specialise in hire-purchase, paying shopkeepers promptly and then collecting the instalments, with interest, from the purchasers, either direct or through the shops.

The advantages of hire-purchase to many customers are obvious. Many of the things listed above would be completely beyond the reach of many people if they could be bought only for cash. From the point of view of the retailer this means a greater turnover. There is a danger, however, that hire-purchase may make buying too easy for some people, who in consequence take upon themselves more commitments than they can afford. An article priced at 50p a week appears to cost only a trifling sum in comparison with a cash price of (say) £50. In the early days of hire-purchase the more unscrupulous salesmen often took advantage of this weakness of many consumers, who in the end found that they had very little money left out of their weekly wages after making the various payments to which they were committed. As a result many of them failed to keep up with their payments and the goods were reclaimed by the seller.

In 1938 a Hire Purchase Act was passed to protect consumers who wish to buy in this way. This stated the following.

(a) If a customer wishes to cease paying for an article he can return it to the retailer provided that he has paid at least half the purchase price.

(b) If more than one-third of the amount has been paid and the consumer then finds that he cannot continue with his payments, the article can be reclaimed by the retailer only if a court order to this effect is first obtained.

(c) The cash price for all goods has to be clearly shown so that the customer can calculate, if he wishes, the extra cost of paying by instalments.

The Act, however, related only to goods up to the value of £100, but in 1954 the maximum value was raised to £300 and in 1964 to £2,000. To commodities of greater value than this the Act does not apply, its aim being mainly to protect poorer people. In 1964 additional protection was given to the consumer against over-persuasive salesmen, the purchaser in certain cases being allowed four days to think over a hire-purchase agreement after signing it, and if within that time he changes his mind the agreement can be cancelled. Further protection was given to consumers by the Consumer Credit Act 1977 which introduced a system of licensing for retailers and others who wish to grant credit to their customers.

Hire-purchase has certain drawbacks to the retailer. If payments are spread over two years it may mean that a customer has to pay a hundred visits to the shop in connection perhaps with the purchase of a single article. The retailer, too, must keep records of all payments that are made. If the retailer himself undertakes the financing of hire-purchase he will require much more capital. As already noted, there are, however, a number of finance companies now which specialise in this sort of business. During the period over which payments are spread the retailer generally has to undertake the servicing of the article.

Another problem associated with hire-purchase trading arose from the desire of post-war governments to control consumer spending in order to curb inflation and divert resources into exports. This led, from time to time, to government regulation of the size of initial deposit payments on hire-purchase sales transactions and to limitations on the period of repayment of the instalments. At the end of July 1982, however, all restrictions on hire-purchase transactions under these two headings were removed, thereby giving a boost to retail sales over a very wide field of different goods.

9 Trading stamps

Trading stamps or coupons are bought by retailers from stamp companies and given to their customers in proportion to the value of their purchases. The stamps can be exchanged later for goods listed in the stamp company's catalogue, or, since 1965, for cash (though generally only at half their 'gift' value). Stamp trading, therefore, is just another method of allowing customers a discount, usually of about 2½ per cent. They are mainly used, however, to foster customers' loyalty, and many independent traders use them as a means of competing against the supermarkets. Coupon trading, operated by manufacturers of branded goods, was in vogue on a small scale in Britain before 1914 and during 1925–30, especially for cigarettes, but the use of stamps or coupons became much more widespread during 1963–75 in spite of considerable opposition from people who regarded stamp trading as an undesirable method of attracting customers. Since 1975 there has been a sharp decline in the popularity of trading stamps, cash discounts generally being preferred.

10 Consumer protection

Although a buyer is protected at law against wrongful representation by a salesman, he is expected to examine carefully every article that he purchases and judge its quality for himself. During the nineteenth century little was done to protect consumers, apart from a series of Weights and Measures Acts (the first in 1878) and the Sale of Goods Act 1893. The 1878 Act insisted on standard weights and measures being used in the sale of goods, inspectors being appointed to make checks. The 1893 Act (amended in 1973) gave consumers a degree of protection against inferior quality, and laid down that goods must agree with a sample or description. Regulations were also introduced to cover the handling of food. It is only during the past twenty years, however, that a serious attempt has been made to protect consumers against inferior goods, and the unscrupulous methods employed by some salesmen, especially in the case of hire-purchase transactions. In addition to the Hire Purchase Acts of 1954 and 1964–65 the following Acts to protect consumers have been passed: (a) Consumers Protection Act 1961; (b) Misrepresentation Act 1962; (c) Trade Descriptions Act 1968; (d) Unsolicited Goods and Services Act 1971; (e) Fair Trading Act 1973; and (f) Consumer Credit Act 1977. The Trade Descriptions Act prohibits the use of misleading descriptions of goods or services or misleading representation of price reductions. The Fair Trading Act established a Consumers' Advisory Committee, appointed by the government, and an Office of Fair Trading, independent of the government. These two institutions replaced the former Consumers' Council. Thus in recent years several bodies have been established to watch over consumers' interests, one of the best known of the independent ones being the Consumers' Association, which periodically conducts tests of commodities (and some services) and compares the products of different manufacturers, the results of these tests being published in its journal *Which?*

Questions

1. What are the main functions of the retailer?
2. Account for the great increase in the number of shops relative to the population in Britain during the past two hundred years.
3. What factors would you have to take into account if you were selecting the site for a retail business?
4. Argue the case for and against a retailer either giving or receiving credit.
5. Consider the advantages and disadvantages of hire-purchase to: (a) the retailer, and (b) the consumer.
6. What services does the retail trade render to the public? Do you think the services are rendered in greater or lesser degree according to: (a) the

commodity sold, and (b) the neighbourhood in which the trade is conducted?
(RSA)

7. Describe the services which an efficient retail business should provide for its customers. Illustrate your answer by reference to: (a) a retail grocer, and (b) a retailer of radio and television receivers and other electrical equipment. (RSA)

8. Why is it that one-third of independent grocers now belong to voluntary chains? (RSA)

9. When the manufacturer sells direct to the retailer, what are the advantages and disadvantages: (a) to the manufacturer; (b) to the retailer?

10. (a) Give *four* main features of the independent type of retail organisation. (*4 marks*)

(b) Describe the system of self-service which such an independent shop might use. (*4 marks*)

(c) Explain how such self-service arrangements can help to promote the sale of goods. (*6 marks*)

(d) Explain briefly *two* methods of selling goods other than self-service.
(*6 marks*)
(RSA Elem.)

17 Large-scale Retail Trade

1 Large-scale manufacturing

A feature of industrial development during the past hundred and fifty years has been the tendency for the size of the business unit to increase. In manufacturing there are many economies to be obtained when production is carried out on a large scale, and the attempt to secure these economies has generally been the motive for expansion. One of the main advantages which the large manufacturing business has over the small is that it can introduce greater specialisation and employ more machinery, and, as a result, fewer workers in proportion to its output. Greater specialisation will make possible the employment of more experienced and more efficient workers in charge of each of the firm's activities. The large firm will be able to buy its raw materials in larger quantities, and therefore more cheaply, than the small firm, and its selling costs – advertising, for example – will be less per unit of output. If the large firm borrows from the bank it will most likely pay a lower rate of interest on its loans than the small firm. There will probably too be economies in administration for the large firm.

2 Large-scale retailing

There has also been a trend towards large-scale retail trade. This has not, however, been so pronounced as in manufacturing, since many of the advantages that accrue to large-scale manufacture are less applicable, if not completely inapplicable, to retailing. For example, the cost of administration often increases much more rapidly as a retail business expands, this being clearly seen in the case of a large group of multiple shops. Like the large manufacturing company, the large retailer can buy more cheaply than the small, for he will be able to purchase his stock direct from the manufacturer instead of from the wholesaler, but much of this gain may be lost if he himself has then to distribute it among several hundred branches, as is the case with a multiple-shop organisation which has to undertake the business of wholesaling itself and provide warehouse accommodation for its stock. This also applies to some extent to department stores, since their costs are increased by their being housed in palatial buildings on expensive sites in the main shopping centres of large cities.

Large-scale retailing does, however, make possible the employment of expert buyers, and if the firm has customers in all parts of the country, advertising in the national press becomes possible. Large-scale retailers, like the larger manufacturing firms, can borrow from the bank more easily than their smaller rivals.

The chief obstacle in the way of large-scale retail trade is the fact that retailing involves a personal service, which is less easily provided by large concerns. There are over fifty million consumers in Britain, and they are scattered all over the country. It is not easy, therefore, to achieve economies in the personal aspect of the work of distribution without some loss of service. The concentration of retailing at a small number of large centrally situated town shops would reduce the cost of distribution, but it would entail considerable inconvenience to many customers. It would also reduce consumers' choice of retailers, and as a result would probably reduce to some extent the retailers' incentive to give the best possible service to their customers. Apparently most people are willing to pay slightly higher prices for the things they buy in return for the privilege of being able to choose their suppliers and for the convenience of having shops close at hand.

There are several forms of large-scale retail trade – the multiple shop, the department store and hypermarkets. In addition there are the co-operative societies and mail-order houses. Co-operative societies vary in size from place to place and include within their ranks a number of societies with as many branches as some multiple shops, while others operate single shops no larger than those of many sole proprietors. Mail-order business, in spite of its increase recently, still forms only a small fraction of total retailing.

For a long time, therefore, the difficulties of securing economies in retail distribution slowed down the development of retail trading on a large scale, and so the small independent trader was able to survive. However, although retailing is still mainly operated as a small-scale industry, the tendency towards large scale is present, as in other forms of production, and some notable developments have taken place. By taking advantage of economies in running costs (as, for example, in the self-service shop) and by buying in large quantities, large-scale retailers can cut their prices in order to try to attract more customers to their shops.

3 Multiple shops

The feature of this type of retail trade is a large number of shops all under the same management. It is not easy to decide how many shops must be under one firm's control to qualify it for this designation. In most large towns small groups of shops under one control are to be found, their general management being directed from the head shop, the others being branches which the firm has opened from time to time during its expansion. These cannot really be regarded as multiple shops – although many of them had this sort of origin – because in the case of the true multiple shops there is no head shop, the central direction being undertaken not from a shop at all but from headquarters which may be simply administrative or may include a warehouse.

The large multiple-shop organisations number their branches by the hundred – one of the largest now has over fifteen hundred branches – and they cover the whole country; some of the smaller organisations limit their activities to particular areas – north-east England, south Lancashire or the Midlands. Sometimes an attempt is made to distinguish between multiple shops and chain stores, but the terms are really synonymous, the description chain store merely being the term more popular in the United States.

The earliest multiples appeared on the retail scene in the 1890s in the grocery trade. The extent to which multiple shops have invaded the field of retail trade can be judged from the wide variety of commodities in which they deal. They are particularly well established in the boot and shoe trade, in the sale of ready-made clothing and in the grocery trade. Multiples are also to be found selling fish, meat, furniture and bicycles. In the case of multiple chemists the sale of drugs and other pharmaceutical products has become only one side of the business. Examples, too, can be found of multiple jewellers and booksellers and stationers.

Because of the large amount of capital required for this type of business, multiple-shop organisations are usually public limited companies, administered from central headquarters. The largest of these firms often find it necessary to decentralise the administration by dividing the country into a number of regions, each in charge of an area manager or district inspector. The central headquarters generally take the form of a warehouse, unless the warehousing is decentralised and under the control of the area managers, in which case the administrative centre will consist of offices.

4 Types of multiple shop

There are three main types of multiple shop.

(a) Some are owned and operated by manufacturers who use them primarily for the sale of their own products. Sometimes they stock only goods of their own manufacture, and in such cases the manufacturers undertake all three functions of producer, wholesaler and retailer. Some of them have found it necessary to stock other lines in order to attract more customers by giving them a wider choice.

(b) Some are retailers only and obtain their stock direct from the manufacturers instead of from wholesalers.

(c) Then there is the variety chain or 'bazaar' type, selling a great variety of goods at low or moderate prices. At one time these shops were fixed price stores, no goods having a price above a certain stated maximum. Before 1914 there were Penny Bazaars, and during the period 1919–39 one well-known shop had two prices only – threepence and sixpence, but the almost continuous rise in prices since 1939 has made it impossible to continue a policy of fixed prices.

5 Features of multiple-shop organisation

Standardisation is the keynote of the organisation of multiple shops.

(a) *Appearance.* Except for those of the bazaar type, multiple shops are usually of about the same size as the average shop of the sole proprietor. In order to attract customers from one branch to another they used to adopt a standardised design for their premises, so that they could be recognised more easily by their customers even when they were in a strange town. More recently, however, this policy has not always been followed in the case of new branches, especially those in new towns.

(b) *Stock.* In the case of shops owned by manufacturers and selling only their own products, the purchase of stock is greatly simplified. In the other type of multiple shop it is usual for the entire buying to be undertaken by expert buyers at headquarters, although the former fixed price stores sometimes permit their local managers to undertake a certain amount of buying. With the possible exception, therefore, of this type of shop, the same sort of goods – the same brands, the same quality – are found in all the many branches of a multiple-shop organisation. Their policy of making bulk purchases from manufacturers is responsible for this. Whether Mrs Smith shops in the Wolverhampton branch or the Portsmouth branch she finds the same kinds of goods displayed. This makes it possible to keep the main reserves of stock at the central or regional warehouses, thereby enabling the local branches to carry less stock than an independent trader would regard as a reasonable minimum. Multiples too tend to concentrate on lines in wide demand.

(c) *Prices.* These too are usually fixed by the management at headquarters, but they may vary between different localities. In many branches of trade the prices of goods are lower than at independent shops. The aim of the multiples is summed up in the phrase 'small profits, quick returns'. Prices, therefore, are cut in order to achieve as rapid a rate of turnover as possible.

(*d*) *Control.* All the branches are under a unified system of control from headquarters, although in the case of the larger organisations the general manager may exercise it through regional or district managers. Little initiative is left to the local branch managers, who generally merely carry out instructions sent to them, and make the regular daily or weekly reports required of them. The takings are usually put in the bank daily – multiple shops generally selling only on a cash basis – and at least once each week a report of the daily takings has to be returned together with a weekly stock return. Goods are usually invoiced to the branches at selling prices, and so the branch managers often do not know the mark-up on the things they sell, and indeed are often little more than foreman assistants.

In large concerns, whether in manufacture or distribution, organisation and control tend to become bureaucratic. This is inevitable if a uniform general policy is to be carried out. A firm operating hundreds of shops must also protect itself against possible dishonesty on the part of its branch managers, and inspectors regularly visit the shops, not only to study local conditions and to see that the company's policy is being maintained but also to check the stock and the manager's return.

The multiples have shown themselves to be the most progressive retailers of today. Since the 1960s they have increased their share of retailing and improved their efficiency by their integration of retailing and wholesaling and by restricting consumers' choice to the best selling lines. They were quick to take advantage of the ending of resale price maintenance in 1964 and, though they were not the first to introduce self-service, they were the first to develop the idea to its fullest extent, thereby reducing their labour costs by half.

6 Department stores

The distinguishing feature of a department store is that it is really a collection of shops all under the same roof, each department dealing in a particular branch of retail trade. Very large premises are required, and these are frequently almost palatial in design and occupy central sites in the main shopping centres. At one time it would probably have been true to say that department stores were single-unit shops without branches. At the present time, however, some firms operate department stores in a limited number of large cities. In addition, there has been a tendency for department stores to amalgamate, possibly to secure greater economies in buying. Since the stores usually continue to do business under their old names – on account of the goodwill appertaining to them – the ordinary shopper generally does not know whether two department stores which appear to be competing against one another are in fact competitors or really different sections of the same firm.

Since the overhead expenses of this type of retail business are very great, a large turnover is essential, and so these shops are to be found only in large cities which serve as shopping centres for wide areas. As is only to be expected, most of them in Britain are located in London, but examples – though usually smaller than those in the capital – are to be found in Leeds, Manchester, Birmingham, Edinburgh and other large cities, each of which attracts customers from a wide area, known as its 'shopping hinterland'. There development has been assisted by recent improvements in road transport as a result of which it has become possible for greater numbers of people in the surrounding districts to do their shopping in these large cities. The shopping hinterland of Leeds, for example, reaches almost to Sheffield in the south, to the Lancashire border in the west, almost to Hull in the east, and far up into North Yorkshire in the north. Manchester, too, draws its shoppers from a wide area, including most of south Lancashire, a large part of Cheshire and north Derbyshire, and overlaps to a considerable extent with the shopping hinterland of Leeds in West Yorkshire.

Department stores had their origin in France, the first being Bon Marché established in 1852. They are well established both in that country and in the United States. In Britain many of them developed out of drapery businesses, and in many of the smaller ones the drapery department is still the main centre of the business. In their early years especially one of their attractions was that they charged lower prices than did the independent traders who in those days offered their customers the maximum amount of service and personal attention and in consequence had to have a high mark-up on the goods they sold.

7   Features of the department store

Department stores vary considerably in size, from over three hundred departments in the case of one of the largest in London to fewer than ten for some of the smaller provincial ones. In the very largest every branch of retail trade may be represented, so that the entire shopping for a whole family could be carried out in one establishment. The essential feature is that each department is run independently of the others and under the direct control of its own manager, who is usually known as the buyer. If this definition is rigidly adhered to, many of the large shops in towns of medium size and which resemble department stores in selling a fairly wide variety of goods do not really qualify for this description. Most large department stores also have a mail-order department (*see* p. 239).

Within the department the layout is very carefully planned to make one purchase suggest another, just as people entering the store to buy from one department often end by buying from others also. People are encouraged to walk round and no pressure is put on them to buy anything, but the assistants are for ever on the alert for the casual stroller, who may at any instant suddenly feel an impulse to buy something.

To encourage people to do all their shopping in one store the management sets itself out to cater for their comfort while they are there by providing rest-rooms, writing-rooms, a café-restaurant, a general information service, lifts and escalators to all floors, and bright and pleasant surroundings. The provision of the maximum amount of service for customers is an important feature of all department stores and one of the ways by which they seek to overcome the drawback which they have for many people who have to travel long distances to visit them.

Sometimes in order to attract people to the store one of the departments may be used as a 'loss-leader', that is, it may be run deliberately at a loss. This practice is more common in the United States than in this country, although it is said that some British department stores are content if the restaurant only just pays its way.

Non-selling departments. Every department store has a number of non-selling departments. Foremost among these are the administrative and accounts departments, for in a large business of this type the work of administration is immense. The secretary is head of the general administration, and the chief accountant is in charge of the accounts side.

Then there is the publicity department, which is responsible for all the firm's advertising in the press, the issue of circulars and the organisation of window displays. All matters relating to comfort of customers will be in the hands of the amenities department. The traffic department, under a traffic manager, is in charge of the delivery of customers' purchases. A large store will also have its own maintenance staff of electricians, plumbers and joiners who carry out any repair work that may be required. Matters appertaining to the staff may be left to a staff manager or personnel officer. Most of the non-selling departments are under the control of managers, whereas the head of a selling department is usually known as a buyer.

Selling departments. In a very large department store the departments may be grouped in sections, each under a section manager. For example, a women's clothing section may include a number of separate departments each concerned with a particular variety of women's clothing. Each department is under the control of a buyer who, as his name implies, is responsible for all the buying of his department. The buyers have very wide powers – in contrast to the branch managers of multiple shops. The main restrictions on a buyer's activities are as follows.

(a) He must not buy goods outside the range of the branch of trade with which his department deals.

(b) He generally has only a limited amount of money to spend during each month.

(c) He must conform to the general policy of the management

with regard to the quality of the goods he buys. In this respect all departments must keep in line, since the aim is to make one department draw people to others. This purpose would be defeated if in (say) the men's clothing department the stock was of cheap, poor quality, while in the department concerned with house furnishings the goods were of a very high quality, for particular people tend to keep very nearly to the same quality, whether they are buying food, clothing or house furnishings. The departments must, therefore, keep a uniform quality for all the various kinds of goods they sell.

The buyer is an expert in his own particular branch of trade, and since his orders will usually be large, he generally buys home-produced goods direct from the manufacturers. Unless a department is being deliberately run at a loss, as in the case of the loss-leader, the buyer is expected to show a profit on the working of his department. In calculating the profit of a department, a deduction – generally, but not always, in proportion to its turnover – is made to cover a share of the general expenses of the store and the running of the non-selling departments.

At one time all the business of a department store was transacted on a cash basis, but some stores now permit customers to open monthly accounts. In the sale of more expensive articles, like furniture, most department stores will also permit the customers to buy on hire-purchase terms.

Mail-order business. Many of the large shops have mail-order departments. This enables them to widen greatly the range of customers upon whom they can draw, but extensive advertising in the national daily papers and by means of circulars is necessary in order to bring their goods to the notice of these people. By this means dwellers in the more remote parts of the country, such as the West of Scotland, the Hebrides, the Shetland Islands or central Wales, can shop on almost equal terms with people living in the large cities. The COD (cash on delivery) system is a good method of payment for this kind of selling.

Firms which undertake mail-order business only and have no shops must advertise as widely as possible in newspapers and magazines. Orders are often placed through part-time agents, goods being selected from illustrated catalogues and delivered by post to the door. On account of the difficulty of choosing goods from catalogues most mail-order firms will send goods on approval. Credit is often allowed to customers, and where payment is made by instalments these are collected by the agents. The value of mail-order business in Britain increased from £35 million in 1950 to £500 million in 1968 and to £1,800 million in 1977, this increase being only partly accounted for by the steep rise in prices during the period. It now accounts for 5 per cent of total retail trade in Britain.

8   Retail discount houses

Generally located a short distance from town and city centres, retail discount houses offer their customers a fairly wide range of goods although, like the multiples, they only stock the best-selling lines. They purchase their stock in bulk direct from manufacturers, and by keeping their costs as low as possible they are able to give their customers substantial discounts. Thus, the discount houses could make little progress until the abolition of resale price maintenance. Sales are always on a cash basis, and self-service in the widest sense is a feature of the discount house, delivery rarely being provided even for bulky articles, and so purchasers of such commodities usually come in their own cars. It would seem that shoppers attracted to discount houses by their low prices rarely take into account the cost of having to provide their own transport.

9   Co-operative societies

Although co-operation in production has made little progress in Britain, it has achieved a considerable measure of success in distribution. The oldest existing society is the Rochdale Co-operative Society, which was founded in 1844 by twenty-eight weavers who provided the capital with which to open their first shop. By 1865, 300 societies had been established.

The early societies were established by groups of working people in an attempt to protect themselves against what they regarded as excessively high costs of distribution due, they thought, to the presence of too many middlemen between producer and consumer and the monopolistic practices of large-scale organisations which were responsible for high prices. They felt, too, that many consumers were weak and inexperienced buyers who were easily persuaded by the skilful salesmen employed by the large retailers to buy things which they really did not want.

Many of the early co-operative societies had a great struggle to survive, but slowly their membership increased until by 1880 it reached a total of half a million. By 1901 the number of societies in Britain reached its maximum of 1,438 but membership continued to expand until 1964 when it reached 13 million.

In the period since the end of the Second World War the co-operative movement has faced new problems. Rising personal incomes and living standards have meant important changes in patterns of retail demand. As well as better qualities in essential lines such as food and clothing, the retail trade has expanded enormously in the direction of consumer durables such as cars and household items such as TVs, washing machines and electrical appliances of many kinds. This has compelled the co-operative societies to enter new fields of retailing. Clearly also the movement has had to face increasing competition from the discount stores and supermarkets, whose lower prices have competed strongly with the dividend distributed by the co-operatives.

In 1958 the Gaitskell Commission reported on the problems faced by the co-operative societies and made recommendations intended to provide a guide to greater efficiency. The Commission considered that there were too many societies and that these ought to be reduced to less than 300 in number. This could be done by amalgamation and would bring in its wake the opportunity to benefit from such economies of scale as bulk buying and more specialised management. In 1967 a plan was announced for the total reorganisation of the movement into fifty regional societies but, as late as 1974, there still remained 242 separate societies in Britain.

Since the late 1970s, however, major revision of the structure and organisation has been undertaken. The results of this are clearly reflected in the following table.

Retail Co-operative Structure, 1978–83

Year	Number of societies	Number of outlets	Number of employees (000)	Turnover (£ million)
1978	202	10,207	153	3,004
1979	101	9,450	149	3,404
1980	191	8,556	139	3,869
1983	115	6,433	90	4,441

It will be seen that the number of societies has now fallen well below the level recommended by the Gaitskell Commission, and that this has been accompanied by sharp reductions in the numbers of outlets and employees. In its search for enhanced efficiency to meet the various problems of present-day retailing, the movement has merged many small societies and increased the scale of its operations. Thus, although membership has somewhat declined in recent years, turnover, as the table indicates, has been maintained despite the wholesale reduction in outlets and societies. As against retail sales in general, however, the co-operatives have lost ground. Between 1978 and 1982, for example, the index of all retail sales moved upwards by 55 points whilst that of the sales of the co-operative movement in the same period rose by only 36 points.

An examination of the present structure of co-operative retailing suggests an impressively large scale of operations in some directions. At the end of 1983 there were, for example, fifty-eight superstores (over 25,000 sq. ft.), 135 major supermarkets (10–25,000 sq. ft.), and 1,436 supermarkets (2–10,000 sq. ft.). At the same time there remained some 2,098 self-service grocery shops of less than 2,000 sq. ft. so that the large store is by no means universal throughout the movement, and significant variations in size and scale remain. Co-operative retailing is now divided into four regions: Scotland, North of England, Midlands and London, and it is probable that, under this geographical organisation, amalgamation and increased scale of operations will be further pressed.

The capital is provided by the members who usually have to pay a small entrance fee and also purchase at least a single £1 share. At meetings – unlike shareholders in limited companies – each shareholder, however many shares he may hold, has only a single vote. A co-operative member may, however, purchase a maximum of £5,000 worth of shares and in addition he may hold any amount in the form of unit loans. The members elect a Committee of Management and a President to take responsibility for the formulation of general policy. A full-time paid secretary undertakes day-to-day control.

The profits of co-operative societies are distributed quarterly or half-yearly among the members in proportion to purchases. Some system of recording purchases has, therefore, to be operated and this increases the work of assistants.

The retail societies are linked through the Co-operative Wholesale Society (CWS), founded in 1863 to supply the retail side, and the Scottish CWS (SCWS). In 1973 the CWS and SCWS were amalgamated. Although the wholesale societies were set up to eliminate the profits of private enterprise wholesale suppliers to the retail societies, the latter today receive only about two-thirds of total supplies from the wholesale societies. Control of the CWS is by the retail societies who elect a board of thirty-five directors who serve on a part-time basis for three years. Voting power depends on the extent of a retail society's purchases from the CWS.

CWS activities are on a very wide scale. These include the manufacture of foods and other goods, banking, insurance, farming, hotels and travel, printing and even the raising of tea on its own plantations in India.

A further organisation of great importance to the movement is Co-operative Retail Services (CRS). This was established in 1934 firstly to assist societies during the depression of trade and secondly to provide retail services in districts where co-operative facilities did not exist. The CRS has been responsible for taking over a large number of societies until, today, it is the largest retail society in the co-operative movement.

10 Features of co-operative societies

Many people became attracted to the co-operative movement because they regarded it as being worthy of support for its own sake. For this reason a strong feeling of loyalty was engendered among the members, and this made for stability of trade. It used to be said that whereas a dissatisfied customer of an independent retailer would change his supplier, a member of a co-operative society would be more likely to air his grievances at a members' meeting but would nevertheless continue to make his purchases as before. The payment of dividend on purchases used to be an attraction to many people, especially in days when the standard of living was much lower than it is today, but in recent years dividends of most societies have been very low. The lower prices offered by the new supermarkets have undermined loyalty to the co-operative movement, especially among younger people who appear to prefer a lower price at the time of making a purchase rather than wait for the payment of a dividend. To enable them to compete against the supermarkets some co-operative societies offer a range of cheap goods on which no dividend is paid, while others issue co-operative dividend stamps.

11 Hypermarkets

These are particularly large supermarkets, officially defined as having more than 50,000 square feet (approx. 6,650 m^2) of selling space, together with a large car park. They are usually situated well away from town centres. Hypermarkets were first developed in the United States.

Britain has fewer shops of this type than almost any other European country, in 1978 having no more than 130 'superstores' and 10 hypermarkets (though many more have been planned), whereas West Germany has over 500 and France more than 300. Opposition to hypermarkets in Britain has come from both planners and conservationists who wish to protect the countryside and keep urban development under control.

12   The survival of the small shop

For a long time the number of shops in Britain tended to be excessive. Some of the reasons for this were as follows.

(a) *Differentiation between shops.* Consumers do not regard all shops in the same branch of trade as being alike. One shop is preferred to another perhaps on account of its more convenient situation, or maybe because one shopkeeper is always pleasant and obliging, while another is glum and taciturn.

(b) *Ease of entry.* The retail trade is one of the few types of business which at the present day it is relatively easy for the man with only a small amount of capital to enter. Nor in most cases is any special training or qualification required, unless he wishes to set up as a pharmaceutical chemist.

(c) *Staffing.* To employ sufficient staff to cope with peak periods means that shops are overstaffed at other times whereas insufficient staff at busy times may mean a loss of customers. In many small shops this is a much less serious problem, since, being family businesses, the proprietor can often call upon other members of his family when he needs extra assistance. The effect of this is to reduce the costs of the small shop.

(d) *Shopkeeping may not be the sole source of income.* Many of the smallest shops are run by people who take up retailing merely as a sideline to their normal occupations. No special premises are required, all that is necessary being that the front room of the house shall be converted into a shop. While the husband is at work during the day his wife looks after the shop; he then takes over in his spare time.

(e) *Resale price maintenance.* When manufacturers could insist on their products not being sold at less than the marked price, the mark-up had to be sufficient to enable the smallest and least efficient retailers to stock and sell the goods in competition with their larger competitors. The ending of resale price maintenance in 1964, therefore, severely affected many of the small, less efficient independent traders and since then their numbers have seriously declined.

Even the larger and more efficient independent traders have found the competition of supermarkets severe. In some cases in the grocery trade groups of retailers have associated with wholesalers, themselves adversely affected by recent developments, to form voluntary chains of retailers who are not in direct competition with one another. In order to reduce their costs such retailers both buy and sell in larger quantities than was formerly their custom, their customers being encouraged to co-operate by the offer of discounts on many commodities. Many independent traders too have re-organised their shops on self-service lines. Others, however, still find that many of their customers appreciate a delivery service and are prepared to pay the higher prices that it involves.

Questions

1. Why has the tendency towards large scale been less pronounced in distribution than in manufacturing?
2. Compare the multiple shop and the department store as forms of retail distribution.
3. Describe the organisation of a department store.
4. Does the co-operative society fall into the same category as (a) the multiple shop or (b) the department store as retail outlet? Give reasons for your answer.
5. State, with reasons, the particular spheres of trade most suited to: (a) the department stores, and (b) the multiple shop organisation.   (RSA)
6. Describe the administration and general organisation of either a co-operative society or a department store owned by a sole trader.   (WR)
7. Explain how mail-order business is conducted. What is the effect of mail-order competition on the small retailer?   (UEI)
8. What are the advantages and disadvantages of the hire-purchase system?   (UEI)
9. What part is played in modern retailing by: (a) the multiple and chain store; (b) the departmental store; (a) the consumers' co-operative store?
          (LCCI)
10. Describe the growth of retail co-operative societies and discuss the advantages and disadvantages of this form of trading organisation as far as the consumer is concerned.   (WJEC)
11. Indicate the advantages of large-scale retailing. How do you account

for the continued existence of the small independent retailer, despite such advantages of large-scale retailing?   (GCE Camb.)

12. Describe briefly the various types of retail outlet in this country, indicating any three that have grown in importance during the past fifteen years.   (GCE JMB)

13. Examine the distinctive features of the supermarket in retail trade.

What are its principal advantages and disadvantages?   (NCTEC)

14. Comment on the special characteristics and importance of: (a) voluntary groups; (b) 'cut price' shops; (c) trading stamps.   (NCTEC)

15. Department stores have not increased their trade since 1950 to the same extent as have multiple shops and chain stores. Distinguish between these three types of retail business. What are the department stores now doing to improve their trade?   (RSA)

16. Indicate the advantages of large-scale retailing. How do you account for the continued existence of small independent retailers, despite such advantages of large-scale retailing?   (GCE Camb.)

17. Describe the main forms of large-scale retailing and state their particular (a) advantages and (b) disadvantages.   (LCCI)

18. Outline the factors that should be taken into account when deciding the location of: (a) a department store; (b) a small retail shop; (c) a supermarket.   (LCCI)

19. Describe the advantages and disadvantages to the customer of shopping in (a) a supermarket and (b) a small retail shop.

20. (a) What are the distinctive characteristics of the following retail outlets: (i) a department store; (ii) a mail-order company; (iii) a supermarket.

(b) What particular advantages does each offer to its customers?

                                                                    (LCCI)

Part Four
**International Trade and
the EEC**

18 Foreign Trade I: Import Trade

1 Britain's trade with other countries

At one time countries used to trade with one another only if each was able to produce or supply something the other could not. Today, however, most international trade is the result of international specialisation of production.

Not so long ago about 80 per cent of the UK's imports consisted of food and raw materials, the rest being manufactured goods. Since the Second World War there has been a huge increase in the imports of manufactured goods, so that these now account for over half of the UK's imports. In particular, there has been a rapid growth in imports of motor cars, electrical machinery and textiles.

In recent years there have been changes in the relative importance of Britain's import sources, with the Commonwealth countries and the USA having been steadily replaced by the EEC countries as Britain's main sources of imports. Britain's main sources of manufactured imports in 1970 and 1982 are shown on p. 252.

The changing direction of Britain's import sources has been dramatic. For example, in 1970 the USA was Britain's main source of manufactured imports, providing nearly 20 per cent, while West Germany was second with 11 per cent. In 1982 West Germany was the UK's main source of manufactured imports with 18 per cent and the USA was second in importance with 13.7 per cent. The importance of Japan in this respect has greatly increased: in 1982 it provided almost 7 per cent of Britain's imported manufactures,

	1970	1982
EEC	33.0	51.0
Rest of Europe	17.0	14.0
North America	26.0	16.0
Other developed countries	6.0	9.0
Developing countries	12.0	8.5
Centrally planned economies	6.0	1.5
	100.0	100.0

Source: *Overseas Trade Statistics of the United Kingdom.*

ranking fourth in the list, whereas in 1972 the figure was only about 2–3 per cent. The growing importance of the EEC as a source of imports has been further enhanced with Britain's membership since 1973. Even so, it should be appreciated that this trend existed before Britain joined the EEC.

There have also been fundamental changes on the export side. In 1900, manufactured goods accounted for almost 80 per cent of Britain's exports, for example textiles (36 per cent) and machinery and transport equipment (15 per cent). The rest was accounted for by non-manufactured goods such as coal (12.5 per cent). By 1984 manufactured goods accounted for less than 70 per cent of exports. Machinery and transport equipment now accounted for 33 per cent and chemicals for 11 per cent, while textiles now formed only 2 per cent. Non-manufactured goods accounted for the rest, especially petroleum and related products (20 per cent), reflecting the importance to the UK of North Sea oil. Coal now accounts for less than 1 per cent of UK exports.

Today, Britain's main export markets include the USA, West Germany, France, the Netherlands and other EEC countries, Saudi Arabia, South Africa and Nigeria. With the new-found wealth derived from oil exports, a small number of oil-exporting countries have become important markets for UK exports, especially Saudi Arabia, which was forty-sixth in order of importance in 1971 but eighth by 1982, and Nigeria.

Thus on both the import and export sides of Britain's trade, the EEC countries are now very important, while the relative importance of the traditional trading partners such as the Commonwealth and North America has declined. For example, during the 1970s the Commonwealth's share of Britain's trade in manufactured goods fell by about half, from 20 per cent of the total trade to 11 per cent.

These changes in the sources of imports and destinations of exports reflect several factors, for example the introduction of new products, the development of new sources of power (oil replacing coal), changes in tastes, improvements in the standard of living and the emergence of newly industrialised countries such as Taiwan, Hong Kong and Portugal, which have replaced countries with long-established staple industries as the main producers of manufactured products such as textiles and iron and steel products. The development of newly industrialised countries extends the principle of comparative advantage (countries specialise in the production of commodities in which they have an advantage) and so increases the tendency of countries to specialise. As a result, a country's exports and imports of manufactured goods increase, say, as a percentage of Gross Domestic Product (GDP). For example, the UK's exports as a percentage of GDP rose from 21.7 per cent in 1972 to 27 per cent in 1982. However, with respect to manufactured goods, imports have continued to rise as a percentage of GDP while the figure for manufactured exports has been constant. The result is that the UK now has a deficit on its trade in manufactures for the first time in many decades.

2 The balance of payments

A country's balance of payments is its set of accounts recording the following.

(a) *Its trading transactions* with other countries, including overseas companies, individuals, governments and so on, i.e. current transactions. These are recorded in the Current Account.

(b) *Flows of money* between countries arising not from imports and exports but mainly from longer-term financial transactions, for example when a British company invests money in a new factory overseas, i.e. capital transactions. These transactions are recorded in the Capital Account. In the UK this account is called the *Investment and other Capital Flows Account*.

The current account. A country's imports and exports fall into two groups. First, there are tangible imports and exports, such as motor vehicles, raw materials and foodstuffs. Trade in tangible goods constitutes *visible trade*. Secondly, there is trade in intangible commodities or services. This is called *invisible trade*.

(*a*) *Visible trade.* The value of a country's visible imports and its visible exports is set out in the balance of trade. Since British money, i.e. sterling, can be spent only in the UK, no foreigner wants it except as a means of purchasing British goods. Similarly, no one in Britain wants US dollars, French francs or any other kind of foreign currency except for the purpose of buying goods or paying for services from the countries which issue these particular kinds of money. Unless, therefore, Britain exports cars, textiles or other things to the United States it cannot earn the dollars which it requires for the purchase of, say, American cotton. Unless Denmark exports to Britain some of the bacon it produces it cannot import British manufactured goods.

When one country tries to balance trade with another in this way it is known as bilateral trade. The volume of world trade, however, will be much greater if multilateral trade is developed, that is, if Britain, for example, earns the means to buy American goods by exporting manufactured goods to Denmark which exports medical and electronic equipment to the United States. This can be more clearly shown by the diagram below.

Such a triangle was formerly an important feature of British trade. Difficulties in exchanging one currency for another greatly hamper the development of multilateral trade. Only if currencies can be freely exchanged for one another can multilateral trade expand to its fullest extent. In 1981 Britain imported goods to the value of £48,087 million and exported goods worth £51,100 million – an excess of exports over imports of £3,013 million.

(b) *Invisible trade.* In addition to supplying one another with goods, however, countries perform services for one another, and these also have to be paid for. In most years Britain's income from invisible items has been more than sufficient to cover the deficit in its balance of trade. In 1981, for example, Britain's invisible items provided a credit balance of £26,315 million, and when all items, visible and invisible, arising from current transactions were taken into account, there was a credit balance of £6,036 million.

What are these services which give rise to invisible items in the balance of payments? First, there is air and sea transport. Not only are many of Britain's imports and exports carried by British airlines or in British ships, but a good deal of trade in which Britain has no direct interest – for example, between South America and southern Europe – is undertaken by British airlines or shipping companies. At one time most of the goods entering into world trade were carried in British ships. During recent years, however, this country's share in the carrying trade of the world has diminished partly because other countries have increased their merchant fleets but mainly because of the development of air transport.

The banks and insurance companies of the City of London also perform many financial services for other countries, and this results in further income to Britain from abroad. In addition there is the net income from foreign investments (+ £1,257 million in 1981). Another invisible item in the balance of payments is travel. The amount spent abroad by British tourists and holidaymakers is a foreign payment and, therefore, equivalent to an import, while the amount spent by foreign visitors to the United Kingdom is a receipt and so equivalent to an export. Until the late 1960s travel was a debit item for the UK.

The question of balance. If the surplus or deficit on the Current Account is added to the surplus or deficit on the Capital Account, and the value of the balancing item (an estimate of measurement errors or omissions which arise in recording the numerous trans-actions) added, the value of the overall surplus or deficit in the country's current and capital transactions with the rest of the world is obtained. This value is called the *balance for official financing*. It should be noted here that the Current Account, the Capital Account and the balancing item are the three components of the Total Currency Flow Account.

The final account of the balance of payments is called *Official Financing*. This shows how the balance for official financing was 'accommodated' or financed. For example, if the balance is positive (i.e. there was a surplus) Official Financing will show how that surplus was dealt with, for example it may be added to a country's reserves of foreign exchange, or it may be used to repay money borrowed in the past to cover earlier deficits. If the balance was +£1,000 million, Official Financing will total −£1,000 million. The addition of these two values will sum to zero, i.e. 'the balance of payments always balances'. The outline structure of the UK balance of payments in 1981 was as follows.

Total currency flow (TCF)		
1. Current account		£ million
Visible trade		
	Imports (f.o.b.)	−48,087
	Exports (f.o.b.)	+51,100
	Balance of trade	+3,013
Invisible trade		
	Credits	+29,338
	Debits	−26,315
	Invisible balance	+3,023
Current balance		+6,036
2. Capital account		−7,209
3. Balancing item		+328
Balance for official financing		−845
Official Financing		+845

Source: *Annual Abstract of Statistics*, HMSO 1983.

If the balance for official financing is negative, it could be financed by using the country's foreign exchange reserves, by drawing from the International Monetary Fund, or by borrowing from overseas central banks or governments. If the deficit should prove to be persistent and large, efforts will have to be made to remove it, for example deflate the economy, introduce tariffs and quotas, take action to reduce the exchange rate against other currencies, or introduce controls on the availability of foreign exchange. However, there are problems with all these remedies; for example, deflation is disliked because of its immediate effects in raising unemployment; countries which are party to the General Agreement on Tariffs and Trade (GATT) should not use obstacles to imports such as tariffs or quotas; reducing the exchange rate against other currencies, though helping exports (because they are made cheaper), increases import prices and therefore is inflationary.

3   The terms of trade

An important influence on a country's balance of trade is the relation between the prices of a country's imports and the prices of its exports. Movements in these two sets of prices are measured by the terms of trade index, which is calculated as follows:

$$\text{Terms of trade index} = \frac{\text{Index of export prices}}{\text{Index of import prices}} \times 100.$$

If the index rises, e.g. as a result of an increase in export prices, the terms of trade are said to be improving or favourable, so that a smaller volume of exports will purchase the same volume of imports as before. On the other hand, if the index falls, e.g. as a result of more expensive imports (for example, a crop failure) or a fall in the exchange rate, the terms of trade are said to be moving against a country or deteriorating. For example, the terms of trade index fell from 121.1 in 1972 to 93.1 in 1974, reflecting the sharp rise in the cost of oil imports following the quadrupling of the price of oil in 1973–74. After this the UK terms of trade improved, rising to 105.9 in 1978, then they deteriorated again falling to 101.1 in 1982.

4 Customs duties

On many goods imported from overseas, taxes known as import duties, tariffs or customs duties have to be paid. These duties have two purposes: (*a*) to provide the government with tax revenue, and (*b*) to protect a country's industries from imports, either because the industries are in the early stage of their development ('infant' industries) or in decline ('geriatric' industries).

After the Second World War an appreciation of the benefits of multilateral trade and a desire to avoid the 'beggar-my-neighbour' policies pursued by governments in the 1930s, which had deepened the international recession, led to the signing in 1948 of an international treaty called the General Agreement on Tariffs and Trade. From this there developed two sets of conferences aimed at reducing the level and number of important duties or tariffs – the Kennedy Round and, more recently, the Tokyo Round. However, the current international recession has seen several countries imposing tariffs on their imports, i.e. protectionism, which can only further reduce the level of international trade and so deepen the recession.

There used to be a distinction between customs duties (imposed on imports) and excise duties (imposed on home-produced goods and services) in the UK, but with membership of the EEC this distinction came to an end in the early part of 1978. Now duties having as their objective government revenue are called excise duties, whether they are levied on imports or home-produced goods (*see also* below). Duties imposed for protective purposes are called *protective duties*. As the UK is a member of the EEC it operates a common external protective tariff against non-EEC countries' imports. At the same time imports from EEC countries into the UK are free of all customs duties. An association of countries operating a common rate of tariff against non-members, and in which members do not impose duties on each others' exports (i.e. free trade) is called a *customs union* (*see* Chapter 21). By contrast, an association in which there is free trade among members and in which each country retains the right to determine its own rates of import duties on imports from non-members is called a *free trade area*, for example the European Free Trade Area set up by the Stockholm Convention in 1960.

5 Excise duties

Whereas protective duties are imposed on imports from countries outside the EEC excise duties are used mainly to raise revenue and are imposed on both imported and home-produced goods. Though their main purpose is to raise revenue, on occasions they have been imposed to check consumption of particular commodities. The heavy duties on spirits such as gin and whisky are mainly for the purpose of keeping down their consumption. Excise duties are payable also on petrol, patent medicines, tobacco and wine. They were first used in 1643 to complement customs duties.

Licences have to be obtained before dealers can sell intoxicating drinks, petrol and a number of other commodities. Similarly, licences are required before one can carry on the business of hawker, pawnbroker, auctioneer or other person engaged in any form of retailing when credit is allowed to customers. These form another type of excise duty.

Specific and ad valorem taxes. There are two methods of calculating the taxes levied on commodities. One way is to base the tax on the quantity of the commodity purchased, that is, at a rate of so much per pint, gallon (or litre) or pound (or kilogram) by weight, as is the case with beer, petrol and tobacco respectively. These are *specific* taxes.

Alternatively, the tax can be assessed at a certain percentage of the price of the commodity, and in this case it is an *ad valorem* tax. Value added tax (VAT) is an example of such a tax and has been levied at a rate of 15 per cent since 1979.

6 Specialists in international trade

There are three groups of specialists involved in importing and exporting.

(a) *Merchants*. Merchants purchase goods on their own account, i.e. they are principals. For example, an import merchant may buy goods from a manufacturer in one country then transport and sell them in another country for a profit.

(b) *Agents*. Agents are involved in making deals on behalf of others, hence they are not principals to contracts. For example, freight forwarding agents speed up the process of moving exports and help firms to obtain payments for their exports. Similarly, a firm, say in the UK, may authorise a sales agent in Greece to make contracts for the sale of its products there.

(c) *Brokers*. Brokers act as intermediaries bringing together potential importers and exporters, who otherwise might not have traded with each other. For example, an import broker in country A may find a buyer for the produce of a wine grower in country B. Sometimes brokers may also act as agents, for example an export broker may be an agent for a shipping line.

7   Dealing with goods on arrival: the customs examination

Goods are imported on consignment or in response to definite orders. Food and raw materials are generally imported on consignment, and this can be regarded as the normal method by which goods are imported. In this case the goods are consigned by the foreign exporter to an import merchant who undertakes the selling of the goods, for which service he will be paid a commission. Foreign-manufactured goods may be imported in response to direct orders from British merchants, or more probably they will be consigned to the foreign manufacturer's or exporter's own agent or branch office.

Upon the arrival of a ship from overseas at a British port two customs requirements have to be met. Firstly, within twenty-four hours of his arrival the Master of the ship must supply to the port authorities a ship's report giving particulars of the ship, its crew, its passengers (if any) and its cargo. Secondly, the importer must complete one of the three following forms, depending on the nature of the goods.

(*a*) *Entry for free goods.* This document is used when the imported goods are not subject to customs duty. The customs officer compares the particulars given on this form (*see* below) with those on the ship's report, and he inspects the cargo before authorising the release of the goods.

(*b*) *Entry for home use.* This document is for use in connection with goods the duty on which is to be paid at once, for when goods are dutiable the duty can be paid either immediately or at a later date. After the goods have been checked and the duty paid they can then be removed by the importer.

(*c*) *Entry for warehousing.* If the duty is not to be paid at once special precautions will have to be taken to ensure that the goods are not removed without payment of duty. The goods can be removed only under the supervision of customs officers to a bonded warehouse, a special place of storage for goods on which the duty is not to be paid immediately. This warehouse must be named on the entry form.

ENTRY FOR FREE GOODS

Port ....
Dock or station ....
Importer's name and address ....

Examination	Ship's name	Master's name	Date of report	Port of shipment of goods	
	Marks and nos.	No. and description of packages and goods	Quantity	Value	Name of place whence goods consigned

I enter the above goods as free of duty, and declare the above particulars to be true.
Dated this........day of.................. 19.........

(Signed)...
Importer.

8   Dealing with goods on arrival: claiming the goods from the shipping company

Before the arrival of the ship the importer will probably have received the following documents: (a) an advice of shipment, and (b) a bill of lading, to which would be attached a certificate of insurance (covering the goods against loss or damage in transit), a pro forma invoice (serving simply as a statement about the nature of the contract, the goods and their price) and a bill of exchange for acceptance by the importer if this method of payment has previously been agreed upon. Of these the bill of exchange is considered in Chapter 9 and insurance in Chapter 12. The advice of shipment is similar to the advice note used in the home trade.

Other documents include: (a) customs invoices in the form required by the authorities of the importing country; (b) a certificate of origin which is a declaration by the exporter stating the country of origin of the goods in transit; and (c) a consular invoice which is mandatory when exporting to some countries, and consists of a specially printed document issued in the exporter's country, and which has to be filled in to meet various specified requirements and countersigned (visa'd) by the consulate of the importer's country in the embassy of the exporter's country.

Other documents may also have to be obtained by the importer to satisfy regulations in the importing country. These vary from place to place and depend also on the type of goods to be shipped, for example certificates of inspection (non-perishable goods) and certificates of health (livestock and animal products).

The bill of lading. This gives the name of the ship the name of the shipper (usually the exporter), full particulars of the goods (the quantity, their type, special markings on the packing cases, etc.), the port of embarkation and the port at which the goods will arrive. The exporter retains one copy of the bill of lading, which has been signed by the person authorised by the shipowner as proof of receipt of the consignment on board. A second copy is given to the shipowner or Master, who uses the various bills of lading to complete his ship's *Manifest*, which is the document detailing all the goods travelling in the ship for that voyage. A third copy is sent to the importer who will not be able to take delivery of the goods he is importing until he produces the bill. It should be realised that the exporter will not forward the bill of lading until he has been paid or until agreement has been reached about payment in the future.

Since the bill of lading is a document of title – that is, it enables the holder to take possession of the goods – it is very important that the importer should receive a copy before the ship arrives, and in order to try to ensure that he does so an additional copy is often sent to him by a different route from that taken by the ship carrying the goods – for example, by air.

Upon the arrival of the ship the importer can present his bill of lading at the port office of the shipping company (the owners of the ship), and pay the freight charge for the carriage of the goods unless this has been paid in advance. The representative of the shipping company, if satisfied that all is in order, will then endorse the bill of lading and return it to the importer, who can then present it to the Master of the ship.

9 Warehousing of the goods

Having now complied with the various formalities required by both the customs authorities and the shipping company, the importer is in a position to take possession of the goods. His next business is to see that they are warehoused. Ownership of the goods while in store is given by possession of a warehouse warrant, a negotiable document by which the ownership of the goods can be transferred from one merchant to another without their being removed from the warehouse. The production of a warehouse warrant is necessary before the goods can be taken away.

If the goods have been admitted as free goods, or for home use, and the duty has been paid, they can be taken to any warehouse and stored there until they are sold. This is the procedure in the case of raw wool. If the goods are admitted for warehousing – as would be the case with tobacco, tea or wine – they will have to be transferred to a bonded warehouse, the goods then being said to be in bond.

Bonded warehouses. The purpose of this type of warehouse is to enable goods to be stored before the duty is paid. Importers may own their own bonded warehouse, or may hire space in one when required. The owner enters into a bond with the customs authorities for a certain sum of money, which he is liable to forfeit if the business is not properly conducted. To be able to store goods without having first to pay duty on them is a great advantage to the importer, for he need then pay the duty only when he sells each lot. To ensure that payment of the duty is not evaded a bonded warehouse can be opened only when a customs officer is present, and goods can be released only on the presentation of a document showing that the duty has been paid on that particular consignment. Another advantage of placing goods in a bonded warehouse is that they can be prepared for sale while in bond. Thus tea or tobacco can be blended or wine bottled while they are still in bond, the duty not being paid until the goods are removed – this represents a large saving to the merchant concerned.

Bonded warehouses are supervised by HM Customs and Excise and the importer has to bear the costs of warehousing while the goods are in bond.

10 Entrepôt trade

A considerable amount of trade of the type known as entrepôt is carried on by the port of London. This means the re-exporting of goods which have previously been imported. For example, most of the tea which comes to Europe is first brought to London and then re-exported to other countries. At first glance this might appear to be a strange thing to do, but a moment's thought should be sufficient to enable the student to notice that this is really nothing more than wholesaling on a large scale. In London there is the main tea market for Europe, and some of the tea purchased there is on behalf of European merchants. Some tobacco is also re-exported.

Many other ports besides London are engaged in entrepôt trade – Le Havre for most of the coffee for continental Europe, and Rotterdam for many things which have Germany as their ultimate destination. In the Far East Singapore serves in a similar capacity as the distributing centre for neighbouring countries.

Customs drawback. It sometimes happens that customs duty has been paid on goods which are later to be re-exported. In that case it is possible to claim a refund of the duty, known as customs drawback. The payment of duty on goods to be re-exported can be avoided where there is a freeport.

Questions

1. Distinguish between: (*a*) the balance of trade and the balance of payments, and (*b*) visible and invisible items in the balance of payments.

2. For what purposes are: (*a*) protective duties, and (*b*) excise duties levied? Give three examples of each kind of duty.

3. In what circumstances is each of the following documents used: (*a*) entry for free goods: (*b*) entry for home; (*c*) entry for warehousing?

4. Describe the procedure for importing: (*a*) a non-dutiable commodity; (*b*) a dutiable commodity.

5. What is a bonded warehouse? What functions does it fulfil?

6. Write brief notes on: ship's report, bill of lading, warehouse warrant.

7. Explain each of the following terms: *ad valorem* duty; customs drawback; consular invoice.

8. What are the uses and advantages of bonded warehouses: (*a*) from the standpoint of the trading community, and (*b*) from the point of view of governments? (LCCI)

9. Briefly describe the procedure employed in importing goods into this country, listing the main documents and stating the function of these documents. (WJEC)

10. Explain the difference between *ad valorem* and specific duties, giving examples for which each would be appropriate. (LCCI)

11. (*a*) Define the following terms: (*i*) bill of lading; (*ii*) entry for free goods; (*iii*) entry for home use; (*iv*) entry for warehouse.

(*b*) Describe the circumstances in which each is used. (LCCI)

12. (*a*) Explain how changes in the rate of exchange of a country's currency may affect that country's balance of trade, and also bring about changes in the prices of imported goods within the country. (*14 marks*)

(*b*) Choosing *two* kinds of invisible earnings, show how they might offset an adverse balance of trade to give a favourable balance of payments.

(*6 marks*)

(RSA Inter.)

19 Foreign Trade II: Export Trade

1 Importance of exports

Britain is unable to produce enough food for its people or sufficient raw materials for its industries. Exports, both visible (goods) and invisible (services), are required to pay for our imports of food and raw materials. During the nineteenth century the UK expanded its invisible exports – foreign investment, shipping, banking and insurance services – to such an extent that an increasing volume of goods could be imported. As already noted (see p. 255), invisible exports still form an important proportion of this country's total exports. The expansion of production since the Second World War has necessitated a large increase in the import of raw materials. The rising standard of living of the British people too has led to an increased demand for foreign goods. Consequently it has been necessary also to increase exports and great efforts have been made by successive governments to encourage manufacturers to expand their exports.

2 The quotation of prices

We have already seen in our study of home trade that the most usual method of quoting prices is carriage paid or carriage forward, the former comprising the price of the goods including delivery to the buyer's premises, and the latter being the price ex-warehouse or ex-works, and therefore not including delivery charges which have to be borne by the buyer.

In foreign trade a number of other charges arise in connection with the sale and delivery of goods, and so there is greater variety in the method of quoting prices. The basic price of the goods is their

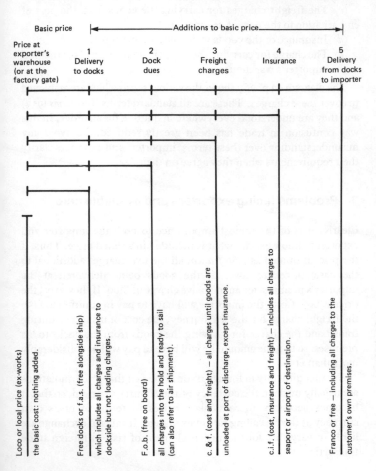

Basic price		Additions to basic price			
Price at exporter's warehouse (or at the factory gate)	1 Delivery to docks	2 Dock dues	3 Freight charges	4 Insurance	5 Delivery from docks to importer

Loco or local price (ex-works)
the basic cost: nothing added.

Free docks or f.a.s. (free alongside ship)
which includes all charges and insurance to dockside but not loading charges.

F.o.b. (free on board)
all charges into the hold and ready to sail (can also refer to air shipment).

c. & f. (cost and freight) — all charges until goods are unloaded at port of discharge, except insurance.

c.i.f. (cost, insurance and freight) — includes all charges to seaport or airport of destination.

Franco or free — including all charges to the customer's own premises.

ex-warehouse price in the country of origin. To this the following five additions have to be made.

(*a*) The cost of carrying the goods to the docks at the port of embarkation.

(*b*) Dock dues and any other charges for loading the goods on to the ship.

(*c*) The freight charges for carrying the goods from the port of embarkation to the port of destination.

(*d*) Insurance of the goods while they are in transit.

(*e*) The charge for carrying the goods from the port of destination to the importer's warehouse.

The diagram on p. 267 shows the various terms which are employed to cover these charges. These are all standard terms (*Incoterms* 1953) and they are understood everywhere in quoting for an order. In this way confusion in trade has been greatly reduced. To avoid any misunderstanding over these terms, importers and exporters clarify their requirements when they agree on their deal.

3   Problems facing exporters and available help

Clearly, it is of the utmost importance to both the importer and exporter to know exactly what is included in a stated price. Thus, if the price is quoted as £160 *franco*, all the five charges additional to the basic price are covered, the goods being delivered at the importer's premises for an inclusive charge of £160. If, however, the price is £150 f.o.b. the importer will have to pay in addition to £150 the freight charge for the sea journey, the cost of insurance during transit and the charge for carrying the goods from the docks to his premises, so that the amount he will have to pay will be considerably more than £150.

Another difficulty in foreign trade is the fact that price quotations are usually made in the currency of the country of origin, so that it becomes necessary to recalculate prices in terms of one's own currency at the prevailing rate of exchange. If rates of exchange are liable to vary this adds a further element of risk to foreign trade transactions.

Other difficulties facing exporters include the following.

(*a*) *Differences in standardised units.* Countries use different units of weight, voltage, length, capacity, etc. The adoption of metric units in recent years has helped British producers to meet domestic and overseas markets.

(*b*) *Language differences.* Exporters may have to translate all the necessary documentation, packaging, marketing literature, etc. into the languages of the countries receiving their products.

(*c*) *The variety of legal requirements.* One example of a legal requirement in the export trade is the licences needed before one country's exports are able to enter another country. In addition, an exporter may need a licence from his own country. Other countries may be imposing tariffs or quotas on their imports in order to protect their home industries from foreign competition.

(*d*) *Risks.* The risks of the export trade are numerous, for example damage or loss in transit. There are also risks that importers may not pay for the goods being imported or that they may be unable to pay for them if the government begins to operate strict exchange controls in order to conserve its foreign exchange reserves. Though it is possible to insure against these risks through insurers or *del credere* agents, premiums may be substantial and so reduce the profits to be earned by exporting, making overseas markets not as attractive as the home market.

Large companies have their own arrangements for dealing with these problems. Smaller businesses have to seek advice elsewhere, for example from the commercial banks or the government's Small Firms Advisory Service set up in 1972–73, which gives advice on such matters as language and currency problems. Advice on language problems is also available from the Central Office of Information. The Export Credits Guarantee Department also assists exporters by helping them to insure against the risks of an importer not paying for his imports (*see* Chapter 20).

Of major importance to exporters is the work of the British Overseas Trade Board (BOTB) which has a variety of services aimed at answering all the questions exporters have to face. For example, what is the best way of selling a product in a particular country? Is there, in fact, a market for that particular product? The range of services provided by BOTB includes the following.

(*a*) Specialist advice on exporting to particular countries, for example on import regulations or labelling requirements.

(*b*) The Statistics and Market Intelligence Library provides information on overseas markets.

(*c*) The Overseas Status Report Scheme can make checks on prospective partners and agents.

(*d*) Assistance with the costs of overseas market research is available through the Export Market Research Scheme.

(*e*) Advice on local standards is available through the Technical Help to Exporters.

(*f*) Help with finding an agent or assessing the potential of a product's overseas sales is available through the Market Advisory Service.

(*g*) The Export Intelligence Service of the BOTB notifies exporters of new export opportunities.

(*h*) The Market Entry Guarantee Scheme provides assistance with taking part in overseas trade fairs and missions and with setting up sales facilities overseas.

(*i*) The Publicity Unit of the BOTB helps to promote products overseas.

(*j*) The Simplification of International Trade Procedures Board (SITPRO) provides advice on delivering goods overseas. SITPRO was set up in 1970 to help rationalise trade procedures and documentation.

An important objective of government economic policy is to stimulate UK exports for balance of payments reasons (*see* Chapter 18) and to help create employment opportunities, hence the amount of assistance government agencies provide to firms already exporting or wishing to enter the export trade.

4 Obtaining orders from abroad

Firms wishing to obtain foreign orders often send out circulars to past and prospective customers abroad. As in the home trade, travellers or commission agents may be employed. Sometimes foreign buyers send their representatives to call upon manufacturers. A firm engaged primarily in the manufacture of goods for export may find it worth its while to open branch offices in those countries where the volume of business warrants it. Industrial shows and exhibitions like the Motor Show, the Toy Fair and the British Industries Fair attract large numbers of foreign buyers, who come to visit them for the purpose of placing orders. 'British Weeks' are increasingly used and involve British companies exhibiting their products in overseas countries. The BOTB is in contact with the Diplomatic Service in British Embassies and Consulates and these, along with the Central Office of Information, draw attention in overseas countries to British goods and services, including Britain's attraction for foreign tourists. Another method of exporting concerns the licensing of overseas producers to manufacture and sell an exporter's product. Even so, many orders from abroad come direct to the manufacturers of the commodities. Finally, in some cases orders are received by exporters.

Indents. Foreign orders are known as indents, although the term is more particularly applicable where orders are placed with agents or exporters. An indent may be open or closed.

(*a*) *Open indent.* In this case the agent receiving the order can obtain the required goods from any manufacturer he pleases.

(*b*) *Closed indent.* This names the manufacturer from whom the foreign buyer desires the goods to be bought.

5 An export transaction

Let us now consider a transaction in the export trade. Assume that the South Australian Shoe Co. Pty of Adelaide has sent an indent for 1,000 pairs of shoes to J. Smith & Co., export agents of London. It is a closed indent and names R. Rushden & Co. PLC of Northampton as the firm from which the goods have to be purchased. The indent will also state how the goods have to be packed and give instructions regarding the markings to be stencilled on the packing-cases. The required markings might be as follows. If there is more than one the packing-cases will be numbered.

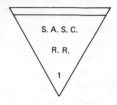

J. Smith & Co. will proceed to obtain the goods from R. Rushden & Co. PLC packed as requested by the foreign buyer, and he will have them delivered to the docks. If the order had been sent direct to the manufacturer the goods would probably have been sent by him to a firm of shippers in London, who would then see to the loading of the goods on the ship. Accompanying the goods a shipping advice note would have been sent stating the necessary instructions.

Having arranged for the delivery of the goods to the docks, J. Smith & Co, will then have the various necessary documents drawn up, as follows.

(*a*) As many copies of the *bill of lading* as are required. This is the main export document and represents the title to the goods while in transit. It is also a receipt for the goods shipped and is evidence of the contract of shipment (i.e. carriage) between the exporter and the shipper. As noted in Chapter 18, it is usually accompanied by various other documents outlined below. If a bank is financing the export transaction, the bill of lading is usually handed to the bank along with a bill of exchange or letter of credit (*see* Chapter 18), the seller's invoice and the certificate of insurance.

(*b*) *The certified invoice.* This document is required for all exports to the Commonwealth by the government of the importing country to enable the duty on the goods (if any) to be calculated.

(*c*) *The freight note* showing the charge for carriage and who is to pay it.

(*d*) *The certificate of insurance* to show that the goods while in transit have been insured with Lloyd's or an insurance company.

Other documents used in connection with an export transaction may include the following.

(*a*) *A certificate of origin.* If it has been agreed that the importing country shall charge the exporting country a lower scale of import duties than that given in its normal tariff, the goods must be accompanied by a certificate of origin, signed by a customs officer of the exporting country.

(*b*) *A customs declaration.* This document is required by the British customs authorities, who keep a record of all exports. It shows the quantity and the f.o.b. value of the goods exported and the country to which they have been consigned.

(*c*) *The National Standard Shipping Note.* This was introduced in 1975 to replace the different shipping notes with a standard form. It is used by exporters when delivering cargoes to British ports and gives details of the goods, the ship to which they will be delivered, and so on.

(*d*) *Air consignment note or air waybill.* The Carriage by Air Act 1961, which revised the rules of the Warsaw Convention of 1929, requires that consignments carried by air have to be covered by an air waybill, which consists of three parts: part one ('For the Carrier') is signed by the consignor; part two ('For the Consignees') is carried with the exports and is signed by the carrier and the consignee; part three is returned to the consignor after having been signed by the carrier. An air waybill includes details of the name of the transporter, point of departure and arrival, weight of packages, names of the exporters and importers, and so on. A consignment meeting the requirements of the Act limits a carrier's liability against losses in transit.

Like a bill of lading an air waybill is a document of carriage, but it is not a document of title. Other documents of carriage, such as a truck receipt or a railway consignment note (railway waybill) are, similarly, not usually documents of title but merely receipts for goods sent.

It is essential that the appropriate documents are completed correctly in order to ensure prompt payment for exports.

Questions

1. What methods are employed to obtain orders from abroad?

2. Mention five different methods of quoting prices in foreign trade, and indicate exactly what each one includes.

3. What documents are used in connection with the export of goods? Describe briefly the purpose of each of the documents you mention. (UEI)

4. Mention the main commodities traded between the United Kingdom and each of the following: (a) Australia; (b) New Zealand; (c) India; (d) West Germany. Explain whether there is any reason for supposing that these patterns will materially alter during the next decade. (GCE JMB)

5. Explain briefly the purposes of trade. In what respects is foreign trade (a) similar to; (b) different from home trade? (GCE Camb.)

6. Explain the use and purpose of the following documents in foreign trade:

(a) open indent; (b) bill of lading; (c) customs specification; (d) consular invoice. (GCE JMB)

7. Explain the role in exporting of: (a) export merchants; (b) factors; (c) shipping and forwarding agents. (LCCI)

8. (a) Explain how (i) export houses and (ii) overseas agents can assist firms seeking to enter the export market.

(b) Outline any alternative methods of exporting which may be available to such firms. (LCCI)

9. Explain four factors an exporter would take into account in deciding the best method of exporting perishable goods. (LCCI)

10. Explain fully the purpose and use of (i) a bill of lading and (ii) a certificate of origin, in relation to the transport of goods overseas. (LCCI)

11. (a) What difficulties, not found in the home trade, may confront an exporter?

(b) Select three of those difficulties and describe how they might be overcome. (LCCI)

12. (a) Safe Toys Ltd. have decided to expand by distributing their products to selected overseas markets. Explain *three* ways in which a foreign government may restrict the company's sales in order to protect their own domestic industry. (*6 marks*)

(b) Identify *six* major considerations an exporter of consumer goods would take into account when deciding whether or not to introduce containerisation. (*6 marks*)

(c) Describe the purpose of certificates of origin and bills of lading in international trade. (*8 marks*)

(RSA Inter.)

20 Foreign Trade III: Financing Trade

1 Methods of payment

Imports and exports have to be paid for. The precise nature of how a particular import or export is financed depends largely on the nature of the commodities being traded. Also important is the degree of competition between countries for export markets. As this competition has increased, so has the role of governments in providing financial assistance to exporters.

There are several methods by which a businessman in one country can make a payment to someone else in another country.

(a) *Cash with order or advance payment.* To the exporter this is the best means of receiving payment for his goods. However, this method is rarely employed as some form of credit to the importer is usually an accepted part of an export transaction. Furthermore, the authorities in many overseas countries will not permit advance payments to be made for imports.

(b) *Open account.* Here the documents of title are sent to the importer who will then pay with his own cheque or bankers' draft or international money transfer or international express money transfer. This method is a risky one as once the exports leave the exporter he loses control of them. As a result this method is only common where there is a very good trading relationship between exporter and importer, or the importer is a first-class company.

(c) *Foreign bill of exchange.* This is usually what is known as a documentary bill, so called because it has attached to it the shipping documents required in connection with the transaction concerned.

(*d*) *Documentary credit.* This method requires the opening of a credit at a bank in the country of the seller. This does not, however, dispense with a bill of exchange.

(*e*) *The bank draft.* This is really a special kind of cheque drawn on the bank of the buyer.

(*f*) *Air mail or telegraphic transfers.* Like a bank transfer, these transfers involve a direct transfer of funds without recourse to a bill of exchange, etc.

These methods are discussed in more detail below.

2 The foreign bill of exchange

In Chapter 9 the inland bill of exchange was examined. The foreign bill is very similar to it – it is drawn by the creditor, accepted by the debtor and, unless it is a bill payable on demand (a sight bill), it allows the debtor a period of credit, while at the same time enabling the creditor to receive payment immediately (less interest on the money for the period of the bill) if he can discount it with a bill broker, discount house or bank. The most usual periods for which bills used in foreign trade are drawn are sixty days and ninety days (that is, approximately two months and three months), the length of the period depending on the custom prevalent in the particular branch of trade in which it is used.

There are two important differences between inland and foreign bills. The date on which an inland bill is due for payment is calculated from the date on which it was drawn, but the period of a foreign bill runs from the date on which the bill was accepted. The reason for this is the interval between a foreign bill being drawn and its acceptance may be considerable, since it may depend on the time taken for the bill to pass from the drawer's country to that of the acceptor. The second important difference between the two types of bill is that the foreign bill is generally drawn in sets of three, although only one of them bears a stamp, and of course only one of them is paid. When documents have to be sent long distances by sea or air there is serious danger of their being lost. As we have already seen with bills of lading, several copies are made, so that one can be sent by one route and one by another. It is for this same reason that several copies of a foreign bill are drawn. As with other documents required in foreign trade nowadays, one copy is usually sent by air mail and another either by a later mail or by sea.

The specimen first copy of a foreign bill of exchange is shown below. This is a foreign bill in its simplest form. In this example R. S. Hoover of New York has purchased goods to the value of $80,000 from J. W. Hinton of London. Hoover would suggest to Hinton that payment should be by a bill for ninety days. Hinton agreed and drew the bill below, which he then sent to Hoover for acceptance. Afterwards it was returned to Hinton. As with the inland bill, there are now three courses open to Hinton: (*a*) he can hold the bill for ninety-three days (including the days of grace) and then present it at Hoover's bank for payment; (*b*) he could use it to pay a debt of his own if his creditor were agreeable, the bill in such a case requiring his endorsement first; (*c*) he may be able to discount it with a bill broker or discount house. Whether he can adopt the third course will depend on whether the acceptor's name is well regarded in London. If not, Hinton will first have to take it to an acceptance house such as Rothschilds, and in return for a fee have it accepted by them – which they will do only if they are satisfied with Hoover's creditworthiness. Whichever course Hinton decides upon, he will probably not deal with it himself, but instead he will instruct his bank to undertake this service for him. Banks also supply exporters with information regarding conditions of trade in foreign countries and give advice on suitable foreign markets for goods.

$80,000

Thames Wharf,
London,
10 February 19—.

Ninety days after sight of this FIRST of Exchange (second and third of the same tenor and date being unpaid) pay to my order the sum of Eighty Thousand dollars, value received.

J. W. Hinton.

To R. S. Hoover,
Thirty-second Street,
New York.

---

3 The documentary bill

At the present day it is most unlikely that a bill of exchange would be used in the simple form described in the previous paragraph. In its place, what is known as a documentary bill would probably be employed. This is nothing more than a bill of exchange with the various shipping documents – the bill of lading, the insurance certificate, the consular invoice, etc. – attached to it. By doing this the exporter can make the release of the documents conditional upon either (a) payment of the bill if it has been drawn at sight, or (b) its acceptance by the importer if it has been drawn for a period. Since the bill of lading is a document of title to the goods, this means that the importer would be unable to claim them until he had complied with the exporter's conditions with regard to payment. Once the documents have been released, the bill can then be negotiated and discounted in the usual way.

4 The documentary credit

This is the surest and quickest method of obtaining payment from the importer. If this method is selected it is still necessary for a bill of exchange to be employed, but the distinctive feature of the documentary credit is the opening by the importer of a credit in favour of the exporter at a bank in the exporter's country. Let us assume that J. Smith of London has arranged to sell a consignment of goods to C. Reed of New York. The terms of the deal having been agreed upon, the stages by which the transaction is carried through will be as follows.

(a) C. Reed, the importer, will instruct his bank, the National City Bank of New York, to open a credit in favour of J. Smith, the exporter, at the London branch of this American bank. Smith will then be informed by a letter of credit from this bank that it will pay him a stated sum in exchange for the bill of exchange and shipping documents. If Reed's bank confirms the credit this means that it guarantees that Smith will be paid, provided that he fulfils his side of the agreement. If the foreign bank had no branch in London it would appoint some other bank to act as its agent there.

(b) Smith now proceeds to draw a bill of exchange on the American bank to which he attaches the bill of lading, the insurance certificate and any other documents which may be required, and the goods will then be despatched by ship to New York.

(c) Smith next presents the documentary bill to the London branch of the National City Bank of New York, and if all the documents are in order he will receive payment, less interest in the case of a bill not payable at sight. The bank, too, will make a charge for its services.

(d) The London branch of the American bank then sends the documentary bill to its New York office for payment by C. Reed in the case of a sight bill or for his acceptance in other cases. When the bill is paid C. Reed's account will be debited by the amount. Everything being in order, the banker will release the bill of lading from the bill to enable C. Reed to claim the goods on their arrival at the port of New York.

The development of this method of making payments in foreign trade has greatly reduced the importance of the acceptance houses of the City of London (see Chapter 10). At one time their main business was the accepting of bills of exchange which otherwise would not have been negotiable because the original acceptor's name was not known to the money market. In the case of the documentary credit, used in the transaction outlined above, payment did not depend on C. Reed, a merchant possibly not known in London, but on the National City Bank of New York, an institution both well known and highly respected. The bill of exchange drawn by Smith can therefore easily be negotiated without the addition of the acceptance of an acceptance house. The decline of acceptance business has compelled many of the merchant bankers of London to develop ordinary banking business to supplement the 'merchant' banking for which they were originally established, and for which they were once famous.

There are two types of credit, as follows.

(a) *Revocable credit*. This can be cancelled or amended at any time without the exporter's prior knowledge. This type of credit is rarely employed.

(*b*) *Irrevocable credit.* This is widely employed at present. Here the importer's bank, called an *issuing bank* (not necessarily his own), gives its unalterable undertaking to guarantee payment *only* if all the terms of the credit are met. The issuing bank can only modify or cancel the undertaking if all the other parties concerned agree. If an exporter should wish to increase his security he can have the irrevocable credit 'confirmed'. Under this another bank in London (called the advising bank) can add its undertaking to that of the issuing bank. Hence the credit will be honoured whatever happens to the importer or the issuing bank. The advantages of the irrevocable credit to the exporter are that he has an undertaking from the issuing bank that he will be paid and without delay provided that the documents are in order and he has met the credit terms. Hence this is a very secure method of obtaining payment and provides the exporter with quite substantial benefits. As a result, exporters often agree to meeting the costs of this method themselves or offer a discount if the importer is prepared to deal on these terms.

Where documentary credits originate in countries with severe exchange rate problems, the credit may contain a clause allowing for the documents to be released to the importer against a deposit by him of the required amount of currency. The importer's bank then applies for an equivalent amount of sterling to be remitted to the exporter's bank – this may be several months later.

5   The bank draft

A bank draft is a cheque drawn on a bank instead of on a customer's personal account. It is an acceptable means of payment when the person tendering it is not known, since its value is dependent on the standing of a bank which is widely known, and not on the creditworthiness of a firm or individual known only to a limited number of people. Bank drafts are sometimes used in home trade in cases where a personal cheque is not regarded as a satisfactory means of payment.

The bank draft is more frequently met with in foreign trade. If Brown, a British importer of wine, wished to make a purchase from Daudet et Cie, a firm of exporters of Bordeaux, a bank draft might be used in payment. Suppose the amount due to be 50,000 francs. The British merchant would go to his bank – say, Barclays – and ask for a draft for this amount, Brown paying Barclays for it with his own cheque, the amount depending on the rate of exchange prevailing at the time between French francs and sterling. In addition, he would have to pay the bank's charge for the service. Thus, Brown pays in sterling and receives a draft in the currency of the country from which he is making his purchase. Daudet et Cie of Bordeaux will be agreeable to this method of payment, for, the draft being drawn on a bank, they are not dependent on Brown having a sufficient balance in his current account to meet it.

The draft is now sent to Daudet et Cie, and at the same time Barclays' agent in Bordeaux, perhaps Crédit Lyonnais, is informed. At the Bordeaux branch of Crédit Lyonnais copies will be kept of the signatures of the officials of Barclays Bank who are empowered to sign foreign drafts, so that these can be compared with the signatures on the draft.

6   Telegraphic and air mail transfers

Just as the telegraphic money order makes it possible to transfer a sum of money expeditiously from one person in (say) Aberdeen to another in (say) Plymouth, so in foreign transactions the quickest methods of payment are by telegraphic or air mail transfer. In principle these are similar to the bank draft, the importer paying his bank in advance at the current rate of exchange between the two currencies, together with the cost of the cable or air mail and the charge made by the bank. If Brown had used this method instead of the draft a cable would have been sent by Barclays Bank to the Crédit Lyonnais at Bordeaux instructing them to pay 50,000 francs to Daudet et Cie. The cable would be in code, and as a further precaution there would be the insertion of some word or number previously agreed upon by the two banks.

The employment of bank drafts and telegraphic transfers for making payments in foreign trade strongly resembles the use of cheques in home trade, in that they all enable bank deposits to be transferred from the banking account of the debtor to that of the creditor, but whereas the cheque has almost completely ousted the inland bill of exchange, the advantages to be obtained from the use of the bill in connection with a documentary credit have enabled it to survive in foreign trade, even though it is not used as much as it once was. Neither cheques nor bank drafts, however, offer the debtor a period of credit, as do bills of exchange other than sight bills. The increasing use of bank drafts and telegraphic transfers has greatly reduced the number of bills coming on to the London money market.

7 Export Credits Guarantee Department (ECGD)

Established in 1919, the ECGD is a government department concerned with assisting exporters of goods and services in two main ways.

(a) *Insurance services*. The department provides several different types of insurance policy to cover the risks of not being paid by the importer because he defaults on payment for some reason(s) under his control or not under his control, for example insolvency, civil war, a change in government policy or expropriation. It is concerned essentially with insuring against those risks not covered by ordinary commercial insurance. Thus the insurance offered covers two broad classes of risks: the creditworthiness of the importer and the 'political and economic risks' of the country concerned. On the other hand, it is not concerned with the risks normally covered by other insurers, for example marine risks. Exporters are required to share in the risk of a transaction so that the extent of cover provided is less than 100 per cent, usually 90 per cent.

(b) *The guarantee service*. Exporters generally provide credit to importers and so it is some time before exporters receive payment. In the meantime the exporters may have to borrow from banks in order to be able to continue with their operations. However, banks require security for the loans they make to help finance trade. If the exporter can obtain a guarantee that he would be able to repay the loan, even if the importer defaulted, then the exporter's problems of raising finance would be greatly lessened and, further, the costs of that loan would be reduced, that is, he would obtain loan finance at a preferential rate. The ECGD therefore exists to provide exporters holding suitable ECGD policies with unconditional guarantees of 100 per cent repayment to banks. As a result, the clearing banks are more prepared to help their customers involved in exporting with short and medium-term loans and long-term finance in the case of exports of capital goods, for example machinery and power stations.

The ECGD thus helps exporters to reduce the risks involved in exporting, for example an importer's creditworthiness, thereby allowing them to enter new export markets, and to provide importers with credit – a very important service which exporters have to provide in order to help win contracts when dealing in highly competitive markets.

Although it is a government agency, the ECGD operates commercially, applying the principles of insurance underwriting to provide a full export credit insurance at a reasonable price — exporters pay relatively small premiums to cover the various risks associated with exporting. It should be noted that the ECGD does not provide finance to exporters, nor does it guarantee the exporter in the event of default by the importer if the exporter fails to meet all his contractual obligations to the importer.

In 1982 the ECGD insured over £17,000 million of exports and paid out nearly £300 million in claims. Bank guarantees of all types were in excess of over £3,000 million, covering export contracts varying in value from a few pounds to tens of millions.

Questions

1. What are the chief features of the foreign bill of exchange?
2. Explain carefully the differences between a documentary bill and a documentary credit. Describe the procedure to be adopted in the case of each

if William Jenkins of London wishes to make a payment of 250,000 lire to R. Mantalini of Naples.

3. What is: (a) a bank draft; (b) a telegraphic transfer? How are they used for making payments in foreign trade?

4. Show how the business of the London money market has been affected during the past thirty years by the development of new means of payment in foreign trade.

5. What are the chief methods by which foreign trade is financed?

(GCE Camb.)

6. Describe three of the standard ways for obtaining payment for exports.

(NCTEC)

7. Explain any three of the following terms used in the overseas trade: indents, documentary credits, Export Credits Guarantee Department, c.i.f., bill of lading.

(RSA)

8. Describe (a) the use and (b) the importance of bills of exchange in foreign trade.

(LCCI)

9. Explain how the interests of exporters are served by *four* of the following: (a) export agents; (b) forward and shipping agents; (c) commercial banks; (d) Export Credits Guarantee Department; (e) export merchants.

(RSA Inter.)

21 The European Economic Community

1 Development of the EEC

As a result of a variety of political and economic factors, such as the need to avoid another major European war and a desire to enjoy the benefits of economic integration, West Germany and France signed the Paris Treaty of 1951 setting up the European Coal and Steel Community (ECSC). They were joined by Belgium, the Netherlands and Luxembourg, which had already in 1948 formed a customs union called Benelux. Italy also joined the ECSC. On 25th March 1957 these six countries signed two further treaties – the Treaties of Rome – setting up (*a*) the European Economic Community (EEC – the 'Common Market') and (*b*) the European Atomic Energy Community (Euratom). The EEC's objectives are set out in Articles 2 and 3 as follows.

Article 2.

The Community shall have as its task, by establishing a common market and progressively approximating the economic policies of Member States, to promote throughout the Community a harmonious development of economic activities, a continuous and balanced expansion, an increase in stability, an accelerated raising of the standard of living and closer relations between the States belonging to it.

Article 3.

For the purposes set out in Article 2, the activities of the Community shall include, as provided in this Treaty and in accordance with the timetable set out therein:

(*a*) the elimination, as between Member States, of customs duties and of quantitative restrictions on the import and export of goods, and of all other measures having equivalent effect;

(*b*) the establishment of a common customs tariff and of a common commercial policy towards third countries;

(*c*) the abolition, as between Member States, of obstacles to freedom of movement for persons, services and capital;

(*d*) the adoption of a common policy in the sphere of agriculture;

(*e*) the adoption of a common policy in the sphere of transport;

(*f*) the institution of a system ensuring that competition in the common market is not distorted;

(*g*) the application of procedures by which the economic policies of Member States can be co-ordinated and disequilibria in their balances of payments remedied;

(*h*) the approximation of the laws of Member States to the extent required for the proper functioning of the common market;

(*i*) the creation of a European Social Fund in order to improve employment opportunities for workers and to contribute to the raising of their standard of living;

(*j*) the establishment of a European Investment Bank to facilitate the economic expansion of the Community by opening up fresh resources;

(*k*) the association of the overseas countries and territories in order to increase trade and to promote jointly economic and social development.

The EEC began to operate on 1st January 1958.

The UK did not join the EEC; instead in 1960 it signed the Stockholm Convention (along with Norway, Sweden, Denmark, Austria, Switzerland and Portugal) setting up the European Free Trade Association (EFTA). Europe was now divided into two trading blocs. Finland joined EFTA in 1961 as an associate member.

Unlike the EEC, EFTA was essentially a commercial arrangement and it did not have long-term political and economic objectives, such as a common agricultural policy or a political union.

In July 1961 the UK applied to join the EEC. Negotiations continued into 1963 when Britain's application was rejected. The UK made its second application in May 1967, when Ireland, Denmark and Norway also applied. However, again the UK's application failed owing to French opposition. The six EEC member states agreed to reopen negotiations with the UK, Eire, Norway and Denmark in December 1969. Negotiations began again in June 1970 and the terms of Britain's accession to the EEC were set out in a White Paper, *The United Kingdom and the European Communities* (Cmnd. 4715, July 1971). Similar agreements were reached with Eire, Denmark and Norway. However, in Norway in a referendum held in January 1972 a majority voted not to join the EEC and so Norway withdrew its application. Thus on 1st January 1973 the EEC was enlarged by the addition of three new members: the UK, Eire and Denmark – the 'six' (population 188 million) became the 'nine' (population 251 million).

With the return of a Labour government in 1974 the UK's terms of entry to the EEC were renegotiated. The UK's position was set out in the White Paper, *Renegotiation of the Terms of Entry into the European Economic Community* (Cmnd. 5593, April 1974). Parliament voted for continued membership in 1975 and this decision was confirmed by a national referendum in the same year.

In June 1975 Greece announced its decision to join the EEC. This was followed in 1977 by the applications of Spain and Portugal. After lengthy negotiations Greece became the tenth member of the EEC on 1st January 1981. Spain and Portugal increased the size of the EEC to twelve members in 1986.

Today EFTA consists of Austria, Iceland, Norway, Sweden, Finland and Switzerland (Denmark and the UK having left in 1973 on accession to the EEC). It now offers free trade in industrial products between member states (since 1966) and between EFTA and the EEC (since 1977).

2 Institutions of the EEC

(*a*) *The Council of Ministers*. This is the Executive of the EEC and consists of one minister from each member state. The presidency rotates every six months. The Council considers proposals from the EEC Commission and is able to make decisions on such proposals alone. It usually consists of each member state's Foreign Minister but other ministers may attend when the Council is discussing matters which concern them, for example agricultural or finance ministers. Decisions giving rise to disagreements are taken by a majority vote, but all must agree on fundamental matters, for example the admission of another country.

The Council gives effect to its decisions by issuing the following.

(*i*) *Regulations*. These are the laws of the EEC. They are binding on each member state and do not have to be passed by individual parliaments.

(*ii*) *Directives*. These are also binding and each country decides for itself how to implement them.

(*iii*) *Decisions*. These are binding only on those to whom they refer.

(*iv*) *Recommendations*. These are merely Council opinions and are not binding.

Members of the Council are limited in the amount of time they can commit to its proceedings, so they meet together only occasionally. In the meantime much of the Council's work is performed by the Committee of Permanent Representatives consisting of the ambassadors of member states.

Though the Council decides how the EEC is to operate, it cannot do anything without the Commission since the Council cannot make any rules unless the Commission has proposed them.

(*b*) *The EEC Commission*. The Commission draws up proposals for policies and forwards them to the Council, executes them after acceptance by the Council, enforces EEC regulations, acts as 'guardian' of the Treaties, and represents the interests of the EEC in international negotiations. It is the outcome of the *Merger Treaty* signed in 1965, under which the various executive bodies of the

EEC, ECSC and Euratom were replaced by the present Commission. Each member state appoints one or two members, each of whom has to be independent of his government – they must act as Europeans, not as British, French, etc. In this way the Commission's members are concerned with the well-being of the *whole* Community and not just with that of their own particular country. Each member has his own special responsibility, for example agriculture or transport. Before the Commission's proposals are sent to the Council, they are sent to the European Parliament.

The Commission is located in Brussels and is supported by a staff of over 10,000 – the 'Eurocrats'.

(*c*) *The European Parliament*. This was originally the Assembly and became the European Parliament in 1962. Before 1979, it consisted of representatives chosen from national parliaments. Since that time, it has consisted of 410 members directly elected (Euro MPs), rising to 434 on the accession of Greece in 1981. The Parliament has powers over the EEC budget, and, while it debates Commission proposals, it is not bound to accept them. It can even dismiss them by a two-thirds majority vote. The powers of the European Parliament are, nevertheless, not as great as those of a national parliament; for example, it does not make laws, neither does it impose taxes. The second set of elections to the European Parliament took place in 1984.

(*d*) *The Court of Justice*. This is the supreme court of the EEC and sits in Luxembourg. Its jurisdiction extends to disputes between member states, corporations and institutions, breaches of the Treaty of Rome, the legality of EEC regulations and civil matters such as sex discrimination. Its rulings have precedence over national law (in theory).

(*e*) *Other institutions*. There are four institutions which control and distribute EEC aid: the European Social Fund, the European Regional Development Fund (ERDF), the European Agricultural Guidance and Guarantee Fund (known as FEOGA, the French abbreviation) and the European Investment Bank. In addition, there exists an Economic and Social Committee, set up to involve pressure groups such as trade unions, employers and consumers in the work of the EEC and the operation of the Social Fund.

3   The EEC budget

The EEC's budget has often been in the public eye in recent years, for example in regard to the size of the UK contribution and the effects of one of its major items of expenditure, on agricultural policy, on UK food prices. Many billions of pounds sterling, marks, francs, lire, etc. are transferred across frontiers to the EEC (i.e. its income) to be redistributed in accordance with the objectives of the various policies of the EEC (i.e. its expenditure). The EEC's budget represents less than 1 per cent of the ten member states' Gross Domestic Product (GDP).

EEC revenues. The EEC raises revenue by means of the 'own resources' or 'direct income' system. This has the following three elements.

(a) The common external tariff on manufactured goods (customs duties on goods from outside the Community).

(b) Import levies on agricultural goods from outside the EEC to bring their prices up to the agreed EEC threshold prices.

(c) The proceeds of a common percentage rate of each country's revenue from VAT. The table opposite shows the relative importance of these sources of income in 1983. Note that a common unit of account is employed, known as the *ECU* or *European Currency Unit*, which is a weighted average of the basket of European currencies. The value of one ECU varies from day to day as the relationships between the exchange rates of the member states' currencies fluctuate. By 1984 the ECU was rapidly developing into a major traded currency, mainly because of the large volume of common market transactions being made in it. It can be expected that use of the ECU will continue to grow.

This system, it is argued, tends to penalise the UK as it is a large importer of food and manufactured goods from outside the EEC.

EEC expenditure. The various revenue allocations are as shown in the table opposite, which relates to the year 1983.

EEC Resources (income) in 1983

Total budget (ECUs million)	19,328	(1 ECU = £0,565 at 31st August 1983)
of which:	(%)	
Customs duties	32.5	
Agricultural levies	12.7	
Value added tax	53.9	
Total own resources	99.1	
Other revenue	0.9	
Total	100.0	

Source: *Bulletin of the European Communities Commission*, 1983.

EEC Resources (expenditure) in 1983

Total expenditure (ECUs million)	22,896
of which:	(%)
Agriculture	60.81
Fisheries	0.37
Regional policy, regional fund	15.01
Social policy, social fund	10.34
Research, energy, industry and transport	3.23
Repayments and reserves	2.93
Development aid to non member states	2.27
Total	94.96
Staff and administration	5.04
Grand total	100.00

Source: *Bulletin of the European Communities Commission*, 1983.

It can be clearly seen that the Common Agricultural Policy (CAP) dominates EEC expenditure. This reflects the open-ended support accorded to this type of activity by the Community.

Much of the expenditure is in the form of grants, such as those provided by the European Regional Development Fund. The budgetary system has created a number of problems. The inequitable distribution of budget contributions among the member states, particularly the UK and West Germany, has raised many calls for reform. The pattern of spending is heavily weighted towards the CAP, leaving little for other policies. The present sources of EEC income have also failed to provide for an *increasing* revenue.

4   The Common Agricultural Policy

One of the objectives of the EEC was to construct a number of common policies, the implementation of which would be binding on all members. Despite very great efforts, the number of areas in which common policies have been achieved is limited. The best example of a common policy is that relating to agriculture – the Common Agricultural Policy (CAP). Though the Treaty of Rome envisaged a common agricultural policy, it laid down guidelines only for a single system of price support for agriculture to replace different national policies. The considerations affecting the formation of the CAP were as follows.

(*a*) The need to establish a common market in which prices would be stable and reasonable, with a common price for each product.

(*b*) A desire to ensure that those employed in agriculture would enjoy a standard of living comparable to that of workers in other industries.

(*c*) The need to rationalise agriculture to improve efficiency.

(*d*) A wish to make the EEC more self-sufficient in foodstuffs.

Elements of CAP. There are two main elements in CAP policy: the protection of the EEC market against fluctuating prices in world markets, and the guaranteeing of minimum prices for agricultural products through *intervention prices* or direct payments to producers, i.e. subsidies.

Operation of CAP. Each year the Council of Ministers sets a price for each agricultural product. These are known as *target prices*. They are not guaranteed prices but, rather, price objectives, which act as estimates of what would be a fair return to farmers for their produce. As these prices are often higher than elsewhere, food in the EEC is often more expensive.

The EEC, in the shape of the European Agricultural Guidance and Guarantee Fund (FEOGA), will buy from farmers if they have to sell below target prices as the result of an exceptional harvest. The prices at which FEOGA will buy surpluses are the intervention prices, set about 8 per cent below target prices. Surpluses so obtained are destroyed, stored at great cost or sold off cheaply to countries outside the EEC. In years of poor harvest, surpluses would be sold inside the EEC to stabilise prices. Hence, FEOGA is really a stabilisation fund.

As intervention prices are effectively minimum prices, they repeatedly encourage overproduction, resulting in 'butter mountains' and 'milk lakes'. In 1979, for example, the EEC held surpluses of 440,000 tonnes of milk, 1 million tonnes of skimmed milk powder and 250,000 tonnes of butter. About 30 per cent of the EEC budget is devoted to dealing with these food surpluses.

Countries outside the EEC cannot send in food at lower prices owing to import levies which vary from time to time and prevent imports being sold below target price. When prices are revised upwards in this way they are known as *threshold prices*.

CAP is the sole fully developed common policy in the EEC, and it has brought the national agricultural policies of ten states into a single system based on free trade in farm products, common levels of support, joint financing and a common policy towards non-member states. The result is that almost all of the major decisions concerning the agriculture of a large area of Europe are taken by the EEC rather than by national governments. Furthermore, most national expenditure on agricultural support has similarly been taken over by the EEC.

Problems of the CAP. The operation of the CAP has raised a number of problems. As is clear from the table above, EEC expenditure is dominated by the demands of the CAP. The subsidised surpluses are growing, and with them, the problem of their disposal. The benefits of the CAP are very unevenly distributed relative to the contributions of individual members to the EEC budget. In particular, the UK, which is major contributor, argues that it enjoys few benefits under present arrangements. Consequently, in 1983, the Commission made proposals for the reform of the CAP, including the introduction of output quotas. It is unlikely, however, that there will be any radical reforms of the CAP in the short term.

5 The UK and the EEC

Britain's accession to the EEC has affected her in several ways, including the following.

(a) *Trade.* As was seen in Chapters 18 and 19, the relative importance of the EEC as a source of imports and as a market for exports has risen steadily. By 1982 the percentage share of non-EEC trade (imports and exports) in total trade for the UK had fallen to less than 60 per cent (from about 70 per cent in 1972). This reflects the fact that the EEC is a customs union within which there are no tariffs. As a result, countries are able to trade freely with each other, i.e. there is a common market in goods and services.

(b) *EEC aid.* The UK has received a considerable amount of financial assistance from the EEC, for example as a result of its Social Fund set up in 1961 to assist with retraining and relocating unemployed workers; the European Regional Development Fund set up in 1975 to provide the economically less favoured areas of the EEC with financial assistance (e.g. the North-West, Clydeside, South Wales); and FEOGA to help modernise agriculture. Between 1975 and 1983 the UK received over £900 million from the ERDF, and between 1973 and 1981 it received £706 million from the Social Fund.

(c) *The tax system.* As a condition of joining the EEC the UK abolished purchase tax and selective employment tax to replace them with value added tax (VAT), a new form of tax on spending (consumption).

(*d*) *Consumer protection.* In 1975 the Council of Ministers adopted a consumer information and protection programme. Since then several steps have been taken to implement the programme. For example, directives have been issued regarding foodstuffs such as one laying down rules for their presentation and labelling (labels must include ingredients, quantity and a 'use by' date), and one concerning quality standards in fresh meat. Directives have also been issued concerning cosmetics (for example, regulating the contents, labelling and packaging), textiles (labels must indicate the relative contents of mixed fibre products), the safety of cars and toys, the use of toxic substances (for example, pesticides, inks, glues), and so on. These requirements and several others have had major implications for the wholesale and retail trades as well as for manufacturing industries.

(*e*) *Common policies.* The UK has also been subject to directives emanating from the various EEC 'common policies', such as environment policy (for example, the use of lead in petrol), energy policy, competition policy, transport policy and fishing policy. Perhaps the most famous of these policies to affect Britain has been the Common Agricultural Policy (CAP), examined above, which has fostered an enormous increase in Britain's agricultural output, for example grain, milk and butter.

(*f*) *Banking supervision.* (*See* Chapters 10 and 11.)

These are only a few of the more obvious ways in which the UK has been affected by membership of the EEC. Besides profoundly altering UK commercial activity, membership of the EEC has also affected the UK's economic, legal and political systems, details of which are beyond the scope of this book.

When attempting to assess the advantages of the EEC membership one should consider the *qualitative* as well as the *quantitative* advantages of membership; for example, membership of the world's third major economic power, peace within Western Europe and new trading opportunities as Britain's colonies went their own economic way following the granting of independence. One can safely predict

that the operation of the UK's commercial system will continue to
be greatly influenced by the development of the EEC in the years
ahead.

Appendix I
Some Abbreviations used in Commerce

1 Commercial abbreviations

AAR	Against all risks
A/C	Account
Ad val.	In proportion to the value
AGM	Annual General Meeting
AOB	Any other business
appro	Approval
B/Dft	Bank draft
b.e.	Bill of exchange
b.f.	Brought forward
b.l.	Bill of lading
b.p.	Bills payable
b.r.	Bills receivable
bros.	Brothers
b.s.	Bill of sale
CA	Chartered accountant
Carr. Fwd.	Carriage forward
Carr. Pd.	Carriage paid
cat.	Catalogue
c. & f.	Cost and freight
c.d.	Carried down
cert.	Certificate
cf.	Compare
c.f.	Carried forward

chq.	Cheque
c.i.f.	Cost, insurance and freight
C/N	Credit note
Co.	Company
COD	Cash on delivery
C/P	Charter party
Cr.	Credit
C/R	Company's or carrier's risk
$A	Australian dollar
deb.	Debenture
del cred.	*Del credere*
dept.	Department
disc.	Discount
div.	Dividend
D/N	Debit note
Dr.	Debit
D/W	Dock warrant
E&OE	Errors and omissions excepted
enclo(s).	Enclosure(s)
et seq.	And the following
ex div.	Excluding dividend (ex = without)
exors.	Executors
exs.	Expenses
f.a.a.	Free of all average
f.a.s.	Free alongside
fco.	*Franco*
f.o.b.	Free on board
f.o.r.	Free on rail
FPA	Free of particular average
fwd.	Forward
GA	General average
GB	Great Britain
HP	Hire-purchase
id.	The same
i.e.	That is
IMO	International money order
inv.	Invoice

L/C	Letter of credit
Ltd.	Limited
max.	Maximum
min.	Minimum
MO	Money order
MS (plur. MSS)	Manuscript(s)
NTP	Not to press
ord.	Order
O/R	Owner's risk
PA	Particular average
p/c	Prices current
pd.	Paid
per pro.	On behalf of
pkg.	Package
PL	Partial loss
P/N	Promissory note
PO	Post Office, postal order
ppd.	Prepaid
Pro forma	Taking the form of
q.v.	Which see (cross reference)
R/D	Refer to drawer
re	With reference to
recd.	Received
ref.	Reference
regd.	Registered
s.a.e.	Stamped addressed envelope
SEDOL	Stock Exchange Daily Official List
sgd.	Signed
S/N	Shipping note
std.	Standard
Tel.	Telephone
Tel. Add.	Telegraphic address
TL	Total loss
TMO	Telegraphic money order
TT	Telegraphic transfer
UK	United Kingdom
VAT	Value added tax

viz	Namely
wgt.	Weight
W/W	Warehouse warrant
x.d.	Excluding dividend

2 Institutional abbreviations

ABCC	Association of British Chambers of Commerce
ACA	Associate of the Institute of Chartered Accountants; also Member of the Association of Certified Accountants
ACGI	Associate of the City and Guilds Institute of London
ACMA	Associate of the Institute of Cost and Management Accountants
ADB	Asian Development Bank
Af.D.B.	African Development Bank
AIA	Associate of the Institute of Actuaries
AIB	Associate of the Institute of Bankers
AICS	Associate of the Institute of Chartered Shipbrokers
ALA	Associate of the Library Association
AMBIM	Associate Member of the British Institute of Management
AMF	Arab Monetary Fund
ARSA	Associate of the Royal Society of Arts
ASEAN	Association of South East Asian Nations
BA	British Airways
BACIE	British Association for Commercial and Industrial Education
BENELUX	Belgo-Netherlands-Luxembourg Economic Union
BETRO	British Export Trade Research Organisation
BIS	Bank for International Settlements
BR	British Rail
CA	Member of the Institute of Chartered Accountants of Scotland
CAP	Common Agricultural Policy
CBI	Confederation of British Industry
CMEA	Council for Mutual Economic Assistance (Comecon)

Cmnd.	Command (official government papers are given 'Command' numbers)
CSE	Certificate of Secondary Education
CTT	Capital Transfer Tax
CWS	Co-operative Wholesale Society
DM	Deutschmark
EAGGF	European Agricultural Guidance and Guarantee Fund (often cited by its French initials 'FEOGA')
EBI	European Investment Bank
ECU	European Currency Unit
EEC	European Economic Community (European Common Market)
EFTA	European Free Trade Area
EMS	European Monetary System
FACA	Fellow of the Association of Certified Accountants
FAO	Food and Agriculturel Organisation (a department of the United Nations Organisation)
FBI	Federation of British Industries
FCMA	Fellow of the Institute of Cost and Management Accountants
FFI	Finance for Industry
FIA	Fellow of the Institute of Actuaries
FIB	Fellow of the Institute of Bankers
FLA	Fellow of the Library Association
FREconS	Fellow of the Royal Economic Society
FRSA	Fellow of the Royal Society of Arts
GATT	General Agreement on Tariffs and Trade
GCE	General Certificate of Education
GLC	Greater London Council
HMSO	Her Majesty's Stationery Office
IBA	Independent Broadcasting Authority
IBRD	International Bank for Reconstruction and Development
ICA	International Co-operative Alliance
ICSA	Institute of Chartered Secretaries and Administrators
IDA	International Development Association
IDAC	Import Duties Advisory Committee

IFC	International Finance Corporation
ILO	International Labour Organisation
IMF	International Monetary Fund
I.o.B.	Institute of Bankers
ITO	International Trade Organisation
LAFTA	Latin American Free Trade Association
LCC	Lancashire Cotton Corporation
LCCI	London Chamber of Commerce and Industry
LDCs	Less Developed Countries
MCAs	Monetary Compensation Amounts
MGI	Member of the Grocers' Institute
NI	National Insurance
OECD	Organisation for Economic Co-operation and Development
OPEC	Organisation of Petroleum Exporting Countries
OTC	Overseas Trading Corporation
PAYE	Pay As You Earn (income tax deducted from current earnings)
PLA	Port of London Authority
RC	Royal Commission
RICA	Research Institute for Consumers' Affairs
RM	Royal Mail
RPM	Resale Price Maintenance
RSA	Royal Society of Arts
SCWS	Scottish Co-operative Wholesale Society
TUC	Trades Union Congress
TUCC	Transport Users' Consultative Committee
UNESCO	United Nations Educational, Scientific and Cultural Organisation
UNO	United Nations Organisation
WHO	World Health Organisation (a department of the United Nations Organisation)

3   The Department of Trade and Industry (DTI)

This is the public department which has most to do with matters concerning British trade and commerce. The parliamentary head of the department is a member of the government of the day of Cabinet rank, and, like other ministers, has to answer questions in Parliament relating to problems which affect his department.

The DTI has a wide range of activities. At one time they were even wider, but new departments have been created to deal with expanding branches of the work, e.g. the Ministry of Labour (now known as the Department of Employment) and the Ministry of Transport (now the Department of Transport). The DTI has a Mercantile Marine department, which is responsible for the administration of laws relating to merchant shipping. For example, the overloading of a ship to a depth below its Plimsoll line would be a matter falling within the jurisdiction of the DTI. It also watches over the activities of limited companies and is responsible for the appointment of receivers in the large towns in the event of bankruptcy proceedings. The granting of the right to use trade marks and patents and their registration are other functions of the DTI. It also concerns itself with weights and measures, inspectors being appointed to check periodically those used by retailers.

The DTI has on a number of occasions undertaken a Census of Production, and several times it has carried out Censuses of Distribution, taking a count of the various kinds of retail shops and their turnover. The establishment of the Central Statistical Office has now centralised much of the statistical work of many government departments. The Department also used to be responsible for the organisation of the British Industries Fair.

There are a number of other divisions of the DTI which supply information to exporters and manufacturers who may be interested in foreign markets. For those businessmen who prefer to make personal calls an inquiry office is available. Further assistance is given to exporters by the Export Credits Guarantee Department which was considered in Chapter 20. The DTI also publishes a *Journal* which provides merchants and manufacturers with information on foreign markets and trading conditions in other lands.

4   The British Consular Service

British consuls are to be found in all the chief commercial cities of the world. Their function is to further British trade with the countries in which they are stationed. It is their business to make periodical reports on trade conditions in their districts and to pass back information which they think will be of service to British manufacturers and exporters. They must watch British commercial interests abroad and report, for example, on the misuse by foreign producers of British trade marks if this should occur or any other actions to the detriment of British trade. It is also part of their duty to give any assistance which might be required by British subjects abroad.

Appendix II
Some Commercial
Institutions

1 Commerce and the state

The state, even in those countries where the production and distribution of goods is left to private enterprise, tends to take an increasing interest in matters affecting the economic life of the people. From the fifteenth to the eighteenth centuries governments sought to regulate trade, but in the early nineteenth century Britain adopted a policy of *laissez-faire*, that is, non-intervention by the state in the economic life of the nation. Little by little this policy was abandoned, and before the end of the nineteenth century the state had intervened to protect the workers in the factories and to provide free education for all. By means of tariffs, countries have tried to protect their own producers and manufacturers from foreign competition. In the twentieth century free trade was completely abandoned, a system of national insurance was built up, and the state has gradually extended its activities to production. During both world wars the nation's economic life was largely directed by the state. In most countries the state now takes a keen interest in economic matters.

2 Government departments

In some countries – Canada, for instance – there is a State Department of Commerce. In Britain the Department of Trade and

Industry is the government department which deals with most questions which have to do with trade. Other economic questions fall within the purview of other government departments and agencies: the Health and Safety Commission is responsible for the administration of the Health and Safety at Work Act 1974 and related legislation; employment offices and Jobcentres are run by the Employment Division of the Manpower Services Commission; the Department of Employment watches over industrial relations and compiles the Index of Retail Prices, popularly known as the Cost of Living Index; the Ministry of Agriculture, Fisheries and Food and the Department of the Environment deal with problems affecting the areas indicated by the names of the departments; and national insurance is under the control of the Department of Health and Social Security. The Chancellor of the Exchequer is responsible for finance, including customs and excise duties and other economic matters. The large number of government departments in Britain which are now concerned with economic affairs shows the extent to which the modern state is interested in these matters.

In many countries industries are now state-owned. In Britain the state has operated a postal service for over 250 years, but it is only since 1945 that it has extended its activities to industrial production. Coal-mining, transport, gas and electricity production and the iron and steel industry have all been brought under national ownership. As a preliminary to the nationalisation of these industries the Bank of England became a state institution in 1946. However, since 1979 the Conservative government has been selling off or 'privatising' many areas of nationalised industry (*see* Chapter 5).

5   Trade associations

There are a number of associations which have been established to watch the interests of traders and manufacturers and to give them an opportunity of airing their grievances and taking concerted action to protect their interests. These include trade associations, chambers of commerce and chambers of trade.

Almost every trade and industry has its association. We have already noticed the work of the Liverpool Cotton Association, which includes members engaged in every branch of the industry, and the Corn Trade Association, in the grading of cotton and wheat respectively, so that these commodities can be bought and sold by grade. The Electric Lamp Manufacturers' Association is another example of a manufacturers' association. Sometimes these bodies are mostly concerned to watch legislation which may affect their interests, such as tariffs and taxes.

6 Chambers of commerce

These are to be found in every important town, the largest, as might be expected, being that in London. Their members are merchants and manufacturers. As with other trade associations, their aim is to protect the interests of their members. The first chamber of commerce was established in Jersey as long ago as 1768, the first in Britain being that set up at Glasgow in 1783. The London Chamber of Commerce (now the London Chamber of Commerce and Industry) was not, however, established until 1881. There are now over a hundred of these bodies in Britain. In many towns there are also junior chambers of commerce, their members being the younger business executives.

Chambers of commerce collect information on all subjects likely to be of interest to their members. Like trade associations, they keep a watchful eye on legislation which they think might damage their interests, and if necessary take action to oppose it. Any suggestion – for example, of an increase in postal charges – would immediately arouse their opposition. They discuss all problems affecting trade in the towns and districts in which they are situated. They also give advice to their members regarding foreign markets. The London Chamber of Commerce and Industry has over 9,000 members, including merchants, manufacturers, bankers and people engaged in transport and insurance. Thus all branches of commerce are represented. The London body also has a department which holds examinations, on the results of which it awards certificates to students of commerce. The various chambers of commerce in the country are affiliated to a national body, the Association of Chambers of Commerce. The Junior Chambers of Commerce are affiliated to the Association of British Junior Chambers of Commerce. There is also a Federation of Chambers of Commerce of the British Commonwealth and an international association, representing chambers of commerce throughout the world.

7   Chambers of trade

These are associations mostly of retailers, and they are to be found in most towns. Their purpose is to enable shopkeepers to meet and discuss any problems which particularly affect them, such as the hours of opening of shops or car-parking regulations which they think might inconvenience their customers and so perhaps adversely affect the trade of the town.

Index